"WHERE DID YOU GROW UP?"

BY HARRIET PRISKA

Happy Trails —
Harriet Priska

Table of Contents

Dedication

I dedicate this book to my parents and both sets of my grandparents. Most specifically to Winne Washburn who was my brave mother while my father was engaged as a chaplain in World War II. Throughout all my life Mom gave me unconditional love and encouraged my life as an artist. And to her mother, Olivia Young, who encouraged my writing and art work as I used those gifts to define my life. Both of them were writers and in their eighties published books, so it is only fitting that now in my eighties I am now publishing my fourth book in this past year!

However first and foremost, I dedicate all of what has happened to the Lord, Jesus Christ, and rejoice in His Grip on all things!

John 1:12 As many as received Him, to them He gave power to become the sons of God, even to them that believe on His name.

Introduction

When my remote doorbell rings in my kitchen, I rise quickly from my desk in my office in my home, step outside and walk about fifty feet to my small gallery. Greeting the customers as I approach, I begin to connect with them. "Welcome" I say warmly as I glance to see what license plate is on the front of their vehicle and wonder if it either is their own car or a rental, then I ask, "Where are you folks from?"

After they reply, I welcome them again as I unlock the door to Serenidad Gallery. Going inside, we begin to chat about their trip. I listen to see if we happen to have anything in common like where they are from, which is often the case. After looking at my paintings on the wall, the local petrified wood, a variety of antique and Navajo jewelry, and other items that may catch their eye, they will often ask me "are you from Escalante," or "where did you move from?" or even "where did you grow up?" I reply to the last query, "Ah, The Question!" and I learn if they are in a hurry or have time for me to tell my story and I judge my response accordingly.

Serenidad Gallery today

I begin by telling them that I was born in St. Anthony, Idaho, in 1943, and relate that after returning from WW II my father got a pastorate in Effingham, Illinois where my brother, John, was born. Then my father received the GI Bill to study for His PhD. at the University of Edinburgh, in Scotland where I went to school from 1950 - 1952. Then I relate that when we came back to the

USA we drove across country to Sausalito, California where I entered 4th grade. After my youngest brother, George, was born there in February of 1953, we moved to Idaho Falls, Idaho. Depending on their time, I continue with my saga of my attending 13 schools in 17 years.

If they have time I tell them that when we were in Idaho Falls in the mid 1950's, my father took the family to see his sister in Los Angeles, California on U. S. Highway 89 which was then the way to drive south from Idaho to get to southern California before the Interstates were built. On our way we visited Bryce Canyon National Park. As a child of 12, I was transfixed by the amazing rock formations! As we proceeded on south, my brother John got sick, and my mother decided we would not take the windy road into Zion National Park. As we drove further southwest on Alternate Highway 89, we saw Zion's monumental sandstone formations towering in the distance and my heart broke! I knew that we had missed something very special!!!

The rest of the story is why I decided to write this book to answer the question I am so often asked: "Where did you grow up?"

Psalm 139: 13 – 18

For Thou hast formed my inward parts, Thou hast weaved me in my mother's womb. I will praise Thee, for I am fearfully and wonderfully made: marvelous are Thy works; and that my soul knoweth very well. My substance was not hidden from Thee when I was made in secret, and curiously wrought (the double-helical DNA) in the hidden parts (elements) of the earth. Thine eyes did see my substance (embryo) yet being unperfect (unformed); and in Thy book all my members were written, the days fashioned for me, when as yet there was none of them. How precious also are Thy thoughts unto me, O God! How great is the sum of them! If I should count them, they are more in number than the sand: when I awake, I am still with Thee!

Chapter 1 – ROOTS

My father, Charles Harrison Washburn, had very few stories to tell me about his family when they lived in Ossining, Westchester County, New York. One I recall was that the Washburn family held to the Puritan faith during the Civil War and had refused to fight.

His mother, Gertrude Foshay Washburn, had genealogy records that went back to the Revolutionary War. Her ancestor was Samuel Lyon who also lived in Westchester County. She joined the Daughters of the American Revolution in the early 1900's and thanks to her research I became in a member in 1977. My father finally joined the Sons of the American Revolution later in his life based on his mother's genealogy.

1910 Census records show that his father, Harrison Barnes Washburn, had moved his family to the Los Angeles area. Eventually they resided in Santa Monica, California.

Gertrude married Harrison on April 26, 1893. They had 3 children in New York before moving to California. In the fall of 1915, Gertrude went to a doctor, complaining of abdominal issues and the examining physician advised her she had a tumor. January 6, 1916, that tumor was indeed twins! Isaac and Charles Harrison, my father! Isaac was a blue baby, and in very poor health. By the time the twins reached their teen years a photo showed that Charles was at least two feet taller than his brother. One day they went down to play in the surf at the beach near their home in Santa Monica. They were both caught in a rip tide and Isaac was never found! I believe that tragedy had a profound effect on Charles for the rest of his life!

My mother, Winifred Elizabeth Young, was born in San Rafael, California to George Deming Young and Olivia Rudolph Young. The Rudolph family had traveled west to Illinois, from Worchester County, Maryland, then on to Salem, Oregon, and later south to Lompoc, California. John Caspar Rudoph III owned "Rudolph General Store" in several locations in Lompoc and then moved his family to Alameda, California. He was listed in the 1910 census as "an oil operator" between 1900 and 1910. John passed away at the age of 53 in 1910 from a heart attack while walking down a street in Alameda. He left his wife, Nina Durand Morehead Rudolph, to raise Olivia and her three brothers, plus Nina's mother and her younger brother Edmund who also lived with her. Nina died in 1916.

Jeremiah Young, James Henry Young's father, moved west from Onondaga County, NY, to Indiana, where James Henry Young was born in 1851. Jermiah moved west with his family to Nebraska (he was in Omaha in the 1860 Census) and then to Colorado Springs, Colorado by the 1880 Census, and was working as a carpenter. His son, James married Elizabeth Sarah Neal in 1885 in Colorado Springs. Elizabeth was born in Illinois in 1858. James and Elizabeth moved to Alameda, California where George Deming Young was born, October 7, 1889.

George was the youngest of three children. George and his father repaired brick chimneys in Alameda that had collapsed during the San Francisco Earthquake in 1906! George went on to trade school in the San Francisco studying construction and carpentry.

In the summer of 1912, George and Olivia met while singing together in a church choir in Alameda. George was hired as a soloist because of his fine baritone voice. After three dates, he departed to teach High School Shop classes in Lompoc, California. George and Olivia, who was working as a medical secretary, wrote letters back and forth all fall, sending their mail by the train that went up and down central California.

When George came home for Christmas he proposed to Olivia. They married at their church in Alameda after his school session was completed in May of 1913. George built most of their furniture at the carpentry shop where he taught furniture making, in the Arts and Crafts style for their home near his High School in Lompoc. Later after the birth of their first son, George Deming Young, Junior, in Lompoc, they moved north to San Rafael, California, where George helped to construct Tamalpais High School in Mill Valley, California.

My mother, Winifred Elizabeth Young was born in San Rafael November 11, 1917. In 1918, George obtained a homestead parcel on the Oakland hills and moved his family to Mountain Boulevard. George built a home, a farm, developed Young's Dairy, and taught High School Shop classes in Oakland. They raised two more children there, Jean and Bill.

Charles, or as I knew him, Harry, as a child was dyslexic. He wrote mostly with his left hand and had speech challenges, stuttering profoundly until a teacher at the University of California in Los Angeles put marbles in his mouth and taught him how to speak clearly! He went on to graduate from UCLA with a BA in Architecture. Then he attended Architecture classes at Princeton University for a year before being led to enter the ministry.

Charles had been in Bible Study Classes at Hollywood Presbyterian Church led by Henrietta Mears. After she prayerfully laid her hands on him, Harry chose to go to San Francisco Theological Seminary in San Anselmo. California, studying to be a Presbyterian Minister.

Part of his training included summer ministry experiences in New Mexico in 1939 and in Delta, Utah in 1940. In the fall of 1940, he commuted each weekend to the Fruitvale Presbyterian Church in Oakland, California, sailing across the San Francisco Bay on the ferry to Oakland to conduct Sunday services. There he met Oliva Young the organist at the church. Harry fell in love with her personality and told her if she had a daughter, he would marry her!

As it turned out, she did! Winnie, as Winifred was affectionately called, was studying nearby at the University of Pacific in Stockton, California. She had a goal of marrying a minister and was completing her Bachelor's degree in in Christian Education and Music! That Thanksgiving Harry was invited to the Young's home for dinner. The story goes that Winnie had returned from the

University and was sitting at the kitchen table snapping beans when Harry walked in the door! It was love at first sight! After both finished their degrees, they married on July 27, 1941, in the Fruitvale Presbyterian Church.

Jeremiah 29:11 is my favorite promise: "For I know the thoughts that I think toward you, saith the Lord, thoughts of peace, and not of evil, to give you an expected end."

Painting done of Charles Harrison Washburn when he was ordained a Presbyterian Minister in 1941 by his older sister Dorothea Horbach

Chapter 2 – Idaho Spud

In June 1941, after graduating from San Francisco Theological Seminary in May, Harry drove his trusty Chevy to Idaho to begin his ministry in two churches, known as the "Twin Kirk Parish" in Saint Anthony and nearby Rexburg, Idaho started by Dr. Jessie Baird in 1917.

Doctor Jessie Baird wrote:

"I first became interested in serving a church in the intermountain country in 1915 in my first year at McCormick Theological Seminary after hearing about the planting of churches in that area from George Peacock, a Sunday School missionary who was seeking people to help him start churches in the Upper Snake River Valley. I then helped him in the summer of 1915 riding many miles on borrowed horses and visiting about a hundred families. Then the first of June 1917, I arrived again in Rexburg, Idaho, a correctly educated Presbyterian minister ordained by the Presbytery of Mahoney, Ohio."

After their wedding at the Fruitvale Presbyterian Church in Oakland, California, on July 27th, 1941, Harry and Winnie moved to St. Anthony, Idaho. The Manse, the home provided for a pastor, located beside the church in Saint Anthony, was ready for the new couple. It was here that Harry brought his bride after a long drive from Oakland, California, in their "old Chevrolet" full of their belongings including a large steamer trunk.

Their ministry included outreach to many ranching families who raised potatoes and other crops in the surrounding area. Monte Bauer, a warm and loving farmer's wife, was one of the ladies that kept track of the Washburn's over many years and was a wonderful friend and firm supporter of their work. Winnie became involved with the music of the two churches, possibly directing the choir for adults and children. Summers found them at Sun Valley, Idaho, at the Presbyterian Church Camp. Harry was a young, bright, active youth pastor.

On Sunday, December 7, 1941, after both services at the churches in St. Anthony and nearby Rexburg, as was their custom, Harry and Winnie had two members of the Saint Anthony church to come over for dinner. Here is Winnie's story in her own words:

"We had not yet been married six months, and this was our first Church, a twin parish of St. Anthony where we lived, and just 12 miles south, the other was in Rexburg, both in Eastern Idaho along the Snake River, and just 50 miles south of the West entrance to Yellowstone National Park. It was a beautiful place to live as our first parish. We had a full view of the Grand Tetons from the east side, out of our front room picture windows. Our Manse was old, but very comfortable; the loving Ladies Aid Society had furnished the house with all styles of furniture making it look more like a high-class antique shop. We really didn't mind the potpourri of old-fashioned couches and rockers and filigree curtains. The two story house was homey and comfy; and the Church Family was so very warm and welcoming. All the families in our congregation were either farmers or National Park employees or teachers and administrators at the local Boys and Girls Schools for orphaned High School aged youth; there were a few city employees as well; altogether an upper class intellectual group of about 120 members, which was quite remarkable for a small Mormon town of about 2000 people. Rexburg was even more Mormon in population with its new and growing Ricks College. That congregation was smaller, but with a similar collection of Church members. We were very much in love with our first Church families, I guess mostly because they loved us so much and took care of us even more than we took care of them. These two Churches had been started by Dr. Jesse Baird as his first churches. He was by then the President of San Francisco Theological Seminary, under whom my beloved Harry studied to gain his Divinity Degree in May of 1941.

Well, it was Sunday morning, the first Sunday in Advent, Dec.7, 1941, around 10 AM. We had just finished the first service in St. Anthony; we had a lively group of 8 people in the Bell Choir who performed the lovely old favorite, "Whispering Hope". It was so beautiful; we lit the first advent candle and sang two verses of several favorite Christmas Hymns; Harry's sermon was on the gifts of the wise men. There was snow on the ground outside; nippy dry cold air at the elevation of 4000 ft. But the furnace functioned well, and we were all warm filled with Christmas wonder. So, we had to scurry a bit to say our goodbyes to our first congregation, bundle up in our little old Chevrolet, and carefully drive 12 miles south to Rexburg to start their service at 11 A.M. Before we left, I put a pot roast with all the veggies in the oven so it would be done when we got home about a quarter to one. We had invited two of the Park Rangers to come over for lunch at one P.M. The service went well in Rexburg, more Christmas music, a smaller congregation but equally faithful and loving to us.

When Church was finished, and we drove slowly over the icy road to finally be home about One P.M. The two National Park friends, both bachelors, came huffing and puffing to our front door in a few minutes. The temperature had dropped. The men reported hearing trees cracking and loudly bursting under the sudden freezing of the sap, making long cracks in the trunks of the pines and firs. They said it sounded like rifles being shot off. My pot roast was "done to a tee" when we got home. I had prepared a batch of biscuits, and I popped them in the oven, and I had made a fresh apple pie the day before, so I put it up on the warming oven to be ready for a warm desert (with real whipped cream from the Henry and Monte Bauer Ranch). I made a big pot of fresh coffee, and dropped a few frozen ears of local corn in the boiling water, checked the table for butter, jam, sugar and cream, etc. etc. So, we sat down and rejoiced over a warm little home and a just right homemade Sunday dinner. The Park men were especially appreciative of our company, a homemade dinner, and time to sit and talk away the afternoon, maybe listen to a baseball game on the radio. The Giants were playing somewhere in the warm southland, and Harry and the men wanted to be sure to listen to the game on the radio.

Dinner was sumptuous; we decided to have our hot apple pie in the living room in front of the fireplace and listen to the game there. So about two P.M. we got ourselves settled; brought out a couple of end tables to put our food on, placed another log in the fireplace, and turned on the radio to catch the beginning of a very important baseball game. It was a wonderfully warm feeling to be "at home" with new friends, in our first Manse.

It was the second inning, and the Giants were ahead, everyone was on the edge of their seats as the bases were loaded.... when suddenly with a crackling sound, the radio announcer interrupted with a loud voice, saying," I am sorry to break into this important game, but I have life shaking news!! Earlier today, a **Japanese Kamikaze** air fleet suddenly appeared out of nowhere and **bombed Pearl Harbor in Hawaii!!!** They seemed to have flown below the radar; **they have destroyed all the American warships in the Harbor**. President Roosevelt has just met with his cabinet; they have declared war on Japan. **We have entered World War II !!"**

Harry turned down the volume of the radio a bit; we all were speechless; the two National Park men's faces were as white as sheets; I covered my mouth, and sobbed; Harry kept saying, "My Lord God, no! No!" We listened for a few more minutes to the report of the attack, then our two friends asked to be excused and left hastily for their homes. We pondered what would be the next step for our Nation. Men would have to be called up to form an army; military emplacements were hurriedly posted all along the California and Oregon coastlines; black outs and brown outs were enforced; residents formed home militia, not knowing if the Japanese were prepared to attack the Pacific coast.

Reality struck home when my younger brother, Bill, became a instructor of pilots in the US Army Air Force in Florida. Our two National Park friends enlisted as officers in the Army. Women in California became riveters and workers in the shipyards, quickly making war ships to transport troops and supplies across the Pacific. Japanese fleets moved rapidly south to the Philippines and northern Australia but were beaten back. Hitler had invaded Poland in 1939. The United States finally joined Brittan in a valiant effort to turn back the horrors of Hitler.

This is only a very small part of what happened after Sunday, December 7th, 1941. Winnie's youngest brother, Bob, had just turned 8 years old. His father gave him a good rifle and took him up in the Oakland hills above their farm and taught him how to shoot in case the Japanese landed! Bob became such a good shot, that when he joined the Navy in 1950, the officers asked him to be a sniper! Bob's hate for the enemy was profound!

Harry and Winnie decided that Harry would not enlist as a Chaplain in the Army until after they had had their first child.... I was long in coming!

In 1942, Harry's mother, Gertrude, who had been living with her daughter Dorothea in Pasadena, chose to come and live with Harry and Winnie in Saint Anthony. Her husband, Harrison, had passed away due to heart condition on March 13, 1937, at the age of 65 after a career in Real Estate in the Los Angeles area. Gertrude brought all her worldly possessions with her including her hand painted porcelain dinner plates from the early 1900's, her sterling service and crystal goblets, plus a few of her own works of art including a watercolor, and a hand painted porcelain vase which she did about 1900. All these precious possessions bespoke of an earlier elegant life she had enjoyed. However, in the fall she was diagnosed with a "tumor" and during the surgery, she passed away on September 28th, 1942, at the age of 66.

Harry then had the opportunity to perform his own mother's funeral. Also, perhaps his first? Hence, I never knew either of my grandparents on my father's side, although upon reflection many years later, I found that I had followed in their footsteps in numerous ways!

Doing the math, I figure that I was conceived in October of 1942. It was often relayed to me that mom's pregnancy was lengthy, and I was overdue. Dad said he walked mom up and down the railroad tracks to "get things going!" At that time there was no hospital in Saint Anthony, so I was born in the Rest Home there, late at night, July 28, 1943. Potatoes were a main crop in that area so I was called a real "Idaho Spud!"

Then, my father was free to make the choice to be a Chaplain. He joined the Army and was assigned to the Sante Fe Infantry Division. Harry traveled east in January of 1944, and mom took me west on the train to live with her parents in Oakland, California. She told me that the Blackfoot people traveling on the train were admiring her Papoose! I was inculcated with train sounds at that early age and have been enchanted with riding trains ever since.

Photo of me and my mother taken by grandmother, Olivia Young, in her home of Winnie and Bunky! 1944

Isaiah 49: 13 – 16 Sing, O heavens, and be joyful, O earth: break forth into singing, O mountains: for the Lord hath comforted His people and will have mercy upon His afflicted. But Zion said, The Lord hath forsaken me, and my Lord hath forgotten me. Can a woman forget her suckling child, that she should not have compassion on the son of her womb? Yes, they may forget, yet will I not forget thee. Behold, I have inscribed thee upon the palms of My hands; thy walls are continually before me.

Chapter 3 – What I did not know

When mom took me to live with her parents early in 1944, the Young home on Mountain Boulevard in Oakland, California was warm and cozy. There was a large stone fireplace that her father had constructed with wooden benches on either side so one could enjoy the family atmosphere on a cold winter's night. George and Olivia had two more children by then, Bob, 10, and Marion, 9. So I was in essence their baby sister and they nicknamed me Bunky! While I do not recall any of it, they had fond memories of me!

What I did not know was that my father had joined the Sante Fe Army regiment and was on his way to war in Europe. Nor would I understand the agony my mother must have suffered, not knowing what he was enduring!

Winnie wrote: "After the Japanese attack on Pearl Harbor, on December 7th 1941, the call came for Chaplains for the Armed forces. I knew long before it happened that my Harry would become a Chaplain. He enlisted late in 1943, went to England with the 110th Medical Battalion and landed in Normandy on Omaha Beach, July 7th, 1944. By the Grace of God, he survived after being captured in the Battle of the Bulge Christmas Day, 1944. After 3 weeks they were freed. His division rescued what was left of the prisoners of Auschwitz, Germany. They battled all the way to the Russian border, on the Elbe River meeting up with the Russian troops that finally defeated Hitler. By December of 1946, Harry returned home, broken, deeply emotionally injured, a totally changed man than the one I married a few years earlier."

Meanwhile, to keep herself busy, my mother went to work in Oakland, California, at the Ming Quong Presbyterian Church orphanage for Chinese girls. Eventually, she found a small home for us on Ashby Avenue on the border between Oakland and Berkley. There we lived until it was time for us to move on to our next adventure! One day, her younger sister, Jeanie, whom we called Pont, was coming to visit us with her two boys, Bud, and Ted, who were 4 and 3 years older than me. I was "helping" in the kitchen and had pulled out a towel from a drawer, with flat hands I pushed the drawer shut and the flesh on my left ring finger got caught as I hurriedly closed it! I got a big cut with a flap of skin that healed with a lump which I still have to this day! That is my sole memory of that time.

Much later I learned that in January of 1944, my father went to see his older sister, Gertrude Dow, who lived on Long Island in New York. She took Harry to see President Rosevelt in his Oval Office. He greeted Harry by saying "our mothers were cousins." I tried to verify that and could not, but since the President was an avid genealogist, I take his statement as true.

Then Harry went to Fort Campbell, Kentucky which was established in 1942 as a war-time armor training and mobilization camp for WWII. There he was assigned to the first Negro troops as their chaplain.

He told me that the landing on Omaha beach on June 6th was every bit as bad as the D-Day landing. I have often wondered why this battle is not recognized today. The 35th Army fought their way to Luxembourg and on in the evening of December the 25th, his division was captured by the German troops. " After a day of hard fighting, on December 16th, 1944, the Germans broke through the American front, surrounding most of an infantry division, seizing key crossroads, and advancing their spearheads toward the Meuse River, creating the projection that gave the Battle of the Bulge its name."

Dad told me that the night when he unit was captured, a German officer immediately confiscated the jeep that my father was driving, then he asked him what was in the trailer which Dad was pulling with the jeep. Pointing to the cross on his uniform, he replied that he was a chaplain and there were Bibles in the small trailer. The Germans left it alone. Fortunately, there were also "K rations" which dad and the men in the medical unit ate to barely survive until they were rescued 3 weeks later. Dad told me he got down to 98 pounds and lying on a bed was very painful because of the pressure on his ribs. He said that these Americans were treated well, and the German officers were gentlemen. However, the Germans brought their wounded to the Red Cross tent and expected the Americans to care for them!

Much later as an adult, I had a dream one night, seeing men being pushed into a large pit in the snowy woods, and my dad scrambling out of one side. Then I saw his serial number. I never knew what it was before! Dad did NOT speak about his war experiences! When I told him about the dream, he confirmed the serial number I had seen. Such was the subconscious effect of his trauma on our family!

Liberated by Patten's army three weeks later, Dad's regiment eventually arrived in Hamblin, Germany when the war ended in Europe on May 9th, 1945. The commander of his unit, Colonel Butler, came to my father and asked him to have a regimental sized flag made for Memorial Day since the unit had lost theirs in the Battle of the Bulge.

Harry went to the Catholic Convent in Hamblin and spoke to the nuns. They agreed that they could use their white sheets and blue surge material that their habits were made from, but they did not have any red fabric. Harry recalled seeing a large orange/red Nazi banner hanging in the town, so he went and took it down and gave it to the nuns. They were very hesitant to use it, but finally it was the only option, and they used it and sewed a five by eight foot Regimental American flag.

When Dad went to pick up the flag, he found that they had only sewn the 48 stars on one side as Germans were used to having banners and not flags, so he had them sew 48 stars on the other side as well! He gave them bags of sugar and flour in thanks, and they were delighted because they had not had such provisions for a long time. The "Nun's Flag" was raised on Memorial Day, 1945 in Hamblin, Germany. He took photos of it flying in the breeze.

After the war was over in Europe, the troops were discharged and sailed back to America; however, Harry was sent back to the Army base in Kentucky, and remained there all fall. He was very depressed because he had not been able to go home. His letters showed his frustration. A photo of him in his uniform in front of the Christmas tree in Oakland, confirms that he did come home by then. The expression on my face shows that I was not very happy with this new person in my life!

Psalm 91 is known as the **"Soldiers Prayer"** I can certainly see fulfillment in my father's life!

Thank you, Lord!

Psalm 91 King James Version

1. He that dwelleth in the secret place of the most High shall abide under the shadow of the Almighty.
2. I will say of the LORD, He is my refuge and my fortress; my God, in Him will I trust.
3. Surely, He shall deliver thee from the snare of the fowler, and from the noisome pestilence.
4. He shall cover thee with his feathers, and under his wings shalt thou trust: His truth shall be thy shield and buckler.
5. Thou shalt not be afraid of the terror by night; nor the arrow that flieth by day;
6. Nor the pestilence that walketh in darkness; nor the destruction that wasteth at noonday.
7. A thousand shall fall at thy side, and ten thousand at thy right hand; but is shall not come nigh thee.
8. Only with thine eyes shalt thou behold and see the reward of the wicked.
9. Because thou hast made the LORD, which is my refuge, even the most High, thy habitation;
10. There shall no evil befall thee, neither shall any plague come nigh thy dwelling.
11. For He shall give His angels charge over thee, to keep thee in all thy ways.
12. They shall bear thee up in their hands, lest thou dash thy foot against a stone.

13. Thou shalt tread upon the lion and the adder: the young lion and the dragon shalt thou trample under feet.

14. Because he hath set his love upon me, therefore will I deliver him: I will set him on high, because he hath known my name.

15. He shall call upon me and I will answer him: I will be with him in trouble; I will deliver him and honor him.

16. With long life will I satisfy him, and shew him My Salvation.

Chapter 4 – Blown off the road to get a job!

In the fall of 1945, Harry wrote letters to Winnie while he was stationed in Kentucky as a Chaplain after the war was over. He was depressed because he was still at the Army base and had no idea why he was not discharged. He used his time to search for a church pastorate in the Midwest and finally secured an interview. As he drove north through Illinois on his way to the Chicago area, a blizzard hit, and as a large truck passed him it blew his vehicle off the road into a ditch. Harry was taken to a nearby hospital in Effingham, Illinois. Some people from the local Presbyterian Church came to visit him and eagerly asked him to be their pastor!

Winnie continues to write:

"And yet God's grace provided us with our second church in Effingham, Illinois, where the congregation nursed, and nurtured Harry. Surely our church family gave us far more than we could ever give them. But Harry never really recovered for the rest of his life from what we now know as Post Traumatic Stress Disorder caused by the horrors of World War II. God allowed us to have three wonderful children, who have since grown into caring Christian teachers and businesspeople; but they too have been injured by their father's deep hurts and we have all suffered from Secondary Post Traumatic Stress Disorder."

My early memories of living in the two story Manse next to the big brick Presbyterian Church that faced US Highway 40 include a large garden in back, and a lovely lawn between the house and the church. I had fun making mud pies underneath the grape arbor behind the back porch in summer and snow men on the lawn in the winter. There were little bunny rabbits living in the straw that had been thrown over the strawberry plants for the winter and a fishpond by the church with goldfish. When I lost my first tooth, my father hung my tooth on a sting in a glass of water with a tiny goldfish nipping at the tooth! I even got a puppy dog one Christmas, but it ran onto the Highway and got run over by a truck.

One summer afternoon, in 1947, I was playing out in the back by the garage, and I found a yellow envelope lying on the driveway. I took it to my mother. She read the telegram and hastily told my father that her mother, Olivia, had been run over by a "hit and run" driver in downtown Oakland and her feet were seriously injured. My Uncle Bob said his mother had come to pick him up from school and they were standing on a street corner when she was knocked over. He was rushed away from the scene, so he does not recall much more. My parents and I immediately boarded the train to California. While I do not recall this train trip, I do have the drawing of the train that I did then!

My drawing of our train trip to California in 1947.

The summer of 1948, my parents took a road trip to see my father's family in Ossining, New York. I was sitting in the back seat of the car. We were driving down a hill in Ohio going about 60 miles an hour when I somehow opened the door and fell out! I cannot imagine my parents' anguish! They rushed me to the Children's Hospital that was nearby. I suffered a fractured skull on my left side just above my ear.

Many years later when I was in my 40's, I got very ill one day and had a flash back, seeing the undercarriage of the vehicle. I do not recall the rest of those 3 weeks in the hospital and the remainder of the journey except when we sailed across Lake Michigan on a ferry. The whistle blew several blasts, it really hurt because my left ear drum had been broken in the accident!

We traveled on to Niagara Falls and we were sitting in a restaurant overlooking them on the American side, when a nice man came along and palmed a quarter out from behind my ear! Strange the things we remember!

We finally arrived at our destination, my Great Aunt Harriet's palatial Victorian home overlooking the Hudson River in Ossining, New York. Josephine Harriet also spelled Harriett Washburn was born in 1872 died in 1955, in Gadsden FL. She went by Harriet married in 1890 her cousin from the Ossining area, Charles G. Washburn born in 1861 died in 1930. They did not have children. Charles G. Washburn had a long career in the coal business from 1900 through 1930. After Harriet's father died, her mother, Phoebe Louise, lived with them for a few years.

My memories of Great Aunt Harriet's home have inspired me to paint older homes of that era to recapture the grandeur of that time. My grandparents, Harrison and Gertrude Washburn, lived with Harriet and her husband and raised their first three children there. I was told that their young daughter Gertrude would wander over to Sing Sing Prison, which was nearby, and the guards would call on the telephone and say that she was there and ask if she could stay for dinner! Young Gertrude had long golden locks and was not doubt very cute! West Point was just across the Hudson River.

Aunt Gertrude told me that when General Douglas MacArthur was the director at West Point, he would come for tea with Great Aunt Harriet on Sunday afternoons. There were apparently family ties, but I could never discover them. I was also told that Harriet donated a large stained glass window in the church that they attended.

After my father returned from the war, my mother unfortunately had a miscarriage. I learned about it 40 years later! Sometime later Mom took me to visit a lady in the hospital who had lost a child at birth. When we went home, I composed a short story about an empty rosewood cradle that had been made for that baby, not knowing that in a way I was also grieving the loss of my own sibling!

When I was four, I had my tonsils out in that hospital. By the age of 5, I was in the dentist chair having a baby tooth pulled because the cavity was so bad....sugar... I have had dental challenges ever since! One day, my mother noticed that I was walking the heels of my shoes unevenly, so she took me to the store that sold Buster Brown shoes and the salesman had me put my foot in a small X-Ray machine. I got to see my own bones!!! But the shoes did not solve the issue, I still walk off the sides of my heels to this day!

In 1948 on the 4th of July, the city had a picnic at the Effingham Community Park. There was an outdoor stage. I was invited to go up and sing "Zip-A- Dee- Doo Dah, Zip-A-Dee Aye" We had just seen the movie "Song of the South" made in 1946 by Walt Disney, but I was too shy to sing. Another girl stood up and sang the song. AND she got a little red wagon for her performance. That was the last time I passed up an opportunity to stand up in front of people!!!

Ferris wheels were very popular in the 1940's. My dad took me to the Effingham County Fair one summer afternoon to see the festivities. We sat on the swinging seat of the Ferris wheel and the operator stopped it at the top and let us sit up there because he was not very busy. From there we could see the racetrack below and all the countryside round about! What a wonderful view!

Another time our family went to Springfield, Illinois to the State Fair. They had a double Ferris Wheel, each one rotating and then each one going round the other! It was quite a sight all lit up at night!

My mother's younger brother, Bill Young, flew his red and yellow two seater Cessna airplane over from Indiana to visit us from Purdue University where he went to study after the war. I sat on my mother's lap and up we went! I was amazed to look down on the fields below. I was hooked and have loved to fly ever since!

By 1948, the traffic was getting so complicated in the Oakland, California, and east bay area so the MacArthur Freeway was designed from San Leandro to downtown Oakland with much of it passing along Foothill Boulevard. George and Olivia Young and their neighbors were all evicted and paid for their property!

My grandparents search for a new home led them to Auburn, California where they bought acreage north of town. My Uncle Bob called it "the ranch" because he wanted people to think it was more than just a farm! George built a lovely ranch style home and Olivia cultivated a flower and vegetable garden. George constructed a large chicken coop and sold eggs in the local market, and they raised turkeys. George and Bob irrigated a large field and raised alfalfa.

With the money from the Foothill Boulevard home, they purchased a brand new light green 1949 Chevrolet sedan, George drove Olivia, Bob and Marion east, first to see Bryce Canyon National Park and then went on up Hy 89 to Panguitch to have a "Sanguwitch" Marion later told me. Then they drove all the way to Effingham, Illinois, to see us in the summer of 1949. What a treat to visit with them at last!

In January 1949, my parents sat me down on the couch in the front room and put my hand on my mother's stomach and explained that she was expecting a baby. It would be born early in April. We prayed for all things to go well. I had a large baby doll I named "Jeannie" after my Aunt Jean, so I was in tune with the "baby" situation.

On April 6th, we were all sleeping when my parents were awakened by people throwing rocks at their second story bedroom window in the early morning hours! These people from church knew that the baby was about due. They came to tell my parents that a massive fire had engulfed the large old brick Saint Anthony's Hospital there in Effingham. The newborn infants were on the top floor. All 11 babies and their mothers perished as did a total of 74 patients, nurses, nuns, and a priest.

Of course, everyone was in shock! Fortunately, my brother, John Charles Washburn, made his arrival on April 11th and was born at home. Dr. Webb and the nurse attending the birth both came down with the measles shortly afterwards! I was hurried across the street to stay with a neighbor until all had recovered 2 weeks later. It was the first time I had been away from my mother. It was quite a traumatic experience for me!

Much later, my second brother, George, eventually became an employee for AAA Fire Inspectors in Seattle, Washington. The effect of this tragedy reverberated around the nation and the world bringing in a new fire safety consciousness to the future construction of all buildings! A "Phoenix" did indeed rise out of the ashes!

On a happier note, my father did many interesting things at the church including decorating for Thanksgiving with lots of corn stalks and pumpkins and fall harvest produce on the front the sanctuary. One Christmas he created a nativity scene outside at the top of the steps at the front of the church complete with manger with my baby doll, Jeannie, as the Baby Jesus!

Many a summer evening was spent admiring and catching fireflies! I regret that I tore them apart and made a ring on my finger with their tail light still pulsing!

In the fall of 1948, I entered Kindergarten, and graduated in the spring of 1949, complete with a cap and gown! In the fall of 1949, I walked about a mile down Highway 40 aka West National Avenue, to go first grade at the big brick Elementary School. At Christmas, the teacher had the class do a play which was broadcast on the radio, and I was Mrs. Santa!

In the fall of 1950, the "Boomer" generation hit all the schools in the nation! By then my mother and baby brother and I had moved to a small house on property owned by a member of the church because my father had been accepted to the University of Edinburgh in Scotland and had preceded us to Edinburgh to make housing arrangements and get settled in. The photo below was taken in the late summer of 1950 just before my father went ahead of us to Scotland. At the age of 34 he was already bald, probably due to the stress of his war experiences.

Family Photo taken with Scottish plaid ribbons for each of us just before we went to Edinburgh, Scotland

I started second grade in a room upstairs in the downtown business district of Effingham with about 40 other kids. I attended class there until we left in early December to go to Scotland. If you are counting, these were the first 3 of 13 schools I was to attend in 17 years!

The railroad tracks cross in the center of Effingham, going both north and south and east and west. Our little cottage was just below that crossing. I enjoyed the train traffic at all hours! The day of our departure to go to Scotland, was exciting for all as we boarded the train. A lady from church went along with us to help mom with us kids. John was now 1 ½ years old and I was 7. We rode the Pennsylvania Railroad to New York City. Unfortunately, in all the confusion, the diaper bag got left on the platform in Effingham. The kind conductor phoned ahead for more diapers to be put on the train as we traveled east!

In New York City we took a taxi to the wharf for the White Star Cunard Line and boarded the M.V. Britannic. We three set sail for Liverpool, England, early in December of 1950.

Jeremiah 1: 4 – 8

The Word of the Lord came to me, saying, Before I formed thee in the belly, I knew thee, and before thou came forth out of the womb, I sanctified thee, and I ordained thee a prophet unto the nations. Then said I, Ah Lord God! Behold, I cannot speak; for I am a child. But the Lord said unto me, say not, I am a child for thou shall go to all that I shall send thee, and whatsoever I command thee thou shalt speak. Be not afraid of their faces: for I am with thee to deliver thee, saith the Lord."

Chapter 5 – "It's a Brawd Richt Nicht the Nicht!"

By now you might be wondering who is the main character in this story? I would hasten to assure you that it is God! He created us and had a plan for us from before the beginning of time! He has His hand of protection on us throughout our entire lives. As you have already seen with Harry's war experiences, Winnie and John's near miss at his birth, and my falling out of a moving car, which should have killed me on the spot. WE WERE ALL PROTECTED! Praise the Lord!

In September 1950, Harry sailed on the M.V. Britannic across the Atlantic from New York to Liverpool, England, and boarded the train to Edinburgh, Scotland. He was greeted there by welcoming people who assisted him in finding a place for our family to live at 39 Mentone Terrace. I even remember the neighborhood store down at the end of the block! Because the British Isles were still feeling the effects of the war in 1950, we had ration books when we did our grocery shopping! Our apartment was not far from the University of Edinburgh. The five room flat was on the top floor, and we had to climb up four flights of stairs to get to it. The view of the roof tops and chimneys was like a scene from Mary Poppins!

Harry had begun his Doctoral studies at the University of Edinburgh in Theology. To get to his classes he took public transportation. That fall, he was standing on the median waiting for a tram one morning, when a woman ran into him with her car, knocking him down and causing a serious wound on his forehead. He was immediately taken to the hospital for care. The injury caused him headaches for years! Harry was unable to continue his studies. The country's Socialized Medical system took care of his bills; however, they would not release him until they determined he was well enough to go home, which was over a year and a half after the accident!

Despite the new situation, our parents decided that mom would bring us children to Edinburgh anyway. The voyage in December of 1950 over the Atlantic was choppy. The large ship had been remodeled after being used to bring troops from Europe at the end of WWII. There was First class and economy class. Our low price room was way down in the lowest part of the ship. We had two berths in the compartment. I slept on the upper one and Mom and John slept on the lower bed. There was a family of boys in the cabin next to us and we heard them singing "Rudolph the Red Nosed Reindeer" through the thin wall all the way across the Atlantic for eight days!!!

We arrived in Liverpool, and I saw my father with a bandage on his forehead! This was the first time I knew of the accident! We boarded the train for Edinburgh. The compartments on European passenger cars have a door that opens directly onto the platform. We loaded all the luggage into our space and off we went. At one station, my father determined to get some "Sweeties" for us kids, he was gone a long time. The conductor called "All aboard" and still no dad. The train began to move and finally dad ran alongside and jumped into the open compartment doorway. No Sweeties, but we were so glad to have him back on the train, what a scare!

We arrived in Edinburgh and got settled. For our Christmas dinner, Dad took us to a very nice restaurant. A couple came over after a while and complemented mom and dad on how well behaved we two children were. Later we learned that they had paid for our meal! The best part, however, happened at the end of the dinner when the lights were lowered, and a waiter entered the room with a large silver tray balanced high over his head on his right hand with a flaming "Figgy Pudding!" He marched to some music all the way around the room! He came to our table and served us each a slice! I tried over the years to accomplish this feat of a flaming pudding with varying degrees of success!

In Scottish Schools a student's progress was based on series of tests. When a student passed the exam, they went on to the next level. I came into the middle of this system and was placed with other students at my age of seven and a half. However, it soon became obvious that I was more advanced, so I was moved up to the next level. I walked to school along a main street about two and a half miles each way with a brown canvas satchel on my back for my books.

That spring I was given three colors of chalk, red, yellow, and green. I knelt down on my knees and began to draw on the sidewalk in front of our flat. I discovered that if I spat on the chalk the colors would mix! That was the real beginning of my "Art" career!!!

That summer, Dad found us a lovely apartment to live in facing a park at 10 Eton Terrace in another part of Edinburgh. We had the basement, first and second floors. Mrs. Macintosh lived on the third floor. I called her "Toshie." She would often have me come up for tea and open faced watercress sandwiches! I recall the outside stairway into the kitchen located in the basement. The main floor had a rather grand formal living room. There was a back stairway that led to the second floor, probably used by servants "back in the day." About halfway up there was a small bedroom and that was my room which looked out over the back yard.

Across the road was a marvelous, gated park with the "Water of Leith" flowing at the bottom of the valley. I spent many contented hours enjoying the "green" trees and grass.

My walk to Primary school was about two and a half miles though the residential neighborhood. That fall, I was placed with children my age. I turned eight that summer. They were studying cursive writing which I had learned before I left Effingham. However, in European cursive the tail on the q was left open as opposed to the way I learned to close it in America. When I wanted to do it my way, the teacher reprimanded me by rapping soundly me on the knuckles with her ruler! Ouch!

Once again, I was more advanced than the children my age so was moved up a level. Finally, I felt at home. One day the teacher announced a contest. We were to memorize a Robert Burns poem and recite it.

As each student recited, I noticed that they were missing the final repetition of the lines at the end of the poem. I counted them on my fingers and when it came my turn, I did it perfectly and won the contest.

"John Smith, fallow fine, can ye shoe this horse o' mine?"

"Yes, indeed, and that I can, just as weel as ony man.

Kaw a nail into the tae to help the powny speel the bray.

Kaw a nail into the heel to help the powny pace weel.

Theres a nail and theres a broad

And theres a powny weel shod.

Weel shod.

Weel shod.

Weel shod powny."

And mind you, I did it with a thick accent! I was sent to the principal's office and there on his desk were several prizes for me to choose from. I selected the book "Alice in Wonderland" and was very pleased with it. My father, however, would have preferred me to have chosen the five pound note because that would have paid for a sack of coal for us to burn in our stove in the kitchen.

The school yard was divided between boys and girls. The girls would draw "Hopscotch" diagrams on the pavement, and we would scoot flat tins around with our feet. On the weekends, the boys and girls would draw circles in the dirt and shoot marbles – steelies, clay, and purees - which were clear glass marbles. I have loved marbles ever since.

Every Scottish school child wore a uniform, which included cap and a jacket of a particular color, with a patch on the pocket to identify the school. Since we were not planning to stay in Scotland very long, my mother made me a blue corduroy jacket with a red satin lining, and she did put the school patch on the pocket. One day I was riding a bus somewhere and a man came up to me and peered at the patch and then asked me, "Do you believe that motto?" It read, "*Truth will Prevail.*" I said "yes." I now know that truth is the basis of all life.

Late one summer evening, I had a burst of energy that I did not know what to do with, so I started racing up and down the 15 steps outside to the basement entrance. A passerby warned that I might fall, but I just kept on doing it anyway and finally I did indeed fall all the way down. I dragged myself back up the steps and up the front steps and in the front door. My mother was sitting the entryway talking on the telephone with a friend. I tried to get her attention, and finally threw up. She was afraid that I had reinjured my head and she took me to the nearby Children's Hospital.

I think I threw up twenty seven times. Fortunately, all I had was a concussion. They put me in the children's ward overnight for observation. There were many beds on both sides of the long room. The night nurse came along and told me to drink some orange juice and I told her I would just throw it up. She insisted. I threw it up and had to sleep in a wet bed all night. In the morning I was the spectacle of an "American child." A doctor and student doctors came stood around the bed and observed me, nude. It was quite embarrassing.

While Dad was in Europe during the war, he often wrote to mom that he would like to show her all the wonderful places he had seen. So, they took a trip to the continent and left my brother and me in the care of Bob and Pat Hayward. Bob was a young student at the University of Edinburgh, too. They had no children of their own. One evening, Pat prepared canned peas as part of the dinner. After taking a taste, I declined to eat any more peas. Pat, however, insisted that I clean my plate, and threatened me that I did not she would wash my mouth out with soap! When I maintained my position, she marched me into the bathroom and carried out her threat. It did not change my mind!

Edinburgh is famous for "The Royal Edinburgh Military Tattoo." Due to being located in the far northern latitude the evenings were very long. We were blessed to enjoy the Scottish band march with their kilts parade in front of Edinburgh Castle. The swirl of bagpipes stirred the soul, and the drummers kept a good beat for the marchers as they passed by. My father was inspired to send me to take Highland Fling lessons that fall. However, while the rest of the young girls in the exercise room were practicing ballet positions I had to stand next to a wall and do foot repetitions over and over again…boring. Dad was not impressed with the results and deemed it a waste of money.

At that time, we could purchase savings stamps and paste them in a book. I collected enough stamps to purchase my own kilt in the yellow Macleod tartan!

On February 6th, 1952, our teacher informed the class that King George IV, had died at the age of 56, after battling prolonged cancer. I was always fascinated with the life of Queen Elizabeth II who followed him and saw a movie of her coronation in color with my father in 1953.

At the end of my school year, we boarded the M. V. Britannic and sailed back to New York, arriving in the harbor on Flag Day, June 14, 1952. The sight of the Statue of Liberty was stirring and memorable. As we walked the streets of New York I remarked that it was "Jolly good" to be back in the States. My father abruptly stopped me in the middle of the street and said, "if you say, Jolly once more you are going to be sorry." I did not want to be sorry and did not say it again!

For Your Information - "It's a Brawd Richt Nicht th Nicht!" means "it is a really fine night! "

In Scotland the 23rd Psalm is sung to tune called Crimond. This is the text:

1. The Lord's my shepherd, I'll not want.

2. He makes me down to lie in pastures green; he leadth me the quiet waters by.

3. My soul he doth restore again: and me to walk doth make Within the paths of righteousness, e'en for his own name's sake.

4. Yea, though I walk in death's dark vale, yet will I fear non ill: For thou art with me and thy rod and staff me comfort still.

5. My table thou hast furnished in presence of my foes: My head thou dost with oil anoint, and my cup overflows.

6. Goodness and mercy all my life shall surely follow me And in God's for ever more my dwelling place shall be.

Chapter 6 – Traveling West

After we sailed into the New York City harbor on June 14th, 1952, my father's sister Gertrude Dow took us to her home on Long island. She had a black and white television. The screen was about 10 – 12 inches wide with rounded corners! That was the first TV we had ever seen!!!

One day she took me to Coney Island Amusement Park to enjoy the rides and cotton candy and ice cream! There was a machine that you could speak into and record your voice for you on a 78 rpm record to take home. I recited "John Smith fallow fine." I sounded very saucy when we played it on the record player!

Aunt Gertrude gifted us with a white four door 1949 Ford Sedan. It was equipped with a visor to keep the sun's glare out of our eyes as we drove west! Dad attached a V shaped piece of plastic onto the hood ornament. It was designed to deflect the bugs to keep them from hitting the windshield.

Away we went, first to visit friends in Effingham, Illinois. We arrived there in time for the 4th of July celebrations in the city park with a giant picnic. The Presidential Primary was underway. Republican, World War II Hero, General Dwight D. Eisenhower was running against Democrat, Adlai Stevenson from Illinois! After watermelon and much fun, the fireworks began with many interesting shapes. Among them was a large teetertotter with an elephant on one end and a donkey on the other that went up and down to illustrate the two political parties and all the uncertainties of the coming election! Last of all was a wonderful big American Flag all done in fireworks!

My parents drove on to Colorado to visit friends in Denver, then up to St. Anthony and Rexburg, Idaho to see their former church friends including Henry and Monte Bauer. Finally, we traveled southwest to Auburn, California where mom's parents greeted us warmly. We thanked them for all the wonderful care packages they had sent us in Scotland, and especially the powdered eggs! Dad had decided that we live in Marin City, just north of Sausalito on the northern part of San Francisco Bay so that he could again attend San Anselmo Theological Seminary.

Marin City was developed because of the need for housing in 1942 for ship builders during the war. When we arrived in the summer of 1952 dad was able to rent one of the two story redwood duplexes built on stilts on the side of the very steep hills. I boarded a yellow school bus that September to attend the school just to the south of us in Sausalito I was placed in the 4th grade because of my age. It soon became clear that I was more advanced and was moved to the 5th grade. A special memory I have was drawing a map of South America free hand!

We had a marvelous view of the San Francisco Bay area out our front room window. I recall sitting on my daddy's knee and listening to the radio program: "One Man's Family" written by

Calton E. Morse. The characters were so real to us, that I was sure that if I went to San Francisco, I could pick out the house in the Sea Cliff area where the Barbour's lived!

On February 2nd, 1953, my youngest brother, George Walter Washburn was born in San Rafael. My parents were watching the inauguration of the new US President, Dwight David Eisenhower on TV in Marin City at 11 AM. Then my father drove mom to the hospital and George was born at 12:03 PM!

Shortly after that, dad received a call to be the Associate Pastor to Reverend Jospeh Gulick at the Presbyterian Church in Idaho Falls, Idaho, so we packed up all our suitcases and moved there that spring.

First Presbyterian Church in Idaho Falls, Idaho.

Isaiah 49:1, 6

The LORD hath called me from the womb; from the bowels of my mother hath he made mention of my name.

I will also give thee for a light to the Gentiles, that thou mayest be my salvation unto the end of the earth.

Chapter 7 – Idaho Spud, Again!

We arrived in Idaho Falls, Idaho in the Spring of 1953. I was placed in the 4th grade according to my age in an elementary school nearby. I could barely keep up with the class and the teacher kindly placed me in a desk next to hers so that she could keep an eye on me! This was my 7th school since Kindergarten!!! Now you are beginning to understand why I cannot answer the question, "*Where did you grow up?*"

While he is not mentioned in the brief Presbyterian Church history I found on line, I learned that George Peacock was also instrumental in the beginnings of the Presbyterian church in Idaho Falls started in 1891.

Later, when they needed a larger building: "J.C. Fulton of Uniontown, Pennsylvania drew the plans for our present church. The design selected was in the Greek Classic style and set on a terrace. Ground was broken for the church on July 16, 1918, and the cornerstone was laid April 27, 1919. The dedication Service was held on Sunday April 11, 1920. With the depression of 1921 came a drop in church membership and a debt of $50,000.

Dr. Joseph Gulick came to serve the church in 1923 on a starvation wage, supplementing his income by teaching history at Idaho Falls High School. Between his leadership and the women of the church, who worked tirelessly to raise the money needed, the last payment was made on the mortgage just before the 50th Anniversary of the church. During regular services on Sunday May 18, 1941, the mortgage was burned."

By 1953, Dr. Joseph Gulick was long overdue for a sabbatical leave. So, while Reverend Harry Washburn took on the pastorate, the Gulick's left for about a year. We lived in their Arts and Crafts Style home next to the church. I walked over a mile to school each day crossing a vacant lot on the way and imagined that I was Laura Ingles Wilder in her "Little House on the Prairie!"

That Christmas we had a lovely tree tucked in the corner of Gulick's stairway going up to the second floor. On Christmas morning, John and I both wanted to turn on the Christmas lights at the same time. We dove under the tree from different sides and down came the tree sending ornaments everywhere!!! Dad was furious and took the tree, loaded it in the car with all the presents and took them to a family who had just lost their home in a fire and gave all of it to them. It was a very good Christmas after all!

For Easter, we got tiny chicks dyed various colors. We raised them in the back yard, eventually using our baby brother George's play pen to cage them on the grass and moving them around from time to time. However, when they appeared as our dinner on the 4th of July, I refused to eat them!

When the Gulick's returned, we were offered an Art Deco two story house painted green on 996 S. E. Emerson Ave. It has since been painted white.

The owners, the Marler's, went on a mission to Mexico for a year. So, we enjoyed living in their lovely home. The Kate Curley Park across the street was a great place to go and play, there were big swings that you could fly very high on! Monkey bars and much more to keep us all outside in the fresh air. We 3 kids really enjoyed it. I liked to lie down on a bench and look up into the trees and imagine that they were the roots stretching deep into the ground!

By that time, I was in 5th grade. The spelling bees were very hard for me since I had missed so much of the American system of learning phonics. I also had not learned "New Math." There was a radio program at that time called "Ozzie and Harriet", and I was teased about that when I even liked some boy in the class just a little bit: "Billy and Harriet sitting in a tree K I S S I N G."

The "Marler's house" as we referred to It, had a big driveway in back that adjoined the neighbor's driveway. That was owned by a Mormon family whose children had all grown up, and they were very kind to us kids. I had saved my very first nickel after we came back from Scotland and had been saving ever since to get a bicycle. Those kind neighbors told me there was an old bicycle with balloon tires hanging on a wall in the garage that I could have. But it needed a lot of help, so I took it to a bicycle shop, and got it restored with the money I had saved. Then I painted it a bright Fiesta Yellow! I had wanted roller skates before that, so I always wanted to be on the move somehow!

One day I had ridden my yellow bike to the church and parked it outside. When I went out, it was gone, and English bike with thin tires was in its place! Eventually the police found the yellow bike out on the edge of town in a store's parking lot, and it had been run over. Sad day for me for sure.

On the first floor of the Marler's house was a large glass porch on one side. When we all 3 got Mumps and then Chicken pox, we all had to be isolated out on the porch. My brother John remembers being out there with measles, too. In those days we just passed things around!

When the Marler's returned from their mission, we moved 2 houses down the street to the house where the Johnson's had lived with their 7 sons! It had a nice backyard with a rock fountain and a pond in the front part of it where John and George used to play with their army figurines.

Mom had long wanted a classic Concert Harp. She finally bought one from a lady in Salt Lake City. We drove down to get it. The lady called me "Hat" and old fashioned nickname for Harriet. I did not like it at all! Sometime after that mom also got a grand piano. She taught me how to play the piano and gave piano lessons to students in town. I was the babysitter for my 2 brothers when she gave lessons, so I did not go too far with my piano lessons.

In the fall of 1954, I went into 6th grade. Our teacher had such a wonderful way of bringing out creativity in her students. We did many fun craft projects. One of the boys liked to write plays and the teacher would let a group of us go into a broom closet and practice his plays while she read stories to the class right after lunch. One of the plays was "Prinderalla and the Since" and we had to say everything backward that way. I was the mother and someone loaned me their glasses and as I walked down the aisle toward the front the correction in the lenses was a magnification so they made it very hard for me to walk. By the end of the year, I was certain I wanted to be a 6th grade teacher!

In 1955, I went into 7th grade. When the first frost hit in early October, all the older kids were let out of school to go out in the fields and pick potatoes. We were taken by the local farmers to the spot where we would work. The men drove us all out to the drop off point were swearing up a storm the whole way!

The two girls and I were so shocked by all the bad language that we had to just say everything we had just heard to get it out of our systems! Talk about turning the air blue!!! We had to fill two large wire baskets with potatoes and then pour them into a gunny sack which we stood up so that the farmers could come along the rows and toss them on to their flatbed trucks. There were also workers from Mexico who picked very fast. We were paid by the bag. Eventually, more mechanized ways were invented, and our labor was no longer needed. I used my money at Christmas to buy my parents a new set of Melmac dishes for everyday use.

In the summer we had Vacation Bible School in the church. One of the craft projects was to make puppets which we stuffed with old nylon stockings. I had a bunch of stockings in my hand and a boy came along with a large pair of scissors and thinking he would help by cutting them up. Hr lunged into my bunch and cut my middle finger of my left hand! It was a large cut and did not heal well, so that scar is there to this day! As part of our confirmation class, we were each called into my father's office and asked, "Do you believe in Jesus as your Lord and Savior?" I was stunned that he would even ask and said "Of course!" I had heard about Jesus all my life. It was a no brainer. I truly asked Jesus into my life about 30 years later!

My father's sister, Dorothea Horbach, lived in Southern California, and he took us one winter to see her. Highway 89 was the way one traveled south from Idaho, through Utah and then Nevada into the Los Angeles basin. We visited Bryce Canyon National Park, and I was totally in awe of the amazing red rock formations! Then as we headed south and neared the turn off to go into Zion National Park, brother John got car sick, and mom decided that we would not go there on that windy road. So, we traveled south and turned west on Highway 89A which went around the base of Zion National Park. From one point, I could see the dramatic sandstone formations from a distance. My heart broke!!! I knew that I had missed something special!!! That thought stayed with me for many years.

When my dad grew up in Hollywood in the 1930's he helped to decorate the floats for the Rose Bowl Parade each year by volunteering for Isabella Coleman who was an expert float designer. When we arrived that December, he took us to her Quonset building where she built her floats each year. We helped put orchids on the float based on a theme from the Italian Opera "Aida." The Rose Parade was a grand event and became a yearly family tradition to either attend or watch it on Television!

In the fall of 1956, I entered O. E. Bell Junior High which was kitty corner across the street from the church. It finally became apparent that I had difficulty reading and I was sent to a reading specialist after school. She sat me down to a machine that moved a bar down the page to guide me to keep focused on what I was reading. It was many years later as an adult that I finally understood that I was dyslexic. It was an unknown challenge. This became more evident when I took Geometry. I loved all the fun shapes, but the math was a great mystery to me. Mr. Popovich was very patient with me working after school so that I could finally get a "C" in the class.

In that Junior High, we were required to take Physical Education classes. However, because of my head injury, I was reticent to stand on my head or do anything physical. I opted out to take Orchestra Class instead. I have no idea how I came to play the cello! I was to play it for the next five years. I also sang in the School Chorus and always enjoyed music.

Also in the fall of 1957, I signed up for an Art class. The first day, the teacher told us to take a pencil and draw lines anyway we wanted. I had a lot of fun drawing circles and ovals all over the page. Then we were to color it in and bring it back the next day. I really enjoyed the exercise. We all turned in our work. When it came time to hand the graded papers back, the teacher threw mine in the round waste basket beside his desk, because I did not put my name on it! I was so incensed that I walked out of the classroom and never went back to Art classes for the next 4 years. I have often wondered what my life would have been like if he had given me another chance?

Instead, I signed up for a Drama class and had a lot of fun acting plays on the big stage.

That Christmas, we took another trip to California to visit my mother's parents who had by then sold their ranch in Auburn and moved to the Monterey Bay area. We saw my Aunt Marion in a play there about the English ambassador Disraeli. He was instrumental in building the Suez Canal. For an assignment In the spring of 1958, I did a monologue as Disraeli talking on the phone about building the canal.

However, our lives were soon to change as our father had been accepted as the pastor of the Presbyterian Church in Sheridan, Wyoming! (I was up to 8 schools by then, FYI.)

Psalm 18 – King James Version

1. I will love Thee, O Lord, my strength.

2. The Lord is my rock, and my fortress, and my deliverer; my God, my strength, in whom I will trust; my buckler, and the horn of my salvation, and my high tower.

3. I will call upon the Lord, who is worthy to be praised: so shall I be saved from mine enemies.

4. The sorrows of death compassed me, and the floods of ungodly men made me afraid.

5. The sorrows of hell compassed me about: the snares of death prevented me.

6. In my distress I called upon the Lord and cried unto my God: He heard my voice out of His temple, and my cry came before him, even into His ears.

Chapter 8 – Being a Preacher's Kid in the 50's and 60's

When I learned that we were moving to Sheridan, Wyoming in the summer of 1958 thoughts of cowboys tying up their horses to a wooden hitching post on Main Street sprung to my mind. Somehow the Western movies had implanted this idea of Wyoming in my consciousness and I fully expected this to be the case. We were moving east to go to "the West!"

When we arrived in Sheridan, their Main Street was as civilized as any other small town in the west, and while they did have a rodeo, there were no horses on the paved streets!

The original brick Presbyterian Church building where we served from 1958 to 1965, was taken down in the 1970's, and the stained glass windows shown here below, were transported to the new building. I believe it was here in the original church that I truly fell in love with stained glass!

The first place we lived in was a lady's home on the side of a hill. We had the lower part of her 3 story older home. Eventually we moved to a Doctor's house and lived there on Thurmond Ave the rest of the time Dad had the pastorate in Sheridan. My route to school involved walking down the hill, across the valley floor, through the city park and up another hill to the High School. Perhaps two to three miles each way.

I continued to play the cello through the 12th grade. I took lessons from a gentleman near the school. He helped me purchase a three quarter sized cello because I was too small to play a full sized one. We had contests in the orchestra class to see who would sit in the "first chair." There were two brothers who were bigger and better than I was, so I never got to be "first chair." We did play with the All State High School Orchestra and made a recording of our performance. I really enjoyed singing in the High School Chorus and Church Choir.

In those days, in order to go on to college, which was always an assumption I made, we were required to take two foreign languages. First, I studied Latin for two years and then German for two years, decisions I never regretted, although they were both challenging. One day in Latin class in our text book we were assigned to translate the first chapter of the book of John in the Bible. This is a snap, I thought, as I could translate it directly using a Bible. Sad to say, I looked for the easy way to get things done, and although it is one of my favorite verses today, the Truth did not sink into my soul then. I took the required year of Typing to graduate and am I so grateful that I can touch type to this day, though not very speedily!

As a freshman entering a new High School, I became painfully aware that I knew no one and had to develop some friendships with girls that were not "IN," since most of the students had lived there all their lives, so being accepted was hardly an option. My first attempt to be "popular" was to take several girls to the drugstore on Main Street after school and treat them to "Cherry Cokes." I charged the drinks to my parents' account. When this became known by Mom and Dad, the practice was immediately stopped.

Eventually I had three girlfriends. The first I met each morning, and we walked to school together. She had some infirmities, so her progress up the last hill was always slow. Then a high school boy joined us as we walked. The whole community was totally shocked when we learned that he had taken her out in a field one Saturday and murdered her!!! Sigh…

The other two girls were very intelligent, and we chummed around quite a lot. One went on to the University of Wyoming and got her degree in Pharmacy. The other planned to be an engineer. She wanted to take a trigonometry class but was denied because she was a girl! We went to bat for her and thankfully she was admitted into the class!

A brief membership in the Girl Scouts was quickly ended when my father found me a job each day after school being a "Candy Striper" delivering dinner trays at the local Hospital. So, for the rest of my High School time I served meals to the patients and then picked up the trays and then washed the dishes five days a week. Hence, I did not eat dinners very often with my family and really did not get to know my brothers as they grew up.

In the summers my Dad found me a position at the local "Coil Factory" making electrical resistors as a full time job with older women who were tired but had to work. I learned how to solder the wires to the stems after the ladies wound the coils and also did the color coding. We worked for Westinghouse and other technical companies. It was tedious work, so to amuse myself I decorated the sides of the wooden carrying trays to pass away my boring hours. It was always about saving money for me to go to college.

Every Saturday my father printed up the Bulletins for the Sunday Service, and I folded them, perhaps 100. I was expected to mow the grass with a power mower on the sloped lawn by the church which was sometimes quite difficult. I learned how to operate the buffer to polish the floors in the Fellowship Hall. All of this was gratis labor.

My brother, John, had a newspaper route in the neighborhood. I would help him fold the papers, especially the Sunday Edition, and sometimes helped him deliver them in snowy weather walking beside his bicycle with the heavy canvas bags full of newspapers on the handlebars.

While I was perhaps a better than average student, " A's" were not a highlight of my grades. My favorite class of all was Senior English. Miss Waggner was known to be a strict teacher. For my special project, I drew a map of Shakespear's London, free hand, on a large piece of paper, and then also drew it on a white sheet that could be used as a tablecloth. I got an A! This was not my first map. I had drawn the continent of South America free hand when I was 4th grade in Sausalito, and later I did a Salt, Water and Flour map of Russia in Junior High in Idaho Falls. Maps have been in my life ever since I drew a map of the USA after we drove back across the country in 1952.

In 1950's and early 1960's, women basically had three career choices. They were expected to become a nurse, a schoolteacher, or a secretary. Since the 6th grade, when Miss Eide inspired her class into many realms of creativity, I thought I wanted to be an Elementary school teacher. When I graduated from Sheridan High School in June of 1961, I received a $400 scholarship to Major in Education.

In the fall of 1961, for my freshman year, I attended Sheridan Junior College. Dad found a house around the corner for me to live in while the owners went south for the winter. Because I was studying Education, I took an Art Class. Also, I took another year of German to fulfill the requirement to get a Bachelor of Arts degree. I truly excelled in my Art class and took on each assignment with vigor. I got "A's" both semesters.

As a Presbyterian minister's daughter, I privately assumed that people at our church expected me to go to Hastings College in Hastings, Nebraska, a Presbyterian Church College. For my sophomore year I was accepted there and got a $100 Scholarship for being a minister's daughter. My mother, meanwhile, foreseeing my College tuitions and financial needs, had returned to College and got training in Special Education so she could teach to help pay my way.

In the fall of 1962, I boarded the train and traveled to Grand Island, Nebraska, arriving late at night. Someone met me and drove me south 30 miles to the campus in Hastings and left me at the girls dormitory, Clark Hall. I was assigned a very small room barely big enough for a bed and dresser with a closet across the hall and a bathroom around the corner that I shared with another girl in the very old three story house that had been converted into living spaces for about 30 girls.

This was my first time to be totally on my own, and again not knowing anyone, I was very lonely. I did have a boyfriend going to Medical school in the Chicago area, and he would call me occasionally on the pay phone down the hall. Again, I took an art class because I was going to be a teacher. The class was Beginning Drawing. We learned how to shade with a pencil. One day the instructor hung a white bed sheet up on the wall with many wrinkles and folds in it and said, "Draw it!" Because I had a lot of time on my hands, I spent many hours drawing it! We were also required to do our own drawings in a sketch book and eventually my drawings looked quite realistic.

By mid-November, I was really feeling the depths of my loneliness and went to the clinic on campus with pain that could not be attributed to anything at all. Fortunately, a girl invited me to her home for Thanksgiving in Omaha, Nebraska. That visit helped me a lot. I had an acquaintance in Florida who paid for my train ticket to come and visit her at Christmas, and I also got to see my Aunt Gertrude there.

The land around Hastings was relatively flat compared with the mountainous terrain in Wyoming, and I was still rather depressed, so my grandfather painted me a picture of some mountains to cheer me up.

The classes required for Elementary Education were not inspiring me at all and by the second semester I knew I had to change majors. Early in the spring I sat down on my bed to study the catalogue from the University of Wyoming in Laramie. That school always had a reputation of being a "Party School." I had avoided going there, yet sigh….I had to make a change. Hastings was quite an expensive school, and even though I had a part time job in the Library, as I had also done at Sheridan Junior College, I knew that it was a financial burden on my Mom. I opened the catalogue, and the first section was "Anthropology." I truly had never heard the word before!!! However, they offered a $100 Scholarship to a Junior. I sent off for the application and eventually I was awarded that scholarship. I learned that Anthropology meant "The Study of Man." This would be a real eye opening to one who had led a rather sheltered life! Before I left I broke up with my boyfriend, although we remained friends over the years, and I got a haircut!

Later in the spring, the art instructor hung one of my drawings in the hallway on exhibit with other Art students. He gave me "B's" both semesters. However, then he came to me and told me that he had gone to the board, and they offered me a small scholarship in Art for the next year! This was totally unexpected and very kind of him to do so. I had to decline since I had already made plans to go to Laramie. However, his gesture was a real validation to me of my artwork for the rest of my life!

John 1: 1 – 4 In the beginning was the Word, and the Word was with God, and the Word was God. The same was in the beginning with God. All things were made by Him; and without Him was not anything made that was made. In Him was life; and the life was the light of men. And the light shineth in the darkness, and the darkness comprehended it not.

Chapter 9 – Ragtime Cowboy Joe

In response to the sudden increase in children now called the "Boomer generation" the administration for the University of Wyoming, built two large 6 story dormitory towers at the east end of the campus, Hill Hall and Crane Hall with a large cafeteria between them. I was assigned a room on the 6th floor of Hill Hall facing west and had a marvelous view of the Snowy Range beyond Laramie. The large steamer trunk that had been my parents when they married, later taken to Scotland and back, and then with me to Hastings and back, once again was the logical way to transport my clothes and possessions in those days!

My room had two twin beds on either side of the windows. Cherry Rush was my roommate, my first ever roommate. We eventually called our room "Chariot!" and put that label on the outside of the door. We were both artistic souls and got along well in the beginning. "Ragtime Cowboy Joe" was the theme song for the University of Wyoming Sports events, but I never went to any!

Once settled in, I walked over half a mile onto the main part of the campus to the Anthropology department located in the large imposing sandstone Science building. I walked up to the second floor and found the office of Dr. William Mulloy, the head of the department. His desk was covered with many papers and as we talked, I noted some illustrations he had prepared for a paper he was planning to publish about his work on Easter Island with Thor Heyerdahl. I mentioned that I could do illustrations like those, and he hired me on the spot for a dollar an hour to work for the department.

One of my required classes was Sociology. It was a real eye opener to learn about other societies and cultures around the world. Up to that time, I had lived a rather sheltered life. One of my classmates was Luanne. She was born with Cerebral Palsy, and the doctors did not give the parents much hope for her development. However, Luanne was determined to walk and did so at the age of 4. She went to school and eventually junior college in Rawlins, Wyoming. I do not know how old she was when we met, and by then she had her own apartment, was working at Coe Library on campus, had a keyboard she loved to play on and even did some artwork! Her back was contorted, and she walked with a limp and spoke with a slur. The Sociology teacher did not cut her any slack when it came to taking tests. She was very frustrated because she could not take notes quickly. Finally, I got her a tape recorder so she could listen to the lecture when she got home and eventually, she got a passing grade! She did get her degree and worked at the library for many years.

I enrolled in an art class every semester when I could, and often got credit for the work I did in Dr. Mulloy's laboratory. Once he gave me a slide of the hillside where he had done an excavation with Thor Heyerdahl. I carefully traced the image and began to paint it. The next morning, Dr. Mulloy came in and said, that hillside it a half inch off, move it! So, I did!!! I cataloged of artifacts he had collected in the South Pacific and illustrated some of them. The most challenging object was a wooden sword lined with shark's teeth on both sides. I learned that most of the things in museums and collections are never seen by the public. I was privileged to experience the back room!

Linguistics was another class I was required to take. For my paper, I recorded the Basque shepherds who lived in Buffalo, Wyoming just south of Sheridan and then got recordings from Basque men who lived in Southern California and compared how they spoke. That was as close to doing a "research paper" in the field as I ever came!

By late fall, my roommate, Cherry was coming in later and later at night and drinking a lot. This Dormitory did not have regulated hours. Then her boyfriend broke up with her. She was devastated! Her drinking got even worse. She said she wanted to die if he did not take her back! Finally, I went to the dorm supervisor and asked for another roommate. It was arranged and Cherry went home on a wintery weekend to get things she needed to move into another room. I learned later that she was in a Volkswagen bug in the back seat.

On a long stretch of the highway going west they hit a ground blizzard which is just about six feet high with zero visibility! A large sedan was coming from the opposite direction, lost control and slammed into the Volkswagen. There was a chain reaction and over two dozen cars slid off the road. I met someone years later who was involved in the medical response team. He told me that they spent a lot of time pulling the glass fragments out of Cherry's body. Meanwhile, the Volkswagen driver died. Cherry was sped to the emergency room in Cheyenne. She lived for about 2 weeks on life support. Then one morning as I was walking down a hall to go to a class, I suddenly felt her spirit. It was her joyous self. I later learned that she had passed at that time. I felt very guilty and thought I was responsible for her death. It was many years before I realized it was not my fault.

There was a Presbyterian Church just off campus with a pastor for college students. Al Line was full of ideas on how to engage with the youth. He went with the times and began running a coffee house in the church fellowship hall a couple of nights a week. I helped to serve expresso in fancy cups he had purchased in San Francisco. We felt like we were part of the "60's" movement and even sang "We shall overcome" from the civil rights movement for racial equality. Al organized a trip for some of us to go to the University in Ohio to a youth rally at Christmas time. We sang that song with our arms crossed and holding hands with 5000 other students honoring the inspiration that Martin Luther King brought to the entire country.

In June of 1964, I was given a room at Knight Hall which was right on campus. I was a "senior resident," and that paid for my room. I worked for Miss Meiler, the Head of the girls' dorm who had very strict rules about hours. I worked in the office and assisted her in counting money each day. We had to have all the bills facing the same way and she would count it to me and then I would count it to her and then she would count it to me a third time! I typed for her with 5 copies and carbon paper between each page. Any mistakes, and I made them often, had to be corrected with a heavy eraser page by page! Later, I also got room and board and a nice room with a bathroom all my own when one of the girls with the next position up came back too late one night and snuck in a window and got caught!

My memories of the misery of Geometry in Junior High School gave me impetus to take Statistics in the Summer session because the class time would be shorter! It was required for my Major in Anthropology. Frankly, aside from the Bell Shaped curve of the normal distribution of the probability of things happening, I did not understand any of it. When the tests were handed out, I simply gave random answers in the hopes that I would be right some of the time! I got a "C" in the class.

As I came to the end of my senior year, my father advised me to stay on and get my BA in Education because I would have to support myself eventually. So, I continued in the summer of 1966 and did Student teaching that fall and got a BA in Education in January of 1966. I was also encouraged to do graduate work in Anthropology, so I applied to the San Francisco State College in January of 1966.

Are you counting? That is 13 Schools in 17 years! Roots??? What are Roots?!!!

Isaiah 41:10 Fear thou not; for I *am* with thee: be not dismayed; for I *am* thy God: I will strengthen thee; yea, I will help thee; yea, I will uphold thee with the right hand of my righteousness.

Graduated from the University of Wyoming – BA in anthropology 1965, and a BA Education January 1966

Chapter 10 – Peace Corps

During his inaugural address in January of 1961, J. F. Kennedy helped to create the Peace Corps by saying ***"And so, my fellow Americans: ask not what your country can do for you—ask what you can do for your country."*** JFK electrified the idealism in young Americans as he continued to inspire many people during his presidency.

I was one of them. I signed up to join the Peace Corps as soon as it was created and was assigned a 5 digit enrollment number. Then I was advised to complete my degree before going further. In my senior year at Wyoming, the Peace Corps had all four of my wisdom teeth pulled! Not a fun time. When I enrolled in Graduate school at San Francisco State College, I was put into a Peace Corps program specifically designed for students who would attend Graduate school for a year, then get training in the summer and return to finish their graduate degree before serving in the Peace Corps. .

My parents moved to San Francisco from Wyoming early January of 1965. Dad got a pastorate at the Ingleside Presbyterian Church on Ocean Avenue. Their manse was provided up the hill nearby. My mother was offered a job teaching Special Education in San Francisco Schools within 24 hours of their arrival! She also enrolled at San Francisco State College to continue her studies. Consequently, our college records were right next to each other in the Registrar's office.

After graduation with my second Bachelor's Degree, early in January of 1966, I traveled west putting my steamer trunk and bicycle on the train in Laramie and arriving the next day in Oakland, California. To begin my graduate work, I signed up for a Sociology class at San Francisco State College and then registered with the San Francisco Board of Education as a substitute teacher at Junior High and High Schools I attended the Sociology class. On the other days I substituted at the school the Board told me to go to each morning. My father often took me to the that school and then I rode public transportation home. I enjoyed seeing many parts of "The City" that way.

At midterm, I was required to write a Sociology paper on an assigned subject and when I got the paper back, I was quite disturbed. I went to the teacher after the class and asked about his marks. He had written a "B" at first and he told me that after he had read everyone's papers, he said my work was not as good as others and marked it down to a "C." I was furious! I marched out and withdrew from the class! Deep in my heart I knew that I was not a scholar!

Now that I was no longer in Graduate School I asked around campus to contact someone in the Peace Corps, but no one had an answer. I was advised to go to the place that I was assigned to. So, in June, I flew into O'Hare Airport in Chicago and was taken to Northern Illinois University campus in DeKalb. There were three of us named Harriet! Most unusual. The instructors from Thailand had a hard time saying "H," so we were always amused.

The program was "Teaching English As a Foreign Language," TEFEL classes started, and we were taught to speak Thai and learned about Thai food and how to greet people properly. I began to ask about my situation, and finally after two weeks, a Psychiatrist interviewed me and asked me what I wanted to do in my life. I told him, "just tell me what to do and I will do it! " That apparently was not the answer he wanted, and he removed me from the Peace Corps. They sent me back to Chicago to fly home.

I visited my ex-boyfriend and his wife there for a few days. She took me to Marshal Fields, and I bought a hooked rug kit and then I went home. As we flew over the southern part of Utah I looked down on all the erosion and geology below, I was totally amazed by the scenery.

My father promptly sent me off to be a counselor at a Church camp for a week, and to another for the next week. Then I took the Greyhound bus down Skyline Drive from San Francisco to my grandparents' house near Santa Cruz.

As we passed by the San Lorenzo School District office, I took note of it, After I arrived at my grandparents' home and got settled in, I called the School District office and was offered a job team teaching 5th grade. In those days, you could walk in the door and get a job even mid-summer!!!

Jeremiah 29: 11 – 12 For I know the thoughts that I think toward you, saith the Lord, thoughts of peace, and not of evil, to give you an expected and. Then shall you call upon me, and you shall go and pray unto me, and I will harken unto you.

Chapter 11 – Really on my own!

At long last it was really time for me to buy a car, a red 1961 Volkswagen Beetle! I paid $400 and set off down Highway 1 from my parent's home in San Francisco to the small town of Felton in the Redwoods above Santa Cruz. I had found an apartment. My roommate was Verna, another first time Elementary teacher who taught in Ben Lomond further up Highway 9. I was in her wedding the following spring.

In the fall of 1965, I ultimately spent the $400 education scholarship I received when I graduated from High School on a set of pots and pans, a set of dishes and a set of silverware, so I was all ready for my new life on my own!

The concept of "Team Teaching" had just been introduced at San Lorenzo Elementary School. 5th grade was the first class to implement that concept in the fall of 1966. Three adjoining rooms were remodeled. The Math room was fitted with a large, long window to afford visibility into the center room, which was mine. The wall on the other side was converted to folding doors so that, when necessary, those two rooms could be opened up and all 105 students could bring in their chairs and sit in the enlarged space.

Since I knew ABSOUTELY nothing about teaching 5th grade, I was assigned the middle range students, and the other two teachers took on the higher and lower needs kids. In general, it all went well as the two experienced teachers managed everything . We were teaching New Math, and I often turned to Brenda, a small girl who understood it all and she showed me in the back of the book how to proceed!!!

We had a nice playground area and one day when I was wearing a pair of wooden shoes called "Clogs," I misjudged the height of an overhead bar, and ran right into it giving myself whiplash. The first, I might add in the next few years. I did not wear a collar, but recovery was a slow process.

With all the uncertainty of the new job I had a lot of stress and my ears started ringing. I was diagnosed with Meniere's disease. I had it earlier when I was at Wyoming, but this time it was much worse For part of the diagnosis, the doctor poured ice water in my ears, which was very painful! The ringing has persisted for the rest of my life.

Lastly, I developed a boil on my chest. I went to my grandmother's doctor who lanced it, and while I lay down resting afterwards, he made a pass at me!!! I was very startled and rebuffed him immediately! He prescribed "The Pill" so that the boil would not come back! Thus, I was launched into the "60's" whether I wanted to or not!

My grandparents lived about 20 miles away in a retirement community in Scotts Valley and I often enjoyed visiting them. George Young, my grandfather, had taken up oil painting when they retired in the 1950's and by this time he was a very accomplished artist. My mother asked him to do a large painting of the nearby redwoods and I prize his painting to this day.

I had taken a Chinese Brush Painting class and after instructing the techniques in the 5th grade, several teachers invited me to teach it in their grades. This was followed by a number of other art classes which I gave to various grades over the course of the year.

One day in April, Mr. Evans, the principal, called me into his office and kindly explained that they would not be rehiring me. Sigh… well I was shocked to say the least. Later in the teachers' lounge, one of the 4th grade teacher suggested that I apply for a Junior High Art position that was open at her daughter's school up in Tahoe. I applied to the Tahoe Truckee School district, not knowing that her daughter taught on the South Shore, in the El Dorado School District, and got a job teaching High School Art in Truckee, California!

As I was driving home for the summer, the red Volkswagen "threw a rod!" I went to a used car dealer in San Francisco and traded it in for a 1964 white VW for $600. Then I spent the summer taking Art classes at San Francisco State College to prepare me for my next teaching adventure.

II Corinthians 12: 8-9 I besought the Lord thrice, that it might depart from me. And he said unto me, "My grace is sufficient for thee: for my strength is made perfect in weakness." Most gladly therefore will I rather glory in my infirmities that the power of Christ may rest upon me.

Chapter 12 – On to the Mountains

The Sierra Nevada Mountain range was named by early Spanish explorers. The "Snowy Mountains" are a formidable granite range along the eastern border of California. The jagged mountain range was a great challenge to early pioneers coming west in search of a better life and GOLD in the mid 1800's!

The Donner Party left Springfield, Illinois in April of 1846, but took the "Hastings Cutoff" in Wyoming, which turned out to be not as favorable as they had hoped. They arrived late in October at a small glacial lake on the east side of the mountains just as snow began to fall. They were forced to winter there and only 45 people of the original 89 members of the party survived getting to Sacramento, California the following spring. At Donner State Park located at the east end of Donner Lake is the 22 feet high stone base for the Bronze monument dedicated to the pioneers indicating the depth of the snow that winter where they camped.

By 1863, the town was established as a staging place for the pioneers before they attempted the steep granite grades ahead. The town was named Truckee in honor of the local friendly Paiute Chief.

In 1868 –1869, the Central Pacific Railroad Company was constructing the west end of the Transcontinental Railroad. As they worked their way east they bored tunnels at the summit and then descended the steep grade on the south side of Donner Lake.

In 1895, newspaper man and lawyer, C.F. McGlashan created an Ice Carnival in Truckee to attract tourists to the area. The Ice Palace was the size of a football field right in the middle of town! Snow sculptures, ice skating rink, sled dogs and skiing events all helped to begin the winter sports industry for the whole area.

By the early 1950's Walter Jalene and his wife had settled on the southeast side of Donner Lake next to Donner State Park. Because of the heavy snow they built an "A" frame house to live in and raise their family and then built two more houses next to it as rentals for tourists in the summer and to serve as housing for school faculty in the winters.

My parents drove our family west in the summer of 1952 on the "Lincoln Highway." Highway 40 was the first highway to be constructed all the way across the United States! I remember being enchanted by the "A" frame houses on Donner Lake. The road up to Donner Pass was quite steep and had many deep hairpin turns.

In 1960, the Olympics were held in Squaw Valley northeast of Lake Tahoe. Interstate 80 was constructed to accommodate the tourists coming to attend the Olympics. The new freeway rose above Donner Lake on the north side with easier curves up over Emigrant Pass.

In my day, a girl was expected to be married by the time she graduated from college. With that in mind, Miss Meiler, director of Knight Hall in Laramie, came to me one day in the summer of 1966 and gave me a men's gold wedding ring that someone had left in the Dorm. When I showed it to my boyfriend, he broke up with me immediately! So, I proceeded out into the world unmarried and got a teaching job to support myself as my father had predicted.

After teaching 5th Grade in Felton for one year, I lived with my parents in San Francisco In the summer of 1967. I attended two art classes at SFSC, and then went to a church camp as a counselor for a week. My boyfriend, Richard, was a counselor there, too. We had been seeing each other for a couple of months. He proposed there at camp and I was in "7th heaven!" When we got back home, we went to Sausalito and had a square gold wedding ring made that had holes on the 3 sides. We continued to communicate all fall when I went to Truckee to teach. He came up for Thanksgiving and sat me down and said that after many sessions with his therapist, he decided that he was a "homosexual," so we ended it all right then. The ring was never that comfortable anyway!

Tahoe-Truckee High School was a long modern two story building with glass windows all along the front. The main entry was in the middle. One hall went to the right, and the library was on the right side and then the Home Ec. room and across from them was my art class room, at the end of the hall were double doors to the outside. The next building had the woodshop and auto shop.

Because I had never been in a High School Art class, I had to "Punt!" We did ceramics, firing them in the large upright kiln that I asked the school to order, copper enameling, various creative activities using found objects, and a class for the School Yearbook.

A nice reflex camera was furnished for the Yearbook photos. I loved it because it was the same type of camera my grandmother used for her black and white photography. The Yearbook man supplied the film and printed very good images for the students to use in the publication.

My modified "A" frame house on Donner Lake I rented from the Jalene family was spacious with a lovely big fireplace. 2 other teachers lived upstairs and another in the next unit. It was a nice arrangement for all of us. Sometimes I would ride my bicycle over to the other side of the lake through Donner State Park. Once I rode it all the way around through the trees beyond the park and up to the head of the lake which was about 5 miles long and then back on the Highway.

One day when the lake was frozen, I even walked all the way across it and back to a friend's house. She was quite distressed as the ice was known to be unstable around the edges, but I had no problems because I remembered that in the early days, pioneers would cut out blocks of ice at the east end of the lake for refrigeration!

The Librarian, Roy Baker, had a small hotel "San Souci" on the lake further along. Late in the fall he asked me to be a member of a committee he was forming to begin the Truckee-Donner Historical Society. The Park Ranger, Bert torgerson, was on the committee and we were joined by several interested people from the area. By the following spring we had gotten the Articles of Incorporation written. I was the Corresponding Secretary.

Recently I contacted the current president, and he found copy of a letter I had typed in June of 1968! The organization has now created a museum in the Railroad Station and the first Jail is also open to the public. 55 years later, the Truckee-Donner Historical Society is going strong.

In the fall of 1967, a student told me about a travel group to Europe for High School students. I drove her down to Sacramento to a meeting of the American Institute for Foreign Studies. The presenter, Ilsa Sternberger, explained that a teacher had to assemble at least 11 - 12 students to take on a 6 week tour and that would pay the teacher's way over and back. Unfortunately, we just did not have that kind of interest in AIFS in Truckee, so I thought that was the end of it.

SNOW came in volumes, and we shoveled and shoveled snow off our parking area and into the lake. It was a real winter experience! I got a job on Saturdays attaching lift tickets on the zippers of skier's jacket at the Squaw Valley Ski Resort. Then I could go skiing in the afternoon for free. I had skied a little bit in Wyoming, but just enough to stay upright!!! I liked riding the chair lift and enjoying the scenery! Once I followed an instructor all the way to the top and then had to get down to the bottom of the run, that was the last time I wanted to ski!

After school was over at the end of May 1968, I went home to my parent's house in San Francisco. A week later the phone rang, and it was Ilsa. Did I have a passport? Could I get one soon? A teacher who had created an AIFS group to Aberdeen, Scotland, was unable to go and if I got things in order, I could be the chaperone at the end of June!

I got things ready, flew to London with the group, and stayed in London for a few days and then took the train to Edinburgh, Scotland where I had lived as a child. It was wonderful to be there again and see Princess Street and Edinburgh Castle. Then we traveled north along the coast to the University of Aberdeen for a 4 week stay! I enjoyed the Scottish countryside, visited the fish market, took a bus to see villages up the coast, and learned how to drink good Scottish whiskey!

Then we went to Paris taking a ferry across the English Channel. Paris has such a special feel. I enjoyed exploring it and seeing Versailles, then we flew back to San Francisco.

In the fall of 1968, I returned to the same apartment. The second year of teaching was a bit easier than the first. Some of the high school students who were not in my class wanted to be there anyway, so I would write a pass from their study hall to come in for an hour. I had a fast and firm rule for all my classes, either you are doing what I assign, or you are doing a project we have agreed on. Either way, you will be doing something creative! I let them play music on the radio which made everyone happy!

In October, I took an art teacher's workshop at Clear Lake, California, about 3 hours away. The project was to cover someone with wet white plaster of Paris strips that were used to make a plaster cast for a broken bone. I volunteered and wore a dress I did not want anymore. I lay on a table with my arms folded and my legs crossed. The other art teachers totally covered me with plaster of Paris strips from my neck to my toes and just to the table on both sides of my dress. Then someone cut off my dress, and I got out of it! Later we learned how to do a head, putting straws in my nose, and again just going to the sides of my face. When I got home, I painted the figure with a green dress and flesh colored arms and legs. Then we attached the head and put a green dustmop on top for hair! I leaned it up against my office doorway. Some people actually came and started talking to it before they realized what it was!

One student wanted me to do her, so we covered her seated in a chair, and then later did her head and attached it afterwards. A very small young boy wanted us to cover him, so he got down on his side and leaned his head on his hand with knee bent and the other leg extended. The students had fun doing these casts, however when it came time to cut him out, I discovered they had gone all the way around his arm and since he was very small, I had a real challenge cutting him out of it with wire snips! Later in the winter, the girl we did seated, was getting off the school bus one morning and was struck and killed, cutting off her head. That was a very sad day for all of us!

In February, of 1969, I was recruited to help with timing high school ski races at Boreal Ridge Ski Resort on Donner Pass. We rode way up to the top on the lift, which was my favorite thing to do and view all the mountain scenery, but after the race was over, we were left on our own to get all the way down the hill. Since we had clipboards for the score keeping, I finally sat down on mine and skidded down the hill, reactivating my whiplash!

On trip that spring to see my parents, I threw a rod in the white Volkswagen, and I drifted into a dealership in Sacramento and purchased a brand new green 1969 VW beetle with automatic shift! No more gear crunching! And it was a lot easier on my neck as well!

1968 - 1969 was a very heavy snow winter. We had 6 feet of snow followed by another 6 feet of snow. We shoveled snow off our parking area into the lake until we ran out of places to put it. Some of the students were bussed from the North Shore of Lake Tahoe to come to school, so when the weather was heavy and the roads were impassable, we had to cancel school. All total we had 8 snow days that year!!

This was the "60's" and more and more of the student's art reflected the psychedelic forms! The yearbook committee dedicated their entire 1969 publication to this endeavor, and it was quite colorful!

My classes room grew more and more popular, and students even started forging my signature on pass slips. Eventually in the spring, the principal informed me that no more passes were to be issued and I was not rehired. I felt like I had been stabbed in the heart! I just shut down everything and we just watched movies about art for the last six weeks.

The Librarian, Roy Baker, told me later that he had never seen so much productivity in the art class as the two years I was there which is very gratifying to remember now.

That Spring while visiting my friend, Ilsa, in San Francisco, she asked me what I saw for my future. All I could see was "White!" So knew I needed to move on! There was an ad in the newspaper for students and teachers to travel on charter flights Europe "one way" from San Francisco to London for $99. I bought a one way ticket to depart early in September of 1969. In those days, many students were traveling to Europe and staying in Youth Hostels and living very reasonably.

While I was not a "Hippie," I was inspired by the book "On the Loose" published in late 1968, written by two brothers traveling in the West and enjoying the wilderness.

At the end of May 1969, I took my bicycle and drove my green beetle to San Francisco for the summer. After a week or so, the phone rang, and Ilsa asked me "are you sitting down?" Then she told me that another teacher suddenly had to cancel and did I want to take a group to London. The answer was easy.

My parents had gotten inspired with the AIFS concept and mom had recruited a group to go to Israel that year. They left just before I did. My brother, John, was in the Army in the Vietnam War and had just been transferred to Okinawa. He was serving as a chaplain's assistant. His Chaplain got permission for John to join them in Jerusalem. Flying east, he arrived in San Francisco just in time to board my flight to New York and then hitched various rides and flew on to be with them.

This AIFS group was studying at the Royal Academy of Music in London for a month. We lived in the University of London dormitory right across the street from the Post Office Tower. We traveled to Stonehenge, Coventry Cathedral, and Stratford on Avon to see "Pericles" at the Royal Shakespeare Playhouse.

I was inspired to do Brass Rubbings on the large, monumental brass plaques of graves for the knights in their armor placed on the floors in the cathedrals from the 13th to the 16th century. It was all the rage then and one even had to book them in advance After a while, when the popular ones were all booked up, and I started looking for other surfaces to do rubbings on and noticed that there were a lot of nice manhole covers on the streets of London. Some were coal chute covers and others were utility covers. My favorite one was the "Dirty Water Manhole" cover! Before the end of our stay, I had rubbed old leatherbound books, fronts of pulpits, raised backs on chairs and even all the raised surfaces on a bus we traveled in!

While doing a brass rubbing in the Mary's Chapel beside Westminster Cathedral, Colleen Blake came up and started chatting with me. We became friends and I visited her in her home in the south side of London. We were birds of a feather and had many fun conversations!

Our courier, Ian Cameron was studying Law in London. He was from New Zealand. He took the group to many theaters to see "Mame," "Fiddler on the Roof," "Man of La Mancha," "Hadrian the Seventh," "Canterbury Tales," and "Hair." Ian made sure we saw all the sights and kept track of some 60 students and chaperones. I had to miss the Russian Ballet because part of my chaperone duties was to sit at the reception desk at the dorm one night a week. Our cup was full by the time we left four weeks later!

We sailed across the English Channel from the White Cliffs of Dover to Belgum. Then took the 12 hour train ride on the "Mozart Express" south along the Rhine River in Germany and arrived the next morning in Saltzberg, Austria. We stayed at a Bed and Breakfast run by a friendly older lady.

That afternoon we boarded a bus to tour Saltzberg, but there was no courier! Just then a young man from Vienna, named Tony Presager, stepped on the bus looking for me! He had met my parents on their AIFS Tour at Ostia Antiqua outside of Rome when they were on their way to Jerusalem. They told him I would be in Saltzberg, so he came to see me! Tony graciously agreed to be our tour guide. We rode around Saltzberg, visiting the place where Sound of Music was filmed, and saw Mozart's House and Saltzberg Castle! Later we had an amazing tour of the salt mines in Salt Mountain.

It was the season for the International Music Festival. We enjoyed a concert at the Mirabelle Palace, the Marionette Theatre production of "The Silver Flute," and the opera "Fidelio." The backdrop for the last scene of that opera was a solid mass of people floor to ceiling all done in white plaster of Paris relief just like we had done in my art class in Truckee!

Then we rode the train through the breathtaking Alps to Paris. It was wonderful to be in Paris again and see more of the sights. All too soon, we boarded the plane to fly home to San Francisco. As we took off, we spotted a new Concorde jet on a nearby runway! It had just been built in 1968!

I went to my parent's home in San Francisco and hurriedly prepared to return to London the following week!

Psalm 121: 1-8

I will lift up mine eyes until the hills, from whence comes my help?

My help comes from the LORD, which made heaven and earth.

He will not suffer thy foot to be moved:

He that keeps thee will not slumber.

Behold, he that keepeth Israel will neither slumber nor sleep.

The LORD it thy keeper:

The LORD is thy shade upon thy right hand.

The sun shall not smite thee b day,

Nor the moon by night.

The LORD shall preserve thee from all evil:

He shall preserve thy soul.

The LORD shall reserve thy going out

and thy coming in from this time forth, and even for evermore.

Chapter 13 – "On the Loose"

I celebrated my 26th birthday on July 28th, 1969, while I was in Europe with AIFS. Up to this point in my life almost every moment was supervised in some way and managed by someone else, so the thought of being "*on the loose*" at last was very attractive to me. I transferred the ownership of my green Volkswagen to my mother and gave my parents my pots, pans, and dishes. I withdrew all my money from my Teacher's Retirement Fund which I had saved the past three years, about $2000, and deposited some in a bank account so my mother could send it to me as needed and bought the rest in $50 American Express Travelers checks. . Now I was free to GO!

At that time the weight allowed for a suitcase when flying was 40 pounds. I purchased a large clothback suitcase called a "grasshopper" and attached a system of wheels with a strap tied around the edge of the case that had a handle on the opposite end. I called my memoirs *"Wheels on my Suitcase."*

That day in September, the charter flight was filled with people "getting away from it all!" They would hitch hike and stay in youth hostels, but that was not my "bag.". As we flew across the Atlantic, I calculated my funds and concluded that I could live on $50 a week, excluding major travel expenses. I studied Fromer's book " Europe on $5 a Day" and planned to follow their suggestions carefully. I wrote up a series of guidelines for myself follow: #1. Always carry enough money. #2. Read about the country while traveling through it. #3. Spend time as carefully as you spend money. Later I added: #4. Always allow for delays!

The one way ticket offered to students and educators flying from San Francisco to London cost $99! I was excited to begin my new life! I arrived at Heathrow Airport in London on September 12th. For the first time in my life, I was totally in charge of all my arrangements. I returned to Ramsey Hall, the dormitory where I had stayed that summer. I kept thinking *"Today is the first day of the rest of your life!"* In the morning, I boarded the train to Cardiff, the capital of Wales and after another short train trip arrived at Bridgend around noon. I was greeted by Gwyn, the AIFS courier we had in the summer of 1968, and his girlfriend, Helen.

I was totally exhausted from two solid weeks of travel from London to the States and then a week later back to England again. So, the slow pace in Wales gave me a chance to finally rest and be refreshed, body, mind, and soul. Gwyn wrote for a local newspaper, and he took me on a couple of assignments to gather information for his articles. The most interesting was up in the hills at a coal miner's meeting where we listened to their grievances with their employer.

Gwyn's apartment was in a stone house several stories high with walls three feet thick built in the early 1700's before the United States was even formed! Amazing to experience history in that way. It was located on top of a 200 foot cliff overlooking the Bristol Channel on the coast of

South Wales. I could see English coastline out my window the. The pub "Three Cups" nearby was where we enjoyed several meals and drinks. He taught me how to go "pub crawling" and I saw a lot of local Welch men that way.

Cardiff Castle with its moat was built by the Normans 2000 years earlier. On the first of July 1969, this was the location of the Investiture of Prince Charles to be Prince of Wales. Lots of banners were still flying in the city. I did some shopping downtown. In a bookstore, I bought a J. B. Phillips translation of the New Testament. I visited Gwyn's girlfriend, Helen, at Ely Children's Hospital and saw in the ward where she worked with handicapped children. A very challenging position indeed.

My goal for my entire journey was to visit Art Museums and absorb local art and history. In Cardiff I went to the National Museum of Wales and viewed their Impressionist collection. I was starting to recognize artists and form opinions about their work. I had seen several fine Museums in London that summer. While visiting the London National Gallery of Art I discovered the magnificent work of J. M. W. Turner who became my favorite English artist . He created the drama of the sea and skies with great freedom and his brush strokes were very inspiring to me!

Gwyn drove me to Ewenny Priory nearby. I was delighted to see some interesting memorial brasses and got permission from the Vicar to do some rubbings the next day. My favorite brass was for a young man: *"Ewenny' s hope, Ewenny' s pride, in him both flourished, in him both died."*

After a week it was time to board the train and travel back to London where I purchased my ticket to Amsterdam. I stayed in Ramsey Hall again and in the late afternoon took 3 different buses to the south part of London to have a proper "English High Tea" with my friend Colleen and her family! Salad with homegrown tomatoes, cucumbers, hard boiled eggs, and lettuce, sliced ham, fruit cocktail in stem glasses, jello, fresh sliced apples, pears, and grapes, with whipped cream. Followed by homemade bread and jam or cheese with tea and lastly a chocolate covered cream filled pastry! Her many collections of shells, stones, odds and ends and brass rubbings were a real eye opener to me!

Earlier in the summer I had made a brass rubbing appointment at "All Hallows by the Tower. So I spent 3 hours the next afternoon doing 2 rubbings! Then I had my hair cut quite short. And on to dinner at the top of the Post Office Tower with Fred whom I had met in in the spring Ray's house on Donner Lake! As the restaurant rotated, we had a tremendous view of London on a lovely sunny late afternoon. Finally, off to the Train Station at 8 PM to go to Harwich on the English Channel and boarded a ferry to the Netherlands. We landed the next morning and I got on a train to Amsterdam.

My father was a chaplain at a Boys Detention Facility in San Francisco. In the Spring of 1969, he met Reverend Van Boeyen who worked with troubled youth in Amsterdam. While visiting in San Francisco, he told my father that I was welcome to come and stay with his family when I traveled there in the fall. At 9 AM I found a taxi and arrived at their home with a bouquet of flowers for Mrs. Van Boeyen. They greeted me warmly and she ushered me to the bedroom of their second son who had now moved out on his own. They had five children and each one had their own room which they decorated to their taste. The bed was most welcome after a very short night's rest and I slept until 3 PM.

In order to graduate from High School in the Netherlands, all students were required to take four languages: such as English, French, Spanish and German. So, the family conversed with me in English quite easily, though after a while, they assured me that they were studying English and not American in school!!! The younger teenagers showed me how to go to the Dam which is the center of town. They helped me get acquainted with many of the Museums, such as the Museum of Modern Art, and the Rijksmuseum which was celebrating the 300th Anniversary of the birth of Rembrandt. I visited it several times to enjoy all his work on display for this special exhibit.

The Scheepvaart Museum of Maritime History was fascinating, and I did several rubbings there. The Tropical Museum was about importing sugar, tea, coffee, cocoa, kola, tobacco, cotton, and hemp, by Dutch shipping companies which transported products from many places around the world in the 1500 and 1600's. I got to view work by Van Gogh, Vermeer, Kalf, and other Dutch painters. I went to the house where Rembrandt was born, and Annie Franks' house. I discovered that *"Art was my passion!"*

On a rainy afternoon I was sitting in my room and their grey cat came and decided to go to sleep on my lap, so I did a sketch of him. They called him: "Grimas" or Katze!

One evening a couple of the kids took me up to the 13th floor of a business building and a restaurant to view the city. Contrary to London which has many tall new buildings, Amsterdam's old city is entirely preserved with no new structures along the canals. There were many bridges over the canals and walkways to explore.

Mrs. Van Boeyen drove me on trips into the countryside. We explored the quaint fishing village of Marken where people dressed in traditional costumes and wooden shoes. In the two and half weeks I became quite familiar with getting around on my own and even rode a bicycle sometimes returning through the Vondel Park near their old multistory brick home which they had nicely renovated on the inside and displayed their collections of pottery and paintings.

I attended church each Sunday at an English speaking church with a Scottish pastor where the Pilgrims once worshiped. There was a stained glass window in their memory. Rev Van Boeyen' s service was very dynamic. He supervised 9 different youth groups around Amsterdam with 200 volunteers and 40 staff. He was currently outfitting a Radio Ship in New York which would sail to the Middle East to broadcast "The Good News."

Upon my arrival, I was included in the family routine Breakfast - coffee with milk, a fried egg, potatoes, bread, and marvelous Gouda cheese! Dinner with the family began with soup, followed by potatoes, perhaps sauerkraut and Wurst, homemade yogurt, and apple sauce for dessert. Then Mrs. Van Boyen would read a chapter from the Bible such as 1 Corinthians 13, or Psalm 9 and so forth. I would help do the dishes and then we watched English and America movies on TV. Followed by discussion of the plots, and finally a late-night sherry and to bed! The first night they asked me what I thought of the war in Vietnam! A lively discussion followed.

Family life was getting very comfortable. I thought I had seen more museums than I had than the rest of my entire life, but it was time to proceed further south to Vienna where I hoped to meet some friends, so I purchased my train ticket and headed out on October 12th along the Rhine River in Germany.

Philippians 4:6 Don't worry about anything, and with prayer and supplication with thanksgiving, let your requests be made known to God and the Peace that passes all understanding shall guard your hearts and minds through Christ Jesus.

Chapter 14 – "Wheels on my suitcase"

In the fall of 1969, I was fortunate to stay in 2 private homes. That blessing anchored my first "Step out in Faith!" However, the three contacts I had in Vienna did not offer me any housing arrangements.

I boarded the train in Amsterdam late in the afternoon and munched on sandwiches thoughtfully prepared for me by Mrs. Van Boeyen. I fell into conversation with travelers in my compartment. One of the ladies was kind enough to show me my couchette where I slept that night. It was too dark to see the Rhine River as we traveled along it, however at one station stop I saw a large spiderweb in the light of a lamp post near my window!

We arrived in Vienna early in the morning. Although I had taken 3 years of German in High School and College, when I disembarked from the ferry in Rotterdam, Holland, I discovered that the people spoke Dutch, which seems Germanic to the ear, but not the same. Then when I arrived in Vienna, I learned that Austrian is not German as well, nor did the people in either country particularly like the Germans at that time. So, yet another language to learn, a whole new system of transportation to navigate on my own and another currency to adjust to.

You can see my outfit in my sketch, the fabric sided grasshopper suitcase on wheels, my short haircut, a short dress, sensible shoes, and a black loden cloth cape that I had purchased in Salzburg in the summer. Thus, until I opened my mouth I could be taken for a European. However, I had a lot of cultural lessons to learn, like where to sit on the tram, when to cross the street and many other things that people thought I should know automatically, and they readily corrected me!

To my surprise, "Britan Week" had just begun on October 12th, when I arrived and there were British Union Jack flags and banners everywhere! Red double decker buses driving on the main streets, and English marching bands playing in the parks and Scottish bagpipes could be heard that week all around Vienna!

The lady at the Travel desk at the railroad station gave me the name of a hotel to stay in and sold me a ticket for a tour of the city. A Japanese tourist accompanied me throughout the day and saw me safely to my hotel that night. I was so very tired that I just lay down on the floor and began to cry. I was totally alone and had no plans or real direction in my life anymore. I wept for some time and then the Holy Spirit spoke to me and comforted me and conversed with me all the way into the middle of the next day! I read Romans 12 in the Phillips translation and felt much revived in my spirit.

I got an October schedule of the performances at all the theaters and opera houses. There was a different play or opera every night of the week! I started to circle the ones I wanted to attend and was blessed to see "Hello Dolly" at Theatre Wein. "The Jazz Show" with Lionel Hampton and Duke Ellington which was an interesting evening. For Britan week the English movie: "The Bed Sitting Room" was shown about post WW II London and I really enjoyed hearing something in English!

There are two Opera houses, the Volksoper (The People's Opera) where I saw Die Fledermaus, Faust's Verdammung, and "Die Lustige Witwe" (The Merry Widow.) Both my parents loved Straus waltzes and my mother had once sung the part of the Merry Widow years before so that was very special to me. The Staatsoper (The State Opera) was much more expensive, and I could only afford to go once to see Carmen. I had purchased a sari in London, so I felt very dressed up in it even though I sat in the very top rank in the back of the Opera house.

My real desire was to go to Vienna's Art Museums, and I soon discovered the Albertina. The Albertina is a museum in the "Innere Stadt" of Vienna. It houses one of the largest and most important collections in the world with approximately 65,000 drawings and approximately 1 million old master prints, as well as more modern graphic works, photographs, and architectural drawings.

The key was to know what artist you wanted to view, then fill out a card and go sit down at an enclosed table and the attendant would bring out a large box with various actual works of that artist. I did a copy of Michelangelo's drawing of a hand. It was a real treat with white gloves to carefully handle some prints by Albrecht Durer, Rembrandt, Picasso, and Francsico Goya. I visited several other art galleries and museums and saw more paintings by Turner, Constable, and Gainsborough during "Britan Week! "

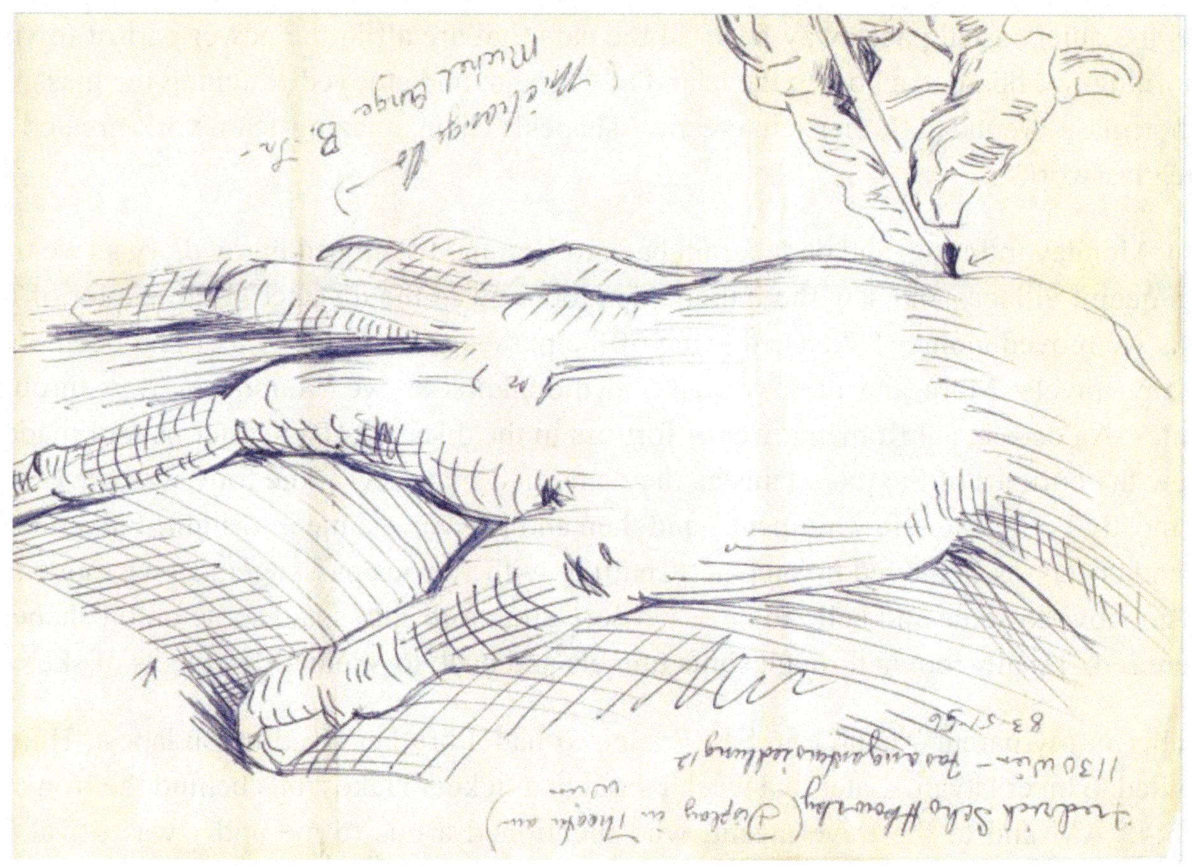

Tony Presager, who had come to visit me in Salzburg that summer, lived in Vienna and was very helpful in getting me oriented and showed me around the city. We took the elevator to the top of the "Donauturm" which is their version of the Seattle Space Needle. We had a nice dinner of cheese, bread, and wine. Pretty classic European eating. Beer or wine was almost always part of the evening meal since I arrived in Wales in September. The Austrian wines were a bit stronger and after several headaches, I decided I could not to drink them again!

Tony advised me to go to Venice for a weekend trip, as the weather was still nice there, so I bought a ticket, left my suitcase at the hotel, and took an evening train south through the Italian Alps called the Dolomite Mountains and arrived early the next morning. I met a young Canadian who suggested a hotel near the train station so I could catch the train returning early on Monday morning. He plus a couple of girls from California and another guy and L spent the day wandering the streets, canals, and bridges of Venezia. We did all the classic touristy things and had spaghetti for dinner which as not anything like American Spaghetti smothered in sauce, we were a bit disappointed. We took a boat to the Lido out on the Adriatic Sea and built a sandcastle along the shore that looked like a Roman Fortification we had seen from the train! There were cats everywhere! Some wanting tidbits, others totally ignoring the wanders! The 15th Century mosaics in the Basilica di San Marco really enchanted me, they are amazing works of art! We sat on the Piazza di San Marco and sipped Cinzano and fed the pigeons. We took another boat to the Basilica di San Giorgio Maggiore and saw a painting of St. George killing a dragon by Capaccio! We enjoyed the quiet casual pace away from all the cars that are all in the newer part of town. The next morning, we boarded a boat to the island of Murano, and enjoyed watching the glassblowers move hot glass around into many interesting shapes! Their amazing teamwork created lovely delicate glassworks.

Up early Monday morning, and on the train back to Vienna, I sketched in my diary as we traveled through quaint villages and saw the Italian Alps looming in the distance. I drew a lot of the tall spires as we moved along. I sketched some of the passengers discreetly as I had been doing all during my travels. More and more vistas, and mountains as we wound our way through the Dolomites. An occasional Roman tower or fortress in the distance, Page after page, I made notes and drew the outlines of the mountains as they emerged into view. The train was traveling very fast so mostly I only had a few moments, and then another view came into sight! Fall colors were bright and cheery as I enjoyed in Vienna. Chatting with various passengers as we moved along, saying goodbye to some and hello to others. More and more spires and some onion shaped ones that were red. Finally, down through some tunnels and back to Vienna! 14 pages of sketches.

A member in my parent's church in San Francisco had a brother lived in Budapest, Hungary. I was invited to meet Istvan. Later that week I bought a ticket to take a bus behind the Iron curtain! Up at 5:45 AM and to the travel agent, who mentioned a bus to me and I was off at 7 AM. However, when we got to the border, the driver asked for my passport, I told him in my best German that he had it. Someone spoke English and asked me where I was going and then informed me that this bus was going to Prague, Czechoslovakia!

Fortunately, at that moment there was a truck driver from Amsterdam driving back to Vienna, so he and his young son took me to the Travel agent. They were amazed at my mistake and sold me a train ticket to Budapest. When I arrived at Hotel Astoria I enjoyed a delicious pork dinner. Then I took a short walk around the city before dark with Christiana who had sold me the ticket! The next morning a Hungarian tour guide took me to see the sights, visiting the National Art Gallery and saw the Rugby stadium which was the first thing to be rebuilt after WW II! We went to the Danube River, and I viewed the buildings on both sides. "Buda" – is the serene side on the far side of the river with various churches along the shoreline. "Pesth" is the business side of the city.

The communists were still in control in 1969. The colors of the people's clothing were grey and black and rather dull. Some musicians the previous evening had asked me for German Marks so that they could escape to the west! I met Istvan at noon for lunch at the hotel. He oversaw the international pricing for Hungarian wine. He spoke excellent English and we had a nice visit. Then the tour started back to Vienna. At the border, the bus was thoroughly searched to make sure that no one was trying to escape. Everyone felt the tension. As we left, we were saddened as we watched the night sky lit up by fireworks to expose anyone attempting to escape across the flat borderlands.

My parents knew the Pastor at the Vienna Community Church, so I attended services all 4 Sundays while I was in Vienna. The music was augmented by the marvelous voices of American opera stars who were singing in "Porgy and Bess" at the Volksoper. Their resonant voices filled our souls. After church service, I got to meet people visiting like me and some who lived in Vienna. One Sunday evening we had a REAL Thanksgiving dinner with Pumpkin Pie which tasted so delicious!

I also met friends of my grandparents who had lived in Vienna for several years, and they took me to dinner at a fancy restaurant across from St. Stephens Cathedral. They treated me to a Salzburger Knockerl, which is an amazing egg soufflé, a traditional favorite in Austria. I wanted to have it for my students in the summer but was not able to arrange it. We toured Stephansdom as the Cathedral is called and climbed up to the top of the spire to overlook the city. Their son gave me a ticket to Spanische Reitschul to watch the training of Lipizzaner horses with very precise movements.

I had the opportunity to meet Gunther Kraus, an artist who several years before had designed four stained glass window walls to enclose a sanctuary of the Parish Church of St. Kapistran. Each wall was 26 feet by 66 feet and they were encased in lead and concrete. It was very inspiring to meet a contemporary artist and learn about all his work. I entered the sanctuary early on Sunday morning and stood next to the vibrant red glass of a side wall as the sunlight streamed through it. I felt a real presence! A modern statement of faith!

Vienna is a bustling city in the southeastern part of Europe. The Austrio-Hungarian empire was defeated in World War I, losing much of an empire's territory which included some of Germany, Hungary, Czechoslovakia, and the Slavic countries. The nation also suffered heavy bombing at the end of World War II and was occupied by the Allies until 1955. Tony assured me that in the end, "the Russians left because the Austrian generals were better drinkers!"

By 1969, Vienna was fully restored to its former grandeur. It was said that if one left Vienna before World War I and returned in the 1960's they would notice very little change. Only the new apartment buildings reflect modern architecture. There was clearly a love of art throughout the city and one percent of any construction project was set aside for some type of artistic decoration such as mosaics or a sculpture.

The Wienerwald, (Vienna Woods,) just outside the city is famous for the Octoberfest with music, dancing, and local beer. Radiant fall colors made a beautiful end to my stay. After traveling along the Daube to see Durnstein Castle where Richard the Lion Hearted was imprisoned during the Crusades, I felt like my bucket list was complete.

My watercolor teacher in California had led classes to the rugged Yugoslavian coast and I really wanted to see the scenery in Croatia, but the Yugoslavian travel agent assured me that November was not the time to go there due to strong cold winds along the coast of the Adriatic Sea. So, I reluctantly purchased a train ticket to Athens, Greece, with resolve to return in the spring. The trip would last 40 hours through Yugoslavia to northern Greece and on into Athens.

As the weather turned colder, and the wind pierced my wool Austrian loden cloth cape I bid fond farewell to the City of Waltz, Wine and Song. I boarded the Orient Express and found my first class compartment on the evening of November 6th. Wanderlust was in my veins once again!

"O Lord our God, grant us grace to desire thee with our whole heart; that so desiring we may seek and find thee; and so finding thee may love thee; and loving thee, may hate those sins from which thou hast redeemed us. Amen "

Anselm 1033 – 1109 AD

Chapter 15 – Sojourn in Yugoslavia

While traveling in the fall of1969, I occasionally wrote home to friends in Truckee, California. Late in December, this is part of letter which was published in the newspaper, the Sierra Sun.

"Greetings from the Happy Wander or the Amerikanker Touriski who came to stay. When I last wrote, I had just completed a culture-packed four weeks in Vienna, Austria and was "full to here" with museums and sightseeing. The evening I left for Athens early in November, was the beginning of a real adventure, unbeknownst to me, which makes it more interesting. First, I was on the wrong car, and it took several moves to get me straightened out. At last, early in the morning I settled into a compartment with several Yugoslavian ladies returning from a shopping trip in Vienna. I was ready to sleep, but no, we must get acquainted. How? in German, and soon we became friends."

In the morning as we traveled over the flat plains of northern Yugoslavia. I passed the time away by showing them some black and white photos I had taken in Truckee, California, which the Yearbook photographer had kindly enlarged and mounted on tag board. All were intrigued with anything American, and I was possibly the first American Tourist they had ever met. Speaking German, I shared that I had really wanted to travel to the Yugoslavian coast to do some paintings, but the travel agent had discouraged me because the weather was too cold by now. The small man sitting next me by the window finally came awake, and said, " will take you there!" Discussion continued for some time. Ziva, a 42 years old peasant type, offered to take me to stay with his sister in a village in the eastern part of Serbia, and then he would go and get his automobile and come back and drive me to Dubrovnik on the west coast of Yugoslavia.

When Ziva stepped out to use the restroom, all the ladies immediately urged me not go with him. He was a "Ciganer!" A half gypsy and not to be trusted! He was swarthy and fit their description of that despised people! I was very torn, I really wanted to go to the coast to paint! Later I went to the restroom. My stomach was churning. I was in great turmoil with indecision! Finally, against all their objections, I got off the train with Ziva at Beograd, the capital of Yugoslavia.

We took 3 commuter trains 100 kilometers east across the flat midlands which stretch north and south along the eastern part of Yugoslavia and into neighboring Romania. We watched workers gathering corn stalks into stacks for winter forage. Other laborers brought in the last of the sugar beets. The fall picture was completed by pumpkins lying in the fields beside cornstalks. We arrived after dark on the border, at the small village called Bela Crkva which in English means "White Church." I was amazed to see a sky full of stars as I deeply inhaled the warm night air.

In 1929 the Kingdom of Serbs, Croats, and Slovenes adopted the name Yugoslavia. After World War 11, in 1946, Yugoslavia became a socialist federation of six republics: Croatia, Montenegro,

Serbia, Slovenia, Bosnia, Herzegovina, and Macedonia. At that time they adopted the name of Socialist Federal Republic of Yugoslavia (SFRY).

Bela Crkva Serbian Cyrillic- Бела Црква, in German, *Weißkirchen*; = White Church is a town in the South Banat District of the autonomous province of Vojvodina, Serbia. The town had a population of 1,300 in 1969.

Friend Ivan, greeted Ziva at the station and easily lifted my suitcase on to his shoulder and accompanied us to Ziva's sister's modern apartment building. We climbed up to the 3rd floor. Rasidorska immediately told us that her husband was in the Yugoslavian socialist military and was not allowed to have foreigners in their apartment over night! So, we went back down to the street and walked to an older part of town. Ivan opened a large wooden gate that led into a courtyard shared by two families. We stepped into his house on the right and were warmly greeted by his family, all sitting on a bed facing a black and white TV watching an American Western with Yugoslavian voice over. I was offered a very small cup of sweet thick coffee. Then came the introduction that I would hear may times "Is California – San Francisco" …"Oh Americanker!" …"Da, Touriski!"

Ivan led us to his mother's house which was not being used in another part of town. Ziva and I spent the night there in the two small bedrooms. In the morning we walked around town to visit several of his friends. Since no one had ever seen an American, I was like a prize being exhibited. I felt like a goldfish in a bowl! Eventually we ended up staying in the home of a young law student, Radisa, with his parents for two nights. On the first day I had been treated to white bean soup, and so I had to get up and go to the outhouse several times that night. The toilet paper was pages of an old catalogue, and eventually I ran out of pages! Breakfast was coffee with sugar, a large slice of bread, and scrambled eggs with sausages. Then a Politzi came to see what I was all about! I had a seven day transit visa, so he was satisfied that I was legitimate! Everyone who came to town was supposed to register with the police.

In almost every home, there was a picture of President Tito, the Yugoslavian dictator, and photographs of family members on the walls. I learned that everyone had lost someone in World War II or in the Partisan struggles that also raged between various Slavic states at that time. In the end, Tito had unified the six states peacefully and he was highly respected.

Ziva arranged for me to live with Izvorka in her spare bedroom. She lived on the same courtyard as Ivan on the left side as we entered. Her mother lived with her, too. "Baba" was dressed like other older widows all in black, a black scarf, a black blouse and a black skirt, with a brown leather vest, black stockings, and shoes. I had my own room and Izvorka prepared meals for us in her small kitchen living area.

The next day Ziva informed me that his friend had wrecked Ziva's car and he needed money to go and have it fixed and then he would return and drive me to the coast. I cashed one of my $50 travelers checks and gave him half of it, and he left. Much later I learned that he really went back to his apartment with his wife Vienna. He did not return! However, I was settling into a comfortable life there, speaking German and learning Serbian. I was drawing sketches of the people and painting watercolors of their houses and flowers that were still blooming and finally resting at last!

Baba with Chenille plant.

Izvorka at her front door with a comforter hanging on the clothesline to air out.

I was having what is now called "an Immersion experience!" NO English at all, and only minimal understanding of their German or they of mine. Each house had electricity and a Television, and No Runing Water. There was a water pump in the courtyard, an outhouse, a garden, a place for animals, and a dovecot on the roof.

I often heard some farm carts with wooden wheels pulled by two horses passing by on the cobblestone streets outside my window. Breakfast was simple and repetitive: Coffee, and hot milk fixed on an electric stove, fresh bread from a nearby bakery, paprikash – a relish made from tomatoes and peppers, with "smoked bacon" - a large slice of fat from a pig recently slain . Later in the day we might drink Sljivovica, a local plum brandy that was very popular. There were grape vines lining the hillsides and their wine was sold throughout the country.

Young people came to teach me Serbian, and I taught them English in return. We started with numbers. t I wrote down what I heard, and got some correctio. I learned how to tell time. Simple words like Molem lepo in Serbian = Bitte Schoen in German = Please. Translating from Serbian to German to English. Havla lepo = Danke Schoen = Thank you.

In the evening of my seventh day there, two young men found a driver for me to go to the Romanian border crossing so I could get my visa renewed. We rode on into Deta, Romania and had a good meal including champaign - Sampaine Romanien. I returned with a 3 month visa stamp on my passport, however my ticket to Athens needed be used by the end of December.

Izvorka woke me on Saturday morning to look at all the wagons going by on their way to the Market = Piatsa. We walked around and observed this free market system inside of a socialist regime. There were lots of vegetables – onions, carrots, parsnips, paprika, dried corn, beans, eggs, cabbage, melons, squash, potatoes, sesame seeds, honey, plus turkeys, geese, and chickens, One man carried a small pig home on his shoulder and another man walked a large pig like a wheelbarrow, with the hind legs in his hands! There were horses and tack items for sale and several flea market stalls and handcrafted items.

More Serbian lessons What did you say?= Kabo Kazati? Eat – Jesti; Work – Rad; Rain = Kisa; Night = Noc. Cyrillic script was very different than English and hard for me to read.

We talked about how to pronounce their words. My new name was Suzy because they could not pronounce an "H."

Occasionally, I would go to a hotel and take a bath! Such a luxury! Otherwise, there was only cold water in the homes where I stayed. To wash my face I got cold water brought in from the well in a bucket and poured in a metal basin. My mattress was stuffed with corn husks. But for a dollar a day, which included meals, I did not complain.

There was a lake at the edge of town, so sometimes I walked over to see the sunset reflected in the water through the trees. It was a European tourist attraction in the summer. I also wandered on the hills and among the grape vines and gazed over to the higher hills in the distance of Romania. There were three large Orthodox churches in town, however none of them were open for services while I was there.

After a week, I was moved to another home. The owner, an older heavy set lady, was dressed as other widows, and we called her Baba. He boyfriend, Labora, had a son in town who did metal work and came to visit occasionally, and we spoke in German. Her 11 year old grandson, Slobodan, also lived with her.

Additionally, a "Soldat," a military man was assigned to board with them, but we did not see him very often. On the other side of the courtyard was my single room and then rooms for her daughter, Nada, and her invalid husband, Dragaloup, who slept most of the time. Next to them was Baba's brother Millet's room. Outside his room was the well. The courtyard had a garden in the back and a yard for two hens and three ducks, and a pen with high fence for a large pig. Two puppies and a cat had free range of the area. The outhouse had two doors, with an old Biology text book used for toilet paper. It was quite a scamper outside to run over to it in rainy weather!

Just before departing in the summer of 1969, I had signed up for a correspondence course with "Famous Artist School" and brought the manual with me so I could follow the instructions and do assignments. I practiced value studies in watercolor and worked on other exercises. I kept busy sketching the people there around me. This helped me become more aware of my surroundings. Sometimes I did cartoons when I had to draw quickly and other times I could do more careful studies when people held still.

I met a young school girl, Cica, and we spoke English together. She took me to her High School English class. It was nice to speak with the teacher who had studied in London. He had me talk with his class about my life in Truckee, California. All were very interested. After a few weeks, I found that I would rather speak English than eat! I also met the High School Art professor and saw his student's work. He invited me to his home to do a portrait of me! He covered over a painting he had done in college using leftover house paints! He first did a sketch of me before he did a painting. I did a couple of sketches of him. He told me that he had exhibited his work in New York and London.

Professor's sketch of me.

My sketch of the Professor sketching me!

Cica lent me a paperback copy of "Lust for Life" by Irving Stone in English about Vincent Van Gogh. Early in his life he lived in Holland among humble people and painted their lives. I really related to his experience and began to draw and paint what I was seeing around me more carefully.

Baba grinding Walnuts and boyfriend, Labora resting. Nada doing the washing and Dragaloup resting.

Mid-December, Baba informed me that she was expecting her family to come and visit for the Holidays, and I would have to move out. I prepared to depart and travel back to Beograd to take the train on to Athens.

I boarded the commuter train early in the morning on December 24th. As we traveled, I heard two ladies chatting behind me and I realized that I understood their conversation. They were talking about Chickens! Six weeks of immersion to understand Chickens!

Psalm 56:8 – 10 and 13 Thou took account of my wanderings… This I know that God is for me. In God will I praise His word…13: For thou hast delivered…my feet from falling, that I may walk before God in the light of the living.

Chapter 16 – "It's Greek to me!"

I arrived in Belgrade, Yugoslavia in the train station, at 10:30 AM, Thursday, December 24th, 1969. When I was enjoying two beef shish kabobs and a cup of Chai in the restaurant I met an American family, a lawyer and his wife and their teenage daughter. We sat and visited while we waited for the Balkan Express which eventually was six hours late due to heavy snows north of us! Two Greek gentlemen joined us, and we shared their festive meal of grapes and homemade bread with feta cheese.

My ticket was first class, and I had a compartment to myself that evening. It was the nicest accommodation I had so far, and I slept well. I woke up on Christmas morning as approached the Greek border. My Christmas Card was a snow covered hillside with a shepherd tending his sheep! Reading the Christmas story in my Phillips Translation of the New Testament, I had a new awareness of a peasants' life in the light of my recent experiences in Yugoslavia. I visited with my American friends in their compartment and borrowed their newer copy of Frommer's "Europe on $5 a Day" 1969 – 1970, to study about traveling in Greece.

Arriving in Thessaloniki, I realized that I could read the Greek word on the sign thanks to 6 weeks reading Yugoslavian Cyrillic letters! We traveled on to Athens, arriving at 11:11 PM, 9 hours late! I found a hotel room with a shower and bathroom down the hall for a very reasonable price. Up Friday morning after a good night's rest and I enjoyed the warm air and sunshine and breakfast with some Americans who paid for my cup of tea, bread, butter, and jam. What a relief to be speaking English again!

The Viking Travel Agency was nearby, and I booked a tour of major Greek archeological sites. I was given a teacher's rate and joined a group of American students from The Hague, Holland, and touring in Greece for Christmas vacation. It was very good to have a travel guide. I will not discuss the tour except to say that Olympia was a very special place, and we all were moved by the serenity of the area. I read Herny Miller's "Colossus of Maroussi" written when he traveled in Greece in 1939 just before World War II, 30 years before I was there. I experienced the "sense of place" that he described then.

I recalled the work of German amateur archaeologist Heinrich Schliemann and his belief in Homer's writings about Troy which led him to excavate the site in Turkey in 1871 – 1873 where he discovered ancient Troy. Then Schliemann came to Greece and excavated Mycenae on the Peloponnese Peninsula in1876. There he discovered the gold funerary "Mask of Agamemnon." My awareness of anthropology and archeology was being amplified by all the antiquities I was privileged to see.

We stopped in Corinth and wandered in the ruins of the ancient city where the Apostle Paul once lived and worked making tents with Pricilla and Acquilla. After five days we returned to Athens. Then I joined the group on a ship bound for the island of Crete on New Year's eve. As we departed the ship began to roll and I headed down to my stateroom as sea sickness overtook me! At midnight, the ship's whistles blasted in the year 1970! What would it hold for me?

We arrived in Heraklion, Crete the next morning and I walked around the town with my new friends visiting the home Nikos Kazantzakis a miner who wrote "Zorba the Greek" in 1946 about Crete. I had seen the movie in 1964 so it was interesting to see those settings on the Island. Sir Arthur Evans, an Oxford Professor and Archeologist purchased land in 1899 on Crete and excavated the ruins of the Minoan palace at Knossos. We climbed through those reconstructed ruins and wandered in the labyrinth of the famed Minoan Bull. In 2011, Gavin Menzies proved that Knossos is the site of "The Lost Empire of Atlantis." A huge Tsunami wave caused by a volcanic eruption 75 miles north on the island of Thera in the Mediterranean Sea swept over the entire island in 1450 BC destroying the Minoan Civilization in what is now called the Bronze Age.

Returning to Athens, I picked up my mail at the American Express some of which had been waiting for me since early November. I walked to the X. E. N. the Y.W.C.A. and got a room with three beds shared at that moment with two Greek ladies. That day, there was a physics teacher, and the other was a bank teller from Veria in Northern Greece who spoke English quite well. Aspa and I got acquainted during the week while she was there taking a refresher course in banking. We agreed to write to one another, and we kept up our correspondence for 40 years!

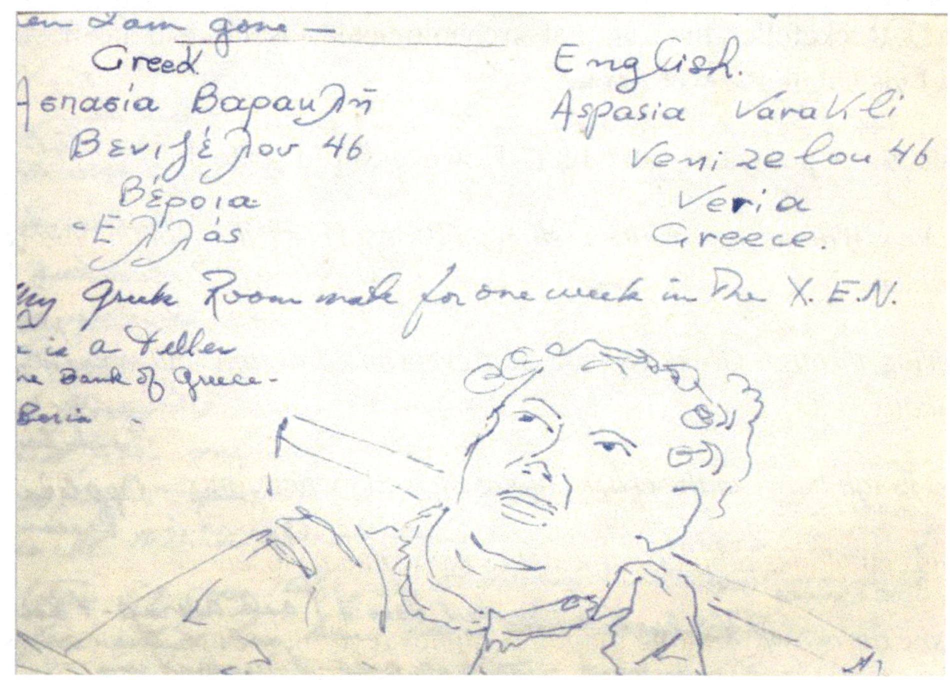

My roommate, Aspa Varakli from Veria.

Others who stayed in the room with me a day or so at a time were American students, Peace Corps Volunteers, and Greek tourists. I learned many things about their traveling life and got a better focus on what I might see and do. The "Y" had a cafeteria with reasonably priced meals, a library, and they offered several classes including an art class where I sketched a male model for several drawing sessions.

Sunday morning, I walked to a Greek Orthodox Church and stayed for their service and a baptism. The air was heavy with incense. Then I walked to St. Andrew's American Church started by a German pastor who had previously started a church in Vienna in1956 and then one in Egypt. The pastor delivered the service in English which he had learned in London. After the service, I met Rachel, an American lady who came to Athens with the Marshal Plan in 1950 as a Home Economist and married Christos, a Greek Lawyer. They invited me to their home for lunch. They had two teenaged daughters. We ate fried chicken and pickled octopus which I learned to love after a while! They continued to invite me to their home, and we became good friends. I met more church members after the service each Sunday and participated in their activities. I had found a new church home!

My days were spent roaming the ruins around the Acropolis and visiting museums.

Since 1957, the Museum of the Ancient Agora has been housed in the reconstructed Stoa of Attalos, which was donated by the King of Pergamon, Attalos II, to the city of Athens. The museum's exhibition featured finds from the excavations by the American School of Classical Studies in the Ancient Agora dating from the Neolithic era until the Post-Byzantine times. Visitors could see important exhibits related to the institutions and function of the Athenian democracy. Funded by John D. Rockefeller, the National Archeological Museum had the most comprehensive collections, and I visited there several times.

Now in retrospect the experience is all a blur. However, I did write this:

"Summary of Days Wanderings while resting and absorbing the Roman Agora which is the ancient marketplace:

Perhaps wandering through Greek ruins is not everyone's dream, but once here in Greece, it comes automatically.

Green grass grows tall between the cracks along the road where once a busy market stood.

Half hidden by green blades a black cat watches me wander closer.

Then suddenly she darts away among the fallen stones leading my eye to a lonely statue standing above fragments of marble columns placed neatly at his feet along the old brick wall.

We face each other – two lone figures on a cool January afternoon.

His masculine shoulders draped with folds of marble warmth.

But only I have eyes to see.

His head sits in some museum, arms and hands long gone, broken from their sockets.

Yet he stands a proud representative of all the ruins which survived the test of time and the folly of man.

The black cat surveys the scene from lofty heights of ancient walls.

She has been here a long time and knows the secrets which the weathered marble holds.

The length and breadth of the temple are her domain.

Alone, with an ancient Athenian ruin, it is balm to the weary soul to know that others also struggled, succeeded, failed, came, and went.

It is winter, and the grey marble is colder than the Mediterranean skies.

The cat will stand guard when I am gone."

This was the area where the Apostle Paul came to discuss the Athenian's shrine to the "Unknown God."

For meals on my own I went to the Plaka neighborhood at the foot of the Acropolis. My choices included the main stays of octopus, shish kabobs, Souvlaki, a salad with Feta cheese, ouzo- a dry anise flavored aperitif, beer, or wine.

To continue my pursuit of Art History, I visited art galleries whenever I could find them and even met an artist or two. My cup was getting full again and I began to study travel brochures and decided to take a ship through the Corinthian Canal to Brindisi, Italy, with a stopover on the Island of Kerkyra – the English name is Corfu.

I departed on January 24, 1969, on a small ship from Piraeus, sailed through the four miles long Corinthain Canal that was cut across the Peloponnese Peninsula in 1893, to the Gulf of Corinth and on north to the Island of Corfu on the west coast of Greece arriving very early in the next morning,

Acts 17: 16 – 34

Now while Paul waited for them at Athens, his spirit was stirred in him, when he saw the city wholly given to idolatry.

Therefore, disputed he in the synagogue with the Jews, and with the devout persons, and in the market daily with them that met with him.

Then certain philosophers of the Epicureans, and of the Stoics, encountered him. And some said, What will this babbler say? other some, He seems to be a setter forth of strange gods: because he preached unto them Jesus, and the resurrection.

And they took him, and brought him unto Areopagus, saying, May we know what this new doctrine is, whereof thou speak?

For thou bring certain strange things to our ears: we would know therefore what these things mean.

(For all the Athenians and strangers which were there spent their time in nothing else, but either to tell, or to hear some new thing.)

Then Paul stood in the midst of Mars' hill, and said, *Ye* men of Athens, I perceive that in all things ye are too superstitious.

For as I passed by, and beheld your devotions, I found an altar with this inscription, TO THE UNKNOWN GOD. Whom therefore ye ignorantly worship, him declare I unto you.

God that made the world and all things therein, seeing that he is Lord of heaven and earth, dwelleth not in temples made with hands;

Neither is worshipped with men's hands, as though he needed anything, seeing he giveth to all life, and breath, and all things;

And hath made of one blood all nations of men for to dwell on all the face of the earth, and hath determined the times before appointed, and the bounds of their habitation:

That they should seek the Lord, if haply they might feel after him, and find him, though he be not far from every one of us:

For in him we live, and move, and have our being; as certain also of your own poets have said, For we are also his offspring.

Forasmuch then as we are the offspring of God, we ought not to think that the Godhead is like unto gold, or silver, or stone, graven by art and man's device.

And the times of this ignorance God winked at; but now commended all men everywhere to repent:

Because he hath appointed a day, in the which he will judge the world in righteousness by that man whom he hath ordained; whereof he hath given assurance unto all men, in that he hath raised him from the dead.

And when they heard of the resurrection of the dead, some mocked: and others said, We will hear thee again of this matter.

So, Paul departed from among them.

Howbeit certain men clave unto him and believed: among the which was Dionysius the Areopagite, and a woman named Damaris, and others with them.

Chapter 17 – El Greco Sky

January 24th, 1970, I boarded a very crowded ferry loaded with cars and many passengers and departed from Athens with the thoughts of staying a few days on the island of Corfu, off the east coast of Greece. The boat was small enough to pass through the Corinth Canal, dug in 1893 when ships were smaller. I met several young people traveling to Italy. We had lunch together and exchanged stories about out travels as we passed through the canal observing the strata and faults that had been exposed.

As we sailed under the automobile bridge 250 feet above us, we waved at kids saying goodbye to some of the men on board who were going to work to in Germany. As the ferry emerged out of the canal, the ground sloped down to the water, and we had the optical illusion of going uphill! We visited all afternoon, had dinner together, then watched a full moon off the bow of the ship and gazed at the stars in the clear night sky.

Finally, I went to my bunk for the night and got up at 6:30 AM as we neared Corfu. As I disembarked, I looked up at the full moon illuminating the clouds and saw an "El Greco" sky! What a sight!

View of Toledo by "El Greco" A classic El Greco Sky!

Dominikos Theotokopolus Oct 1, 1541 – April 7, 1614, most widely known as El Greco, was a Greek painter, sculptor, and architect of the Spanish Renaissance. He usually signed his paintings with his full birth name. He was born in the kingdom of Candia, modern Crete, which was part of the Republic of Venice, Italy at that time. He trained and became a master within the Post-Byzantine tradition before traveling to Venice at the age of 26, In 1570, he moved to Rome where he opened a workshop and enriched his style with elements of Mannerism and the Venetian Renaissance. On 1577, he moved to Toledo, Spain, where he lived and worked until his death. El Greco received several major commissions there and produced one of his best known paintings seen above, “View of Toledo.”

As I stepped off the ferry a young boy offered to lead me to a hotel. After taking a nap, I took a walk toward Garista Bay and found the “Corfu Tourist Services” I met the proprietor, Michael S. Halikiopus, the son of Spyros, the “great fixer” in Gerald Durrel’s book “My Family and other Animals” about an English family who lived in Corfu thirty years before. I eventually read the story. It was fascinating! At the information desk the clerks were Stephanos from Corfu and Mike from Delphi. They kindly directed me to do interesting things and told me about excursions to take around the island. Later I met Stephanos’ sister Mary, who taught English, and chatted with their parents in their upper level apartment in the old town.

During the next days, we often ate meals together and chatted with other travelers. It was not yet tourist season, so we congregated at various favorite eating places such as the Corfu Palace and sipped tea while overlooking the bay. Off in the distance were the mountains of Albania rising out of the water, always mysterious to me.

Corfu Palace Café

Corfu, with Albanian hills across the Ionian Sea.

One evening at an outdoor restaurant, I met Gilles, a young Frech Canadian studying architecture and traveling for a year. We were joined by Stephanos and Mike. For dinner we ate large shrimp recently caught in the waters nearby. We discussed many things and enjoyed animated conversations!

Mike arranged a good rate for me at a hotel right across the street from the Corfu Museum of Asian Art. I visited there and over time toured several other Museums and the two fortresses on either side of the harbor. Thanks to Mike's suggestions to take different bus rides around the island each day, I gave up all thoughts of leaving soon. I took along my sketch book and enjoyed drawing the older part of town built by Venetians.

St Spyridon at the end of a street.

One day on a bus trip out of the city I met a local man, who told me of some Roman ruins in an old orchard. He mentioned that there was a nice mosaic that unfortunately had a large hole in it dug when someone had been looking for water on the property years ago. He got permission for me to visit the site. My archeology preservation instincts came alive, and I immediately wanted to clean it.

Back in town, I told Gilles about the mosaic and we both went out to see what we might do. We weeded, scrubbed, and cleaned it for four days. Gilles did a very precise architectural drawing of the remains of mosaic square by square. In the beginning, the mosaics all appeared to be black and white, but by the time we finished we discovered that there were other colors - orange, salmon, yellow, grey, green, as well as black and white. Lovely designs appeared as I scrubbed away the help of Ajax window cleaner and by the last day I had worn down the bristles of my fingernail brush to almost nothing. I did a pen and ink drawing of it, too. We hoped that the owner would now get nicer tips when he showed it to the tourists who would be coming soon.

My sketch of the mosaic floor we cleaned.

At last, I had found a place where I could do my artwork and enjoy the peace and quiet and explore the island at my leisure. I continued painting assignments in my Famous Artists course. Mary became intrigued and asked me to teach her art lessons, so I gave her instructions from the art course. She worked on them for several weeks and her mother did paintings as well. I found that as I taught Mary various concepts, I understood the instructions better myself! I painted a several watercolors around the island.

One of the many Greek Orthodox Churches on Corfu.

There were 37 Greek Orthodox Churches and monasteries on Corfu. Some of them had crosses on them which were askew! On Sundays, I went to services in one of the chapels. Women with children sat on the left and men on the right. The choir was above the entrance in the balcony. The air was quite thick with incense. Following communion, on February 12th there was a celebration in honor of Saint Theodora and all the girls named after her were recognized. Saint Spyridon was the patron saint of Corfu, and some men were named Spyros in his memory.

Many artists have come to Corfu over the years, most notably, British artist and Naturalist, Edward Lear was there in 1850. I found his limerick and added it to my sketch.

"There was an old man of Corfu

who simply had nothing to do,

Here and there he ran

until he got tan.

Poor old man of Corfu!"

Edward Lear was in Corfu in 1850 and possibly saw it like this then!

My Reflections on Corfu:

"The streets of the old town are narrow, perhaps six feet wide.

They are paved with hewn white stones angularly fitted together with cement filling the cracks.

Steps often led up and down hills and around the high apartment buildings which cut off the sun.

One feels like one is walking at the bottom of a dark slot canyon which may end abruptly at a church door or some older building which preceded the newer street.

Or one may burst suddenly into lighter air of a marketplace or an area where there once was rubble of a building destroyed by the German Blitzkrieg in WWII. There children laugh and play, bouncing a ball against a kitchen wall.

To truly see Corfu, one must walk slowly as a cat stealthily hunts his prey.

Inside each doorsill is a way of life.

A darkened staircase with a keyhole of light at the top.

Patient silversmith soldering links of chain.

Intent shoemaker mending a heel.

The neighborhood barber chatting with his customers about the weather.

An aged grandmother hooking lace.

Fragrant bakery you find with your nose.

Wander down steps with the green moss and the rain, down toward the harbor.

For a moment you are protected from the wind that blows off the water where waves crash on rocks and splash against the ancient fortress.

From the rock sea wall, you can gaze quietly across the water at the distant Albanian hills receding blue, purple, grey and watch the wind leave soft footprints as it scurries along the bay.

Feel the touch of warm spring rain.

Breathe deeply in your mind and let your soul go free.

One wonders how their laundry ever gets dry in this weather.

With the help of a neighbor, lines are strung back and forth across the apartment canyon walls, iron hook to window shutter to rusty peg.

Early in the morning the laundry is hung out to dry and when horizontal space runs out, the clothes are ingeniously pinned one below the other, bright flags to greet the new day!

Another corner round and eight cats are in committee discussing the local rodent population.

Complaining at the interruption, the motion to adjourn is hastily accepted and they slip away silently into their respective places of business.

The secretary with only one eye casts her gaze upon you disapprovingly for having ruined her mousy minutes.

What are you doing wandering around during siesta anyway?"

The rest of the island is equally enchanting. High cliffs and scenic coastlines beguile the tourist and quite beaches lure many sun worshipers to Corfu each year from England, France, Germany, Austria, and America. The hotel manager assured me that no one ever leaves Corfu when they say they will!

Spring was arriving with wild iris, yellow and white daisies by the score on the hillsides and pink and white almond orchards blossoming in the fields. Young sheep romp in the green grass. Peasant women bending over all day long picking up olives beneath their ancient family trees on steep hillsides.

Peasant woman collecting olives on the hillside.

The Old Town of Corfu was ruled by the Venetian nobility from 1386 to 1798. Later the French occupied the area. Unlike the rest of Greece, the Turks never held Corfu for long. After the Napoleonic Wars, the island was under British rule until 1864 when the Ionian Island chain was ceded to Greece. Corfu is rich in history, going back to around the time of Christ.

Roman travelers were Nero, Julius Caesar, Anthony and Cleopatra. "Richard the Lion Hearted" stopped over on his way back from the Crusades just before he was imprisoned in the castle, I visited above Durnstein, Austria. Achillion Palace, the famed summer residence, was built for Empress Elizabeth of Austria and later owned by King William II of Germany. "Mon Repos" the summer palace for Greek Royality, was the birthplace of Prince Philip, Duke of Edinburgh, and consort to Queen Elizabeth II.

My tourism cup was getting full, and my 60 day Greek visa would expire soon, so I went to the travel agent to find out when my ferry would sail to Brindisi, Italy. I was alarmed to learn that the ferry had burned down in the harbor in Italy! At that moment, however, two Australian school teachers whom I had met a week before, were also checking on their ferry tickets to Italy, so it was arranged that we would travel together through Italy. Their airline ticket unfolded to 9 feet long! They were traveling around the world for a year!

My fond farewell dinner was attended by many of my new friends on the evening of February 25th. They wrote memories and thoughts in my notebook. One young man penned "*Only in Corfu have I seen El Greco skies!*"

Isaiah 58:11 and the LORD shall guide thee continually, and satisfy thy soul in drought, and make fat thy bones: and thou shalt be like a watered garden, and like a spring of water, whose waters fail not.

Chapter 18 – "All Roads lead to Rome"

One month after I arrived in Corfu, Greece, I departed for Italy on February 24th at 9:30 AM. As we sailed across the Ionian Sea, I gazed at the old town of Corfu piled high up on the hills between the two ancient stone fortresses guarding the bay. I reflected on the quiet time I had enjoyed there and the opportunity to finally draw and paint, which I had been longing to do for several months. At last, I had a Greek island experience!

Joan Benson was an art history teacher and Deidre Brown was an English teacher at Brisbane Girls Grammar School in Brisbane, Australia. We got better acquainted as we sailed to Italy. They called me Suzy, since the Greek people could not pronounce "H" either, so the name just stayed with me! Our meeting was indeed a Divine Appointment! Joan had done much careful studying and planning to visit all the major art museums, ruins, and galleries on their trip around the world! And by staying with them the price of our hotel rooms was lowered. I could not have asked for anything better!

We arrived in Brindisi in the southeast lower part of Italy late that afternoon. It is the ancient seaport at the far end of the Appian Way /" Via Appia Antica." The road was built in 321 B. C. went 400 miles to Rome. The Roman roads were noted for their straightness, solid foundations, cambered surfaces facilitating drainage and use of concrete made from pozzolana (volcanic ash) and line. The Via/road traversed the lower part of the "Boot" of Italy, west to the Bay of Naples and then north to Rome. We were delighted to find the ancient road several times as we traveled.

Via Appia leads to Rome!

We boarded the train late that evening and arrived in Naples early the next morning. Joan's itinerary began with a trip to Herculaneum, the 6th century B.C. Greek city of at the base of the volcano, Mount Vesuvius. The entire area had been totally covered by ash in the eruption of August 24th 79 AD. Herculaneum was not discovered until the 1600's. We wandered through the excavated remains of this once thriving city and contemplated the sudden disaster. Then we rode up to the rim of the volcano and were awed by the size and depth of the crater. The next day we traveled by train to the see the ruins of Pompei further to the south. The overwhelming tragedy of the eruption was made evident as we saw plaster casts of people with anguish on their faces and even a dog caught by the sudden deadly gas and suffocating dust from the volcano. My art history lesson began as Joan read to us all day as we viewed frescos painted on some of the walls of the remains of the villas and gazed at mosaics on the floors which were amazingly well preserved.

Fresco is a technique of mural painting executed on freshly laid wet lime plaster. Water is used as the medium for the dry-powder pigment to merge with the plaster. As the plaster dries, the painting becomes an integral part of the wall.

Traveling further south on a bus, we enjoyed the charming town of Sorento and the jagged Amalfi Coast. The narrow road was a real challenge for our bus driver as he negotiated many hairpin turns driving up the hills of the peninsula and down the other side. The rock walls along the roadside were six to seven feet high and used to terrace the lemon trees that grow so well there in the Mediterranean climate.

The sea below us was a light blue green along the rugged coastline and steep limestone cliffs jutted grotesquely into the water, A necklace of black volcanic sand beaches was churned by white waves, and yellow lemons glinted in the afternoon sun. Villas and whitewashed homes clung to the cliffs. We noted many fortified stone towers perched precariously above the cliffs along the coast that were once used warn about Turkish pirates by lighting fires on the top of them. Gyrating staircases could be seen on the pathways along rugged slopes dashing seaward. I wrote in my journal that I could paint there for a year, but sadly with our daily tourist schedule, I could not.

.The next day we took a bus north to see the Oracle "Cave of The Sybil," once visited by people who sought guidance like the Greeks did at the "Oracle of Delphi." The town of Cumae nearby was the oldest and most distant colony of Greece settled about 740 B.C. Next, we explored the Roman ruins nearby and were delighted to discover the Appian Way. In Acts 28:14-23 we learn that the Apostle Paul landed nearby at Puteoli on the Bay of Naples and was allowed to stay for seven days and to speak with Jews there before traveling up the Appian Way to the "Appii Forum," a market center where Paul was greeted by Christians walking down about 40 miles from Rome to see him at the "Three Taverns."

March 1st, we took the train to Rome. Riding along the coast we noticed ruins of Roman towers and aqueducts along the way. Rome was founded about 747 BC and rose to be a city state about the 5th Century BC. Built on seven hills, the city was surrounded by one and then two walls. The second was heavily fortified. The Empire began to extend about 50 – 25 BC and fell in the 400's A.D. when invaded by barbarians from the north. Constructed in 126 A.D., the impressive Roman Pantheon originally housed statues of many gods of mythology. The walls are twenty feet thick, and it has a magnificent marble dome looming above it which was one of the largest domes at that time. The building was changed to a Catholic Church in 609 A.D.

Our next two days were filled with morning and afternoon tours with extensive sightseeing around the older part of Rome . The most memorable for me was viewing many large mosaics on the walls in numerous Basilicas recreated to replace the original paintings which were hung at the Vatican Museum.

A special treat was gazing upward at the ceiling of the Sistine Chapel to see the hand of God reaching out to give life to Adam painted by Michelangelo 1508-1512. The Basilica of St. Peter is very spacious and the light streaming in from windows in the dome was awesome. We saw Michaelangelo's Pieta sculpted in 1499 and many other fine works of art. I dated my life as before and after visiting Michelangelo's Artistic Adventure in Architecture! He was seventy years old when he was commissioned by Pope Paul III as the chief architect to design St. Peters! It was the largest church in the world for many centuries.

We viewed the ancient ruins of the Roman Forum and thought of the Apostle Paul walking on those stone paved streets. One street is named the Via Sacra, the Scared Way. The beautiful and intricate mosaics interested me the most and we saw them everywhere.

To make a Roman Mosaic, first a base was created with layered pieces of wooden planks, cut hay, porcelain, gravel, clay and mortar. Then plasters were applied to the surface and before the plaster hardened, stones or pieces of glass were placed in it. Large tiles or flat stones were placed around the edge of the mosaic.

The history of ancient pottery at the Etruscan Museum traced the development of pottery from Crete through Greece and then to early Italian pottery. I visited every art gallery I could. At that time the National Exhibition Hall featured " Romanian Art." The country of Romania was located next to Yugoslavia and became part of the Roman empire centuries before. Joan was diligent about reading guidebooks aloud and giving us descriptions of the sights we saw. My information cup was soon full to overflowing!

.On March 8th, we attended services at St. Andrews Presbyterian Church. The Scottish minister was from Glasgow. I enjoyed singing familiar hymns and the congregational singing was wonderful . Joan and Deidre met some people after the service from Australia. They had already made a point of visiting the Australian Embassy and one of their students who had moved to Rome several years before.

We took the rest of the day off and relaxed on a piazza sipping a cup of cappuccino and watching people go by. There were ladies with their maxi skirts and fur coats, mothers with children, people walking their dogs.

The next day it was back to our schedule starting by visiting the Vatican again and then more museums. I enjoyed the Museum of Folk Art. The traditional handwork was a welcome change from all the prehistoric sites we had been viewing! Finally, we traveled out to the ruins of the ancient port for Rome, Ostia Antica, where my parents had met Tony from Vienna in the summer of 1969. There were more wonderful black and white mosaic floors! After dinner we enjoyed a lovely sunset from the Lido, the wharf on the Mediterranean Sea and rode home on the Metro.

Thursday afternoon, we departed on the train to Assisi. We viewed fertile green fields and vineyards straggling up the foothills. We were just ahead of spring and saw snow on the mountains to the north. Assisi is a stony hilltop village with a number of churches. The Basilica of St. Francis was visible as we disembarked. The town's flavor was distinctively Roman with a thick icing of Tourist traps! Our taxi switched our way back and forth up the narrow cobblestone streets. We arrived at the guest house of St. Anthony, run by the Franciscan Sisters of Atonement.

What a welcome relief from all the traffic in Rome, which was always precarious at best! Our hearts were lifted as we experienced the peaceful atmosphere that pervaded everything.

The American Mother Superior from Modesto, California, greeted us warmly and showed up to our room with a lovely view of the town and valley below from our balcony. The Irish Sister assured us that St. Patrick did not drive snakes out of Ireland, they were simply a symbol for sin! It was so nice to have conversations in English! The next day we wandered through the narrow streets of the old town and visited the Basilica of St. Francis. His message of universal love has inspired many throughout the ages. Joan pointed out frescos and many fine art works throughout the town.

After a few days of wandering the peaceful back streets and visiting the Basilica again, we boarded the train for Florence. Frankly, I had no thoughts about this destination, yet as we approached, my heart began to sing! I was stunned by its beauty and artistic soul.

We discovered the one of treasurers of the Italian Renaissance on our way to our Pensione as we viewed a replica of Michelangelo's "David" in the Piazza Della Signoria. He began work on the 17 foot high block of marble when he was 25. It was hewn out of a large piece of marble that had been set aside for a giant figure! Michelangelo later said he was simply liberating the figure that already existed in the stone! The original sculpture was exhibited inside the Galleria Dell' Academia to protect it from the elements as were a number of works by Michelangelo and other artists.

We visited wonderful museums in the Old City and leaned much about the Italian Renaissance. I took a break one morning to do a sketch of the Russian Orthodox Church of the Nativity completed in 1902. It was quite different to all the other Renaissance basilicas we had seen!

Russian Orthodox Church of the Nativity in Florence, Italy.

Each Basilica had a separate Baptistry, because a person needed to be baptized before entering a church! The Baptistry of San Giovanni/ Saint John has a spectacular set of cast bronze doors covered with gold leaf, seventeen feet high. They were created by goldsmith Lorenzo Giberti. He won the commission in 1424 and labored on them for twenty seven years. The ten large panels depicted scenes from the Old Testament. He used new sculptural techniques and perspective in low relief. Some figures were almost free standing sculptures. Among the twenty-four busts, there is a self-portrait of Giberti and his father. The name the "Gates of Paradise" came from a complement by Michelangelo. A copy of the doors can be seen in San Francisco on Grace Cathedral.

Self Portrait   I still had short hair.

My notes about Leonardo da Vinci's work read: "took a bus to the town of Vinci to Leonardo's birthplace, which was a very humble house of a peasant girl, then to the museum to see replicas made from his sketches. Most were concerned with working gears, levers, and pulleys to get the maximum amount of energy with the minimum amount of effort. The replicas included several war devices such as battlements, rapid firing canons, quickly constructed bridges, and locks in canals using hydraulics, flying machines, printing presses and coinage. Many of the machines in the museum were movable to demonstrate their action. His sketches were written backwards with diagrams similarly labeled. He was a major part of the Renaissance! Because of the multiplicity of interests that spurred him to pursue every avenue of knowledge, Leonardo can be considered, quite rightly, to have been the universal genius par excellence.

Joan was very enamored by Fra Angelico's frescos and went to see everyone she could possibly visit in our week in Florence. I still was most enchanted by mosaics! Fortunately for me, the next stop was Ravenna the following Monday, and unbeknownst to me this was considered the Italian Capital of Mosaics!

Ravenna was built in 500 A.D. as the Capital of the Roman Empire after the fall of Rome in the 400's A.D. The nearby port on the Adriatic Sea connected it to the rest of the Byzantine Empire in Constantinople. The interiors of all the basilicas and baptistries are blazingly decorated with mosaics on their arched ceilings and floors! Stories of Christ's life and ministry are beautifully crafted for all to understand. Many of the figures had golden halos and, in some cases, the entire backgrounds were gold mosaics! We viewed ancient ruins of villas which had mosaic floors. My favorite mosaics were of animals and birds! For many years I carried around greeting cards that

I bought there, one with a dove on the side of a water fountain, another of a lamb symbolizing Christ, and an ornate representation of fruit and leaves.

Venice was 100 miles to the north. A few days later we took a train that arrived late on a rainy evening and found a Pensione nearby for the next few days. Our trip in Italy had been checkered with a lot of spring rain, snow on Mt. Vesuvius, and even hail! The skies cleared the next day, as we took gondola rides around Venice. I was the tour guide for a change!

On "Good Friday" we had more rain, I spent the day catching up writing in my journal, correspondence and reading. I wrote my advice to myself to "just visit Venice once and have happy memories!" Sadly, the whole place seemed much more commercial the second time to me. In between showers, we did more sightseeing and rode a boat out to the coast and to Murano to watch the glass blowing.

Sunday morning, I took a walk on my own and drew a sketch of a lamppost with the Campanili/ Bell Tower of the Basilica of San Gregorio across the canal. It had an angel on the top of the tower. With all our travels, I simply had not had much time on my own to do any sketching! Easter Sunday afternoon, I attended a service at a Methodist Church.

Venice – Campanile of San Gregorio

We were clever enough to book a 30 minute flight to Milan on Alitalia later that afternoon. We had great views of the jagged snowcapped Dolomite mountains, the Italian Alps. We discovered that Monday the day after Easter was a holiday in Italy and everything was closed.

Then we found out on Tuesday that all the guides at the Museums all over Italy had gone on strike! And my feet gave out, nice timing!! I went to American Express and got a lot of mail. Ever since learning about the special student and teacher airline rates at the travel agency in Corfu, I had been negotiating for a flight from London to New York. I heard from the agency when we arrived in Rome and immediately, I wrote for a more definite date. In Milan I got a date in mid-April to depart so I sent off funds for that ticket! Joan and Deidre bid me fond farewell that day and promised to stay in touch when they traveled to California later in the year on their way back to Australia.

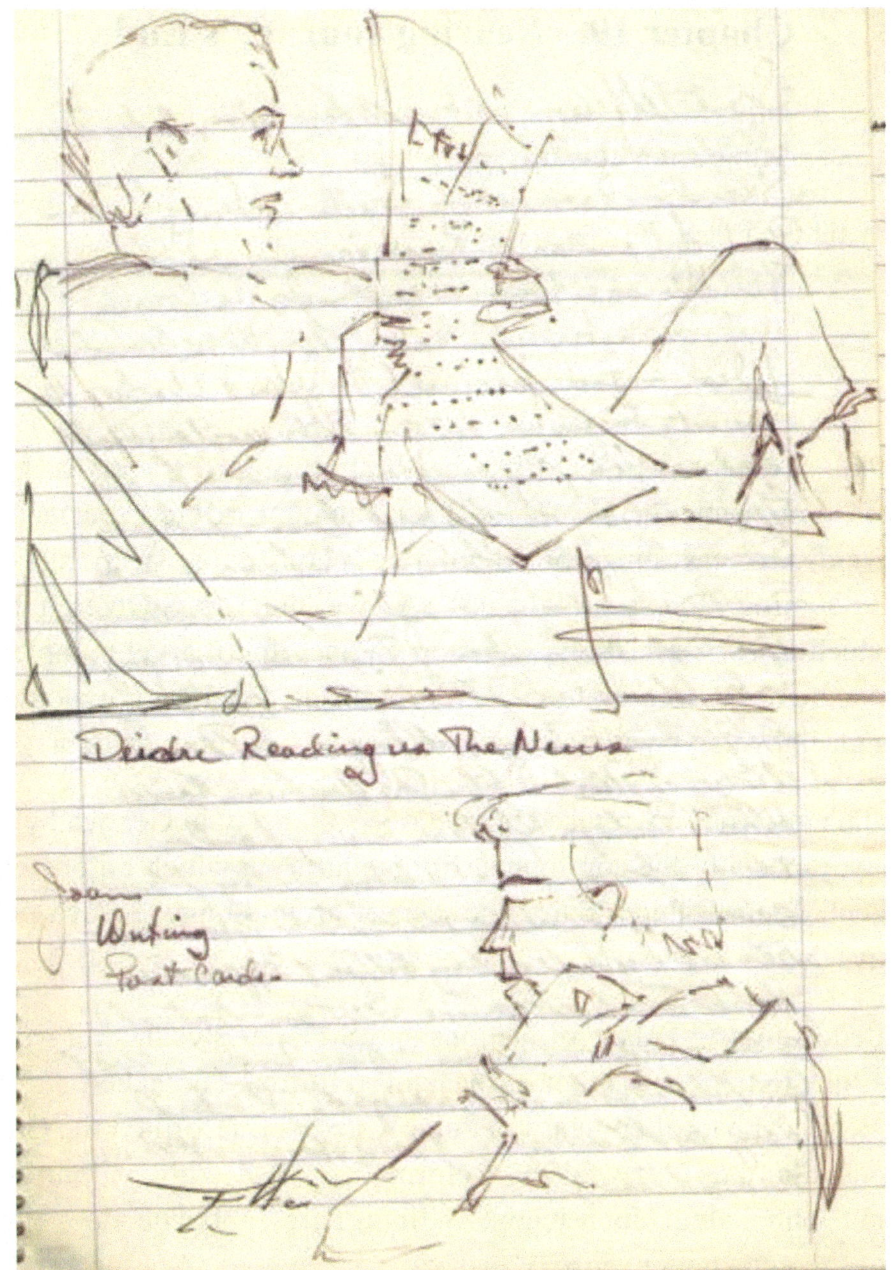

Joan and Deidre catching up on the news.

I wrote these scriptures in my Journal the day I departed for Switzerland:

Matthew 6:34 Jesus said: “do not worry about tomorrow, for tomorrow will worry about itself. Each day has enough trouble of its own

Matthew 7: 1-2 “Do not judge, or you too will be judged. For in the same way you judge others, you will be judged, and with the measure you use, it will be measured to you.”

Chapter 19 – Nearing Journey's End

'It is good to have an end to journey towards;

But it is the journey that matters,

In the end…"

Earnest Hemingway

On March 31st, 1970, I departed from Milan, on the train which travels east and south of the Italian Alps. Lake Como nestled at the foot of the mountains offered spectacular alpine views. Journeying northward, we saw gingerbread villages perched on steep hillsides and steeper mountains beyond shooting almost straight up! As we came to Switzerland, we entered the Simplon Tunnel which is 12.5 miles long. It is an engineering marvel completed in 1906. The double tunnels are some of the longest tunnels in the world. Then we burst out on the other side and traveled along glacial valleys with jaw dropping scenery for over an hour!

I granted myself a holiday from my revised budget of $7.00 a day in Geneva by cashing in all my odd bits of currency, especially the communist Romanian "lei" which no one else would touch! A light wet snow kept Mount-Blanc and the fine scenery around Lake Geneva well-hidden during most of my five days there

. I visited the United Nations – Palace of Nations and St. Peter's Cathedral where in the 1500's John Calvin and John Knox and other protestant reformers preached. My father was a Presbyterian minister and I had often heard of John Knox who reformed the Church in Scotland into the Presbyterian Church. I viewed the Reformation Wall with sculptures honoring many brave men including John Calvin, John Knox, William Farel, and Theodore Beza. I went to the memorial Wall twice to get a better sense of history.

While wandering around Geneva, I met a tall young Japanese student who had been studying classical base violin for a year in Koln, Germany. In his spare time, Tosh washed dishes and saved up enough money to come to Geneva to purchase a Rolex watch. He told me he just kept repeating "Rolex, Rolex" all the time he was working to keep himself focused on his goal! When he stepped up to the sales counter to choose the Rolex he wanted, they were very impressed with his story and that he paid them 1114 Swiss Francs, in cash, so they gave him a 5% discount!

The two of us ambled along Lake Geneva and watched the swans swimming in the water, enjoyed the lovely gardens and explored the old town. I visited many art galleries and museums. I saw a very large radiant scenic canvas painted by Neo-Impressionism artist Georges Seurat that was described by Vincent Van Gogh as having a "fresh use of color with an expansive palette." I wondered how Joan and Deidre were doing in Vienna. I missed all of Joan's commentaries as I visited many interesting sights and saw many wonderful modern art exhibits including a Bible illustrated by Salvador Dali!

Sunday morning, I attended 10 AM services at St. Peter's Cathedral. Bells were ringing as I arrived. The full congregation included both old and young Swiss people, and many were men! The organ music was wonderful! Then I went out in the snow at 11 AM to the Calvin Auditorium next door, where John Knox had followed John Calvin as pastor. A Scottish mister was the guest speaker. The theme was the faith of Abraham as he was sent by God to the promised land, "Not knowing where he was going." I really related to that! My prayer that morning was "Dear Lord, help me to make the best of whatever happens today."

Monday morning, I boarded the train for Paris. I had written to my friend June who was from Bighorn, Wyoming. June Wood had married her cousin in Paris after her husband had passed away. I had her address but had not gotten a response from her. I was hoping that I could stay with them as she had so generously offered some time before.

The train traveled through a long tunnel and then eventually out on to the plains of central France. At one point, we connected to another train with several cars loaded with skiers returning from their holiday in the French Alps. We arrived in Paris at 9:35 PM. I had June's address; however, the Taxicab driver had a great deal of difficulty discovering the location. On the 4th try he finally located their private street and dropped me off just as June was just arriving from the same train! They were with the skiers returning from the ski resort operated by her husband and his brother!

Their living quarters were on the 4th floor of their building. From my guest room I had a marvelous view of the Eifel tower and the Dome of the Invalids that housed Napoleon's tomb. Directly below us was President Pompidou's garden and on the far side of the gardens were more 4 story buildings housing the Italian and Russian embassies. The trees were just starting to bud out. Spring was on its way. Truly an amazing sight!

View of Paris from the 4th floor. The Eifel tower and Napoleon's tomb.

June was a very gracious hostess. The next morning at breakfast she informed me that they served their guests food in the morning and expected them to get their other meals on their own. She had a buzzer under the carpet that she pressed with her toe when she wanted service from the kitchen! On my travels, I had literally gone from the bottom in Yugoslavia to the top in Paris!

I walked over to the Left Bank of the Seine River and met my French Canadian friend, Gilles who had recently arrived from Corfu. He was seated outside a popular coffee shop in the St. Germain quarter chatting with friends. The next few days he gave me a great tour of Paris. Although it was my third visit in 2 years, this was by far my most extensive and informative experience. For me a real highlight was visiting the Auguste Rodin Museum. I had seen a copy of his "Burghers of Callias" and a few of his other works in Venice. I so was glad to have the opportunity to see more of his sculptures especially "The Thinker" and "The Kiss." He was considered the founder of modern sculpture both in marble and bronze.

Our tour included visiting Napoleons Tomb which was strategically located in the lowest part of les Invalides with viewing only from above, so that all were forced to bow their heads to see magnificent marble coffin! The guides at the Louvre were on strike, but I had seen the Mona Lisa by Leonardo da Vinci and other wonderful paintings there the summer before. The Jewel of Saint Chapelle was overwhelmingly awesome with so much stained glass!

Renovations to Notre Dame had just been finished. The scaffolding that was around it last summer was gone. I loved the rose window! We went to every art gallery and museum we could. I had always been enchanted with the artistic atmosphere of Paris Both times I was there before I had wanted to stay longer. We rode the Funicular railway up to Montmartre and chatted with the artists painting "en plein air" along the streets. We climbed the steps of the Basilica du Sacre'- Coeur which can be seen from anywhere in Paris.

Visiting Gilles helped me to realize that I had matured quite a bit since my month at Corfu. My six weeks with Joan and Deidre encouraged me to focus more on works of art and art history. I wrote in my journal about a sermon I heard "Worry not about tomorrow, the day has enough trouble in itself." My prayer was for strength to live one day at a time. I was wondering what I would do when I returned to San Francisco. I thanked the Lord for my ticket to return home in a week.

Saturday morning, June loaned me a nice coat for a special event. She and I walked with her husband and friends to the Hotel de Invalides nearby. We each presented our individual official invitation at the entrance sent by Monsieur Pompidou to attend the *Legion de' Honor* presentation. We walked into the courtyard and stood behind Dominique who was June's husband's Godson. Military bands were playing and there was much pomp and ceremony as the 15 recipients stood opposite their various military representatives. Then President Pompidou arrived in an olive green Citron. As the honorees stepped forward, he greeted each one, presented them with the Medal of Honor, shook their hands, and kissed them on each cheek. Usually, the Medal of Honor is given by a military officer. It was very rare for the President himself to perform the ceremony!

As we walked home, June told me how she met and married her husband in France and that all their children were first cousins! We celebrated Dominique's special event with champagne, and met his fiancé.

At last, it was time for me to pack my suitcase and prepare to take the train to the port of Calais on the English Channel, at noon on Sunday. I did a painting for June and wrote this poem for her in thanks for my stay.

L' Ame de" Paris

What haunting voice just whispered
"Thow cares away
come paint with me
live an artist's life
in gay Parie."

And how do I know

As I wander down
Some ordinary street
Just where I am-quite suddenly
Tho I've never heard this beat?

I cannot find the answer
In gaily stretching branches
Promising but bare,
Nor in Parisian faces
Hurrying here and there—

Scenic lines produce no clue
Notre Dame
Champs-Elysees
Tour Eiffel
The Louve—

Then in a quiet moment
When every thought is tried
I turn to my heart
And burning there,
I find
L' Ame de" Paris.

Sunday, April 12th, I boarded the train to Calais then rode the ferry across the English Channel to England. We arrived just below the White Cliffs of Dover. I got on the train to London. It was pleasant to see the English countryside once again! My friend Coleen met me at the station, and we took another train to her home in Southeast London. I was greeted warmly by her husband and two children.

The next few days were spent resting, checking my flight arrangements, and going to downtown London to visit the British Museum. There I enjoyed seeing the Athenian Elgin Marbles from the Parthenon brought from ancient Greece and large seascapes by M. W. Truner. I have always been inspired by his work. Unfortunately, that was all I was able to do during my short stay in London, although I really had wanted to see more.

I wrote a "Characterization sketch" about this atypical British family: "(I wrote the dialogue as Coleen talked and used her phrases whenever I could.)

"Coleen, 32, mother – (not housewife – she informed me- though she keeps the house quite tidy despite itself.) Ron 40 – Electrician – (He is very good at his job, Coleen says, that's why he doesn't have to be at work on time.) Ronald – 8- young boy (manifested by his dislike of going to Cubs, School, and all other such adult sponsored activities.) Louise – 6- Arty and precocious (always handy with a crayon, sticky paper or any other resourceful object that falls into her hands.)

The family lives on the upper two floors of a three story flat in London S.E. 27 aptly named Gipsy Hill. Other occupants are a parakeet, found one day by Ronald. The green bird chats with himself all day long. Also, there were several snails belonging to Loise whose favorite verses in the Bible are about the creation story referring to the blessing of all things that crept upon the face of the earth. And a swarm of tadpoles swimming in a glass bowl around of bit of kidney that Collen tossed in yesterday.

Outside of the central window of the three bay windows a pigeon occasionally takes pause. Once Coleen found a seemingly wounded bird that was taking shelter there. Collen called the children to rush downstairs and catch the poor thing when Mum pushed it off. The entire effort failed when the bird packed up and flew away! Coleen was feeding the birds by setting seed along the window ledge but was forced to stop by the neighbor below who was complaining about the mess they had to clean up.

Ron and Coleen have lived in the flat ever since son Ronald was a baby. They furnished the flat as time went by. The dining room was rather distant from family activities and cold in all but the summer months. I was treated to a special occasion last September when I came to "High Tea." We all sat around the table and helped ourselves to salad, bread, meat, the works! Little did I realize that they rarely sat around that table or any table for that matter. Ron, the children, and I ate off our laps, or on low tables or stools as we watched TV. I did not see Coleen eating at all. She consumes in the kitchen! The kitchen is filled with a small sink, stove, short cabinet, a tall cabinet and a bathtub!"

Apollo 13 was the seventh crewed American mission into space and was launched on Saturday, April 11. All the world was focused on these three men who were to have landed on the moon. However, the lunar landing was aborted after two days due to an oxygen leak in the service module. We were glued to the television to learn news about their return! They did land safely in the ocean on Friday the 17th, as I was departing for New York City!

I took a taxi to Gatwick Airport south of London and departed on the Caledonia Airway charter flight at 10:15 P.M. Seven hours later we arrived at midnight at Kennedy Airport in New York City. After going through customs and having nothing to declare, I discovered that the American

Airline flights to San Francisco were fully booked, so I took a taxi to the large T.W.A. terminal and got a reservation later at noon.

Finally, I stretched out on a seat and slept, sort of, until people started arriving at 5 A.M. There were people eagerly awaiting their friends and family members flying in from the west coast. A mother whose son was returning from Viet Nam burst into tears as he arrived carrying his sack over his shoulder. A young mother with a son born since his father had departed, teaching the baby to say "Daddy!" They eagerly greeted him!

In the swirl of Kennedy airport, I mused that air travel was a necessary means of transportation in America but is only a motion picture dream to my friends in Yugoslavia. They asked me "How much does it cost to fly in America?" "How long does it take?" The possibility of the average American citizen flying must be many thousands of times greater than the average southern European!

I finally walked up the concourse and got on the jet. I had tears of joy as I thought "I will be home soon." I recalled the words: "Home is the place that when you go there, they have to take you in!" I realized I had found the source of happiness that is in my own heart. I had the ability to enjoy life one day at a time and let tomorrow take care of itself.

Genesis 12: 1 - 5 Now the LORD had said unto Abram, Get thee out of thy country, and from thy kindred, and from thy father's house, unto a land that I will shew thee: and I will make of thee a great nation, and I will bless thee, and make thy name great; and thou shalt be a blessing: and I will bless them that bless thee and curse him that curseth thee: and in thee shall all families of the earth be blessed.

So, Abram departed, as the LORD had spoken unto him; and Lot went with him: and Abram was seventy and five years old when he departed out of Haran. And Abram took Sarai his wife, and Lot his brother's son, and all their substance that they had gathered, and the souls that they had gotten in Haran; and they went forth to go into the land of Canaan; and into the land of Canaan, they came.

Chapter 20 – Secretary

Dear Reader, the next three years of my life were a mix of many things that I cannot relate chronologically, so accept this chapter as an "Impressionism painting in words" of the events that transpired. Thank you!

On April 20, 1970, I landed at San Francisco International Airport and was warmly greeted by my parents, Winnie and Harry Washburn, with open arms and tears of joy and relief after our separation of eight months with a lot of uncertainty for them wondering where their wandering daughter was! It was good to be home and back to familiar things that helped me to really relax and unwind.

We drove down to the Santa Cruz area to see Grandma and Grandpa Young. More warm hugs and tears! They sat me down and said: "You are an artist, now what are you going to do with your life?" They were both involved in the art world, and their remarks really encouraged me. Since his retirement, my grandfather had been oil painting landscapes for fifteen years. He told me that my drawings and paintings had vitality. I had often painted with him in my mind. My grandmother informed me that she read my lines of descriptive verse to her poetry classes. They found my writing pleasing and poetic. I had often felt her presence over my shoulder as I wrote.

"My mother is her mother's joy,

Just as I to mine.

Smile by smile we link our hearts.

Across the span of time,

Receiving from each other

The thing we give away -

Hope that springs eternal.

And joy in each new day.

Dr. S. I. Hayakawa was a renowned linguist and scholar. I studied his work in my linguistics class at the University of Wyoming in 1965. He taught at San Francisco State College from 1955 to 1968. In November of 1968 he became the President of S.F.S.C. during difficult times when the students were on strike there demanding that Black Studies be included in the curriculum, and they were picketing against the war in Vietnam. There were several other strikes at Universities at that time, protesting the United States involvement in Viet Nam, most notably the riot at Kent State University in Ohio in May of 1970.

Early in May 1970, I walked into the Registrar's office at San Francisco State College to apply for a secretarial job. I later learned that a bomb had been found in the drinking fountain outside the office door I had just gone through! Thankfully it was discovered and nothing happened. I was hired as a clerk mailing copies of transcripts to schools where students requested their scholastic records be sent. The student's files sometimes got misplaced and there was always great tension when they were not where they were supposed to be. Eventually I was a trouble shooter to find them. I later worked as a graduate evaluator. Those were the days right before the computer was installed. Then it happened, we went to punch cards which created even more problems!

I enrolled in a master's program at S. F. S. C. that fall and took classes there through the Spring of 1972. I earned 12 units in "Museum Practice and Administration of the Arts" assisting with the installation of six different Anthropology displays. The class visited many museums in the San Francisco Bay area. Additionally, I earned six units in Anthropology by re-cataloguing several collections in the Tregenza Museum there on campus.

Perhaps the most valuable lesson I learned was that museums needed to have "pot boilers" or small items for sale at the checkout counter. Those sales helped pay the expenses of the institution. A retail lesson I never forgot!

I rented an apartment with a roommate not far from campus and was on my own again. While visiting my parents one day my youngest brother, George, in his enthusiasm to see me, linked our arms back to back and lifted me up over his shoulders. While it was a loving gesture, he pulled some muscles in my lower rib cage which was quite painful. So, to get in shape I joined the Jack LaLanne Health Spa nearby.

I had kept in touch with the watercolor instructor who had inspired me to go to the Yugoslavian coast. I participated in a workshop with Richard Yip in the summer of 1970 in the California Gold Rush Country of the Sierra foothills. I still loved old buildings. My paintings and drawings consisted mostly of old barns and landscapes on my outings around the S. F. Bay area.

Rough and Ready, California. **Northern California camp.**

One day at the health spa I met a man named Ken Boston in the weightlifting section. We started dating and eventually we married. I moved to his house in South San Francisco. His social interest was the Loyal Order of the Moose where he was the secretary and was required to be there most evenings.

Ken was fifteen years older than me and had been divorced for some time. He had a son Kenny who was five years younger than me and his daughter, Kathy, was six years younger than me. Ken owned a four bedroom house. For some time, his son, Kenny, lived with us while separated from his wife.

Kenny worked for Pan American Airlines and because he lived with us, we could fly standby for 10% of the fare! We took advantage of this opportunity and flew to Hawaii in 1972 then flew to Mexico in 1973. Later we flew to London, Tahiti, the Caribbean, Australia, and Spain.

We also took a cruise up the inland passage to Alaska. The blue of the glacial ice was stunning. I wrote a letter to my grandmother describing the amazing beauty of the blue ice floating in Glacier Bay. I read the letter to the passengers one evening. A pianist accompanied me with music that sounded like ice! My "urge to travel" and desire to see other cultures and their art was being fulfilled!

First trip with Ken to Hawaii.

My younger brother John got engaged to Marjie at Thanksgiving in 1970. Joan Benson and Deidre Brown whom I traveled with in Italy came through San Francisco just then as they were returning home to Australia on their around world tour. They joined us for the festivities that November. John and Marjie were married in June of 1971 and moved to Spokane, Washington where John attended Whitworth College to get his BA in Education, and Marjie had their first child, Willie, there the following year.

That summer, Ian Cameron, who had been my A.I.F.S. tour guide in London in the summer of 1969, visited me on his return trip from London to Australia.

In the spring of 1971, my youngest brother, George, received his "Order of the Arrow" the top award in Boy Scouts. This is the photo of our family: Left to right - John and Marjie Washburn, Harry Washburn, George Washburn, Winnie Washburn, Harriet Washburn. George joined the Coast Guard after graduating from Lowell High School in San Francisco.

John and Marjie Washburn, Harry Washburn, George Washburn, Winnie Washburn, Harriet Washburn.

Ken Boston's family lived in the central valley north of Bakersfield, California, where he had been raised after the family had migrated there from Oklahoma in the 1930's. His mother, Lottie, was still very spry and we hit it off right away. She had collected many things over the years that charmed her. Of particular interest to me was a lovely assortment of red glass plates and stemware.

Eventually I inherited the glass collection and began to do research to find out the name of the pattern. The collectable world was just coming alive with an interest in depression glass. I learned that the name the pattern of was "Cape Cod." It looked particularly beautiful in our dining room with the sunlight shining through it! That is what launched me into the world of collectables as we visited antique shows to learn about this charming red glass. Not much was known about the pattern at the time, but later it was featured on the cover of the Depression Glass price guide!

In my spare moments, my artwork and handwork flourished. I learned to crochet like my grandmother, I continued to hook rugs, enjoyed needlepoint and crewel stitchery, and I became quite inventive and creative even making something out of nothing! I tried out many forms of artistic expression! When inspired, I continued to write poetry.

In August of 1971, I attended another watercolor workshop in the Sierras with Richard Yip painting at Donner Summit, above Truckee, and at the north shore of Lake Tahoe.

Richard advised his students to forget their previous experiences and start a fresh.

He informed us that "all mediums are difficult.

Good paintings depend on the human spirit not on experience.

Put yourself into the painting and sketch things you are afraid of!

Sketch to see.

The character of the object never changes, though the angle may.

Paint a visual statement such as nostalgia."

These words of advice carried me through all my years of painting!

Donner Summit

In November 1971, we ventured north up the Californian coast to the early logging town of Mendocino. I was enchanted by the remote atmosphere and wrote:

"Why must I ever wander to feel at home again?"

Years later I learned that my great grandfather's parents had emigrated to Mendicino from Germany and operated a General Merchandise Store there in Caspar. Their son John was born in Humbolt county in 1858. As a teenager, he took care of the bookkeeping in his parents' store and rode a pony to carry the mail over the mountains!

As an adult, John Caspar Rudolph moved south to Lompoc, California where he owned a General Merchandise Store. That is where my grandmother Olivia was born! She was raised in that mercantile environment and later wrote poetry about her father's transactions with his customers.

In 1966, when I taught fifth grade in Felton, just north of Santa Cruz, I met a couple from Bulgaria. Mable Netoff was a very interesting lady and had created a small retail business in the front room of her home in Capitola south of Santa Cruz with all kinds of wonderful things that they had imported from around the world. I was enchanted with the woven blankets with patterns on both sides and wind proof djellabas or kaftans from Morocco, and her colorful beaded jewelry.

Mable's specialty was "essence of roses" in glass vials encased in carved wooden boxes from Bulgaria. Upon my return to the states, I visited her and continued to be enchanted by her merchandise. Eventually I asked her if I could take some of her fascinating jewelry to my office at San Francisco State and sell it to the gals there. For a while the office manager allowed me to set things out on my desk during our coffee break time, but finally he told me to stop. I paid all the proceeds to Mable, but I enjoyed the opportunity to present fun merchandise!

Shirley Biby was a supervisor in the Registrar's Office. We became fast friends and discussed many subjects. When I got engaged to Ken, she introduced me to her friend Gilda Forster in Pacifica where they both lived. Guilda ran "Boutique Potpourri" in the Sharp Park area featuring her high-end fashion designs for both men and women. My mother had brought home a small length of silk from Hong Kong on her A.I.F.S. tour to the Far East in 1970. Guilda very carefully cut it out to make a lovely dress for my wedding in July of 1973. My grandfather, George Demming Young, passed away in 1972, but my grandmother, Olivia Young, was able to attend. Then Ken and I took our honeymoon trip to Mexico.

Grandma, Olivia Young, at our wedding reception. **Hibiscus in Mexico.**

Psalm 95: 6 – 7 O come, let us worship and bow down: let us kneel before the Lord our maker. For he is our God; and we are the people of his pasture, and the sheep of his hand.

Chapter 21 – "Boston Craftiques"

On the 4th of July 1974, my husband, Ken Boston and I visited his friends in Paradise, California, and enjoyed a marvelous parade with lots of inventive participants including some men who walked along with their hands above their heads a large top hat pulled over them covering their chests. They had eyes and a mouth painted below the hat which they animated by moving their stomach muscles! They were hilarious . We visited several shops in town of Paradise where ladies had incorporated antiques and crafts together. I was very inspired to begin to create things using "old stuff". On the way home, Ken told me that I did not need to work in the Registrar's office anymore because his income was sufficient for both of us. I came home and created my business name "Boston Craftiques" combining crafts and antiques.

Later that summer we sold some things people had given me at a flea market. As I walked around the tables, I picked up an interesting item for twenty five cents and put it on my own table and almost immediately sold it for a dollar! The "Retail "Light went on in my head! That is how I began to be an antique dealer! I was following in the footsteps of my ancestors and their children as entrepreneurs stepping out and creating businesses befitting the times!

Inspired by Mable Netoff selling imported items out of her home, I began my antique and craft business in our dining room. I ran an ad in the local paper, and quickly discovered that I could not make any money on my hand crafts. However, antique dealers came to my sale and bought things that were old. One was a dealer invited to join her at her business "Second Time Around." The shop was in Rockaway Beach on the Pacific Coast Highway in Pacifica. She wanted me to help run the store parttime so she did not have to be there so much. "The Cloth Jungle" with vintage clothing was next door. They both had a good clientele.

That summer, Kenny had moved back in with his wife so now our Pan Am standby tickets cost us 20% of the fare, but it was still a good deal for us, so we flew to London for a couple of weeks. While there I did some shopping and came back with a treasure, an old American metal bank whose hand would put the coin in his mouth.

A Real Find

A treasure from England—Harriet Boston shows the antique mechanical coin bank given to her by a friend during her "antique hunt" in and around London. (See Pat's Column.)

Now that she's "into antiques," Harriet Boston traveled to Jolly Olde England to see about the possibilities of finding some bargains. But to her amazement, "it seems like most of the good antiques are already here—in America."

Harriet reports that her scouting trip to England convinced her, "There is a tremendous wealth of antiques right in our own back yard."

FLEA MARKETS in London come in several varieties. There is the famous Flea Market on Petticoat lane, with all new goods. It is held on Sunday mornings and is known as a "tourist trap."

Another Flea Market is on Portobello road. It has more for antique dealers. However, Harriet found, "It is who you know, rather than where you go."

She did find a Westminster chime clock—but again, most of the clocks are already in the states.

ENGLAND, these days — even with high prices — is still one of the cheaper places to visit. "Can you imagine! Some French come to England to buy groceries. And the French have the British coming over there to buy their liquor!"

Harriet raves about the English pub lunches. "My favorite was lager beer and lime juice with huge sandwiches." According to her, it's easy to get around on public transportation. She even stayed with a family in Greenwich as a "lodger," which gives one a better chance to get acquainted than when staying in hotels.

The collector or antique buyer is likely to be discouraged, according to Harriet. "Prices are prohibitive to buy and then, sell."

Inflation in England has really affected sales.

"IT WAS interesting and I did bring back some things I had wanted," Harriet says, "but I was very happy to come home."

Harriet, who has some of her things on display in "The Second Time Around" antique store at Rockaway Beach, is a Flea Market fiend.

Her corner at the store features kitchen utensils, memorabilia and, lately, old lace.

"A LOT OF the teens and young people are into the costume effect," Harriet says. "They can use the lace to decorate blouses or long dresses."

Other shelves of "In Items" feature old license plates stamped "World's Fair—1939," railroad hats, garters, rhinestone jewelry, labeled containers or glass (there is even a DUZ soap box—remember that commercial, D-U-Z does everything?).

And one of the latest trends to develop is the collecting of posters and photographs of the movie stars we're watching on the old movies—Bogart, Temple and other favorites.

Remember "The Second Time Around" when the visiting foreign students come to town or when the relatives have run out of things to see this summer. It's a fun place to visit. And right next door is "The Cloth Jungle," for another nostalgia trip.

While on a trip that fall into the Goldrush Country, we came across a large outdoor antique business called "You Name it." I discovered that almost anything "old" had a buyer! The item that brought it home to me was a beer bottle opener with the name of the brewery on it. This simple item could be worth a couple of bucks! I also learned that kitchen items were of interest to the collector, especially if the handles were made of the early plastic called Bakelite and also old wooden kitchen items.

People came into the Pacifica store looking for Depression Glass and I was invited to join a Glass Club in the San Jose area an hour south of my home. Eventually, I helped to begin the Bay Area Glass Club for those of us who lived on the San Francisco Peninsula. In order to learn the Depression Glass patterns, the members would flash pages of the price guide to each other to see if we could remember the pattern names! It was a very good memorizing technique which has helped me recall the patterns to this day!

While I only had a very small space in her store in Pacifica that was the size of a single car garage, I did well and soon I was outselling the owner! In exasperation, she asked me to leave! I was bemoaning my fate to my fashion designer friend, Guilda one day and she advised me that she was planning to open her high-end fashion design business on Columbus Street in San Francisco near Fisherman's Warf. She invited me to join her there so she could spend more time in backroom designing and sewing her clothing!

In 1975, "Guilda of San Francisco -Original Designs" opened near Fisherman's Warf. Guilda already had some very interesting customers like Pete Marino, a San Francisco socialite. Pete had obtained black knit jumpsuit that Elvis Presley had worn. He asked Guilda to sew a duplicate for him to wear! He introduced her to many of his San Francisco friends who became her clients.

I gradually developed my antique business. I had a glass display case filled with antique jewelry. However, I came to realize the need for San Fransico themed souvenirs. I mounted post cards of The Cliff House on Pacific coast and antique photos of Victorian homes that dotted the older part of the City on small wooden boxes and also wrapped the postcards around large candles.

One day, while I was sitting the front of the store, a lady came in selling Neo Life Vitamins. Since my ears had been ringing for years, she suggested taking various supplements to address the issue. Eventually I became a distributor myself and even went door to door downtown San Francisco. (I learned that selling door to door was an essential part of becoming a good salesperson!)

In October of 1976 to celebrate the Bicentennial of the United States, Ken and I flew east and enjoyed a Fall Color Tour of New England. Shortly after that my father's sister, Getrude Dow, informed me that I was eligible to be a member of the Daughters of the American Revolution. My grandmother Gertrude Washburn had done the needed genealogy research on our Revolutionary War ancestor, Samuel Lyon, in the early 1900's and all I had to do was prove that my father was her son and I was his daughter. I became a member of the San Adreas Lake Chapter of the Daughters of the American Revolution in the summer of 1977.

Guilda asked me to do crochet work on some of her creations by adding fringe around her ruana's which were a winter wrap for ladies. One day I was working on a ruana when a man came in and started admiring the layout of the small sales area in the front of Gilda's store. He was from Hollywood and was seeking a location like this to film part of a Television program called "Movie of the Week." He negotiated with Guilda to have a TV crew come in and film actors both in the front of the store and in her work area in the back. It was a big production complete with lights and cameras and very exciting for us and the tourists who gathered around to watch the filming. We were on ABC that fall!

Coming Attraction

Look for this sign and this shop on your TV screens--the "Gilda of San Francisco" boutique, owned by Pacifican Gilda Forster, who used to own the "Boutique Potpourri" in Sharp Park, was selected as the location for an ABC "Movie of the Week." The two stained-glass logo designs and lettering pictured here were created by Pacifican Zyg Karchevski, who said the crowds were so large outside the entrance to Gilda's shop last week during the filming he didn't even bother to muscle his way through. Another Pacifican, Lyn Buchanan, crafted the stained glass figures from Karchevski's designs. Tribune photo.

In May of 1977, Ken and I flew to Australia at the invitation of my traveling companions when I was in Italy. Joan and Deidre drove us from their homes in Brisbane on the northwest coast on a tour of Western Australia. It was wonderful to be with them again. In Canberra, I was amazed to see a bronze sculpture honoring General Dragolub-Draza Mihailovic, a Yugoslavian Partisan a World War II hero . I had learned that he was the uncle of my Serbian boyfriend when I was in Bela Cirva in November, 1969!

We traveled to Sydney and discovered that the nationwide air controllers strike was still going on, so we lost our trip to tour New Zealand. We stayed with my A.I.F.S. friends from 1969, Ian and Carol Cameron in their charming old Victorian home until the strike was over a week and a half later

. I was delighted to visit the Sydney Opera House almost every day and we got to purchase seats to see a play there, Ceasar and Cleopatra, because someone was stuck somewhere else in the world due to the strike!

Wandering around downtown one day, we discovered Sydney Antique Market, a large sales area with 100 dealers all under one roof! I was stunned at the concept, since I had only seen one antique dealer in each store I had ever visited in California. I found a few things I could bring home on the plane including some amber glass from the 1930's and some green American Depression glass. When we finally did get on the plane on standby, we were deplaned on the island of Pago Pago while people who had been waiting there for days to leave the island were boarded! Fortunately, there were two seats left after they were all accommodated, and we got back on that night after an hour's wait in that hot muggy tropical climate.

As I continued to expand my antique inventory, I was able to purchase a tall Victorian Ebony Display Cabinet with small shelves on the top part to show decorative items on either side of a large mirror. It added a lot of "atmosphere" to my antique presentation. I had the opportunity to be a dealer at the large antique show at the San Francisco Cow Palace just south of San Francisco and was able to sell there several times. Eventually, I wanted to take the display cabinet along.

Fortunately, my space was near the building's back door so Ken could load it right off the rear of his small pickup truck, a Ford Ranchero, that he drove for work. At the end of the show, we loaded everything up. Ken called the heavy display cabinet the "Black Moriah." It was very bulky and awkward to move. When we got back to Gilda's store late on Saturday night, the key to the store was not on my key ring!!! I never did know what happened to it!!! Finally, we knocked on the door of the man in the upstairs apartment and he and Ken carried the "Black Moriah" and all my other boxes up the narrow stairs.

On our way home, Ken suddenly said to me, "I want a divorce!" I was stunned, and silent for the rest of the long way home. Finally, Ken broke the silence saying, "I do not want a divorce, I just do not to help you with your antique shows anymore ." Phew!!!

That was a real shock to me. I remained silent.

Shortly after that Guilda said that she thought her store was becoming schizophrenic. Sne asked me to leave! Fortunately, I had recently discovered The Great American Collective nearby on Lombard Street in San Francisco. They had a space available, so I moved my merchandise over there right away. It was interesting to discover that the gal who ran this collective was the sister of the owner of the large antique market we had visited in Sydney! Collectives were a whole new concept of selling antiques which this owner had recently introduced to the United States! These sisters revolutionized the antique market in the coming years!

I the fall of 1977, my mother told me that her sister, Pont, who recently passed away of cancer, had gifted her with art supplies for painting on porcelain. Mom contacted Elizabeth Uttinger, a Swiss porcelain painting teacher in San Francisco. Mom asked me if I wanted to take lessons together with her. I quickly agreed as my artistic endeavors had been mostly hand crafts in recent years and I had not done any painting for quite some time.

We climbed up the stairs to the second story of Elizabeth's classic San Francisco home located on a steep hill and sat down at her kitchen table where several other ladies were already working on their paintings of various floral designs.

I was challenged to learn a new medium and soon found that like watercolors one worked from light to dark. We mixed the powdered paints with a special oil and then painted on a glazed surface. Once the item was fired, you could not change your work at all. So, one had to be very careful and deliberate to paint the subject because in the firing the paint became permanently embedded in the glaze. My mother only took four lessons, then gave me all the supplies which my aunt had received from a woman who painted in the early 1900's. I studied weekly with Elizabeth for five years.

Finally, while I was painting a pear and I rejoiced because it really looked like a pear!!! It took a while for me to learn the techniques. I painted flowers and birds on various shapes, some of which were white porcelain items I bought in flea markets and garage sales.

Early in 1979, the King Tutankhamun exhibit came to the de Young Museum in San Francisco and caused quite a bit of excitement. Since my father had been to Egypt in 1952 and again in the early 1960's studying the antiquities, he prepared speeches to give to interested audiences on Egyptology. Guilda's customer, Pete Marino, had acquired a replica of Pharoh's throne that was used in the movie "The Ten Commandments." Pete and dad became friends.

One day I went to visit my parents and dad pointed at a rather large box on the dining room table and said that Pete had left it for me! It was full of a rough fabric, but as I put my hands down the sides to pull the item out, I got a very strange sensation that I could not explain. As I unwrapped the fabric, I discovered a mummy's head!!! Apparently, Pete and a friend had robbed a grave in South America and had only been able to smuggle out the head! PHEW!!! What was I to do with it???

I took the mummified head to the Great American Collective and found a dealer who was selling a plaster replica of King Tut's bust. He was happy to trade it for the mummified head. I presented the King's blue and gilt bust to my dad. Everyone involved was pleased and I was very relieved!!!

Ken was the San Francisco area sales representative and serviceman for the Hoyt Heater Company. The water heaters were manufactured in Reno, Nevada. Plumbers would come to his warehouse to get their water heaters and when needed, Ken would go out on service calls in the San Francisco side of the bay and occasionally further south.

One Saturday Ken told me that he had a service call in Woodside and asked if I wanted to come along. We drove up Skyline Drive through the Redwood trees and came to a private gate for the home of radio author Calton E. Morse. I was excited to meet him because I had listened to his radio program "One Man's Family" on Sunday evenings when we lived in Marin City in 1952. The script was so real to me that I was certain I could find the Barber home in the ritzy Sea Cliff neighborhood in San Francisco where they were supposed to have lived. Carlton and his wife Patricia welcomed us warmly and I chatted with Patricia while Ken worked on the problem with Carlton on the newly installed water heater. Later another visit was required for further correction of the installation in their large home. Patricia called me "Joy" and we kept in touch.

When Carlton and Patricia decided to downsize, they gave me things to sell. I was very blessed by their trust because they did not like to have strangers come on to their large, forested estate. Whenever I told a customer that an item was from Carlton E. Morse, a great deal of excited conversation followed. Sometimes people even told me they named their children after one of the radio characters!

I had the opportunity to visit the Oakland Rose Garden on June 20th, 1979. I did a drawing of a Lucky Peace Rose and later printed the drawing on a blank greeting card to sell. I wrote a poem there in the garden and dedicated it to my grandparents who had lived in Oakland many years before:

ODE TO A LUCKY PEACE ROSE

OF ALL THE BLOSSOMS IN THIS GARDEN

YOUR PINK PEACH PETALS ARE MOST FAIR

STILL HARBORING DROPS OF MORNING DEW

IN YOUR TIGHTLY WOUND THROAT THERE.

YOU BOB GENTLY IN THE AFTERNOON BREEZES

HERE IN THE SECLUDED FRAGRANT VALLEY

TUCKED AMOUNG THE OAKLAND HILLS.

MEMORIES OF MY GRANDPARENT'S COURTSHIP

PASS BEFORE MY MIND

SOMEHOW YOUR AGELESS BEAUTY

IS WITH THEIR LIVES ENTIWNED.

THANK YOU FOR THIS TOUCH OF GLORY

ALONG LIFE'S HURRIED WAY.

THANK YOU FOR THE SWEET REMINDER

THAT WORDS CAN NEVER SAY.

In the fall of 1979, I learned that there were outdoor antique shows held once a month on Sundays in Shopping malls just north of San Jose. I began traveling to Valco Village, a shopping mall in Cupertino and setup my tables and a small glass display case on the last Sunday of each month. I also went to Cherry Chase Shopping center in Sunnyvale to sell on another Sunday. A lot of my customers were dealers because I marked my prices low.

One lady always asked me for buttons for sewing. I learned that Lucille Weingarten had recently moved to the Bay area from New York City. She was the past president of the National Button Society. She told me that next to postage stamps, vintage button collecting was the most popular hobby I the world! When Lucille found out that I had some old porcelain button blanks in the collection of Porcelain painting equipment I got from my aunt, she encouraged me to paint on them with themes that were attractive to button collectors for their competitions. The important thing was that the porcelain blanks had their shanks on the back and were part of the button. I joined the local button collectors club and began to seriously look for buttons to sell collectors and crafters.

By October of 1979, Ken and I agreed to divorce. His life in the Moose Lodge and his nightly heavy drinking was not the way I wanted to live the rest of my life. I found a singlewide trailer in another part of South San Francisco and moved over to it with my small dog, Pepe. I was vastly relived and joyous in my newfound freedom! I got a job for the Christmas season at Rod McLellan's Company famous for developing and selling Orchids. One of the managers had lived in Sheridan, Wyoming when we were there in the 1960's. I enjoyed being surrounded by all the beauty and even painted a few orchids on some of my fun plates. I was rejuvenated and energized by my fresh start in life at the age of 36.

Small bell I painted for my parents in 1979.

Psalm 81:10 I am the LORD thy God, which brought thee out of the land of Egypt: open thy mouth wide, and I will fill it.

Chapter 22 – A New life!

Our divorce was filed late in October 1979 and my move to a trailer park nearby was quick and joyous! I was exhilarated by the freedom from many things, mostly the relationship as a whole. At that time a small 25' trailer next to my 40' singlewide just over the picket fence was being vacated by a lady in her 60's. However, soon Leslie moved into it with his parrot, Lolita, who made life very interesting for us all. She soon learned to chuckle like me and whistle for Pepe whenever she had a chance.

Leslie was a retired college English professor, who with all the rest of the tenants had been kicked out of their tall apartment building in downtown San Francisco because it was going to be demolished. He did not have a vehicle, so sometimes I took him shopping or to refill his propane tank.

I had recently read about "Findhorn," a trailer park in Scotland that had been transformed into a spiritual garden retreat and I was inspired to do some gardening around our two plots to make them into "Findhorn West." At first, Leslie scoffed at the idea, however he finally got on board and painted all our picket fences with white paint, and I planted succulents in our four-inch borders along the driveways that surrounded our trailers.

Winter descended on us with a vengeance. On those chilly nights we listened to heavy rainstorms pounding on our metal roofs. Still all in all it was a joyous time for me, and I did some sketches of flowers and printed up a couple of greeting cards still using Boston Craftiques as my business name.

At the end of January 1980, I set up in my usual space at Valco Village in Cupertino. The space was "L" shaped with a wooden post in the middle of the "L" which I could pound a nail on and hang a small framed etching I had on consignment from a lady who had asked me to liquidate her accumulation of many old things. Some items were interesting and others not so much, but with optimism I took her odd bits to help her get some money out of it all.

Mid-afternoon, a customer came by and asked to see the etching. The subject was the Field Museum on Lake Shore Drive in Chicago. He proceeded to tell me that he had been looking for something special to hang in his bathroom. We chatted for a while and finally he bargained me down from $7.50 to $5.00. Sigh. Such is the life of an antique dealer, always letting the customer win!

The rest of the winter ground on, and I did two shows every month just to keep the bills paid. At the end of April, I was set up at Valco Village Antique Show again. The weather was more pleasant now. Later in the afternoon, that same customer appeared at my table. He recalled seeing me there in January, but frankly, I had met many customers and so did not think much about them unless we started dealing on a regular basis. We chatted for a while and finally he asked me if I would like to join him for dinner. I accepted. He described the route to a Chinese Restaurant in Menlo Park which was on my way home. Then he walked away.

After packing up all my boxes and tables into my brown Pinto station wagon, I drove north up Interstate 280. As I passed the Stanford University campus in Palo Alto on the right, I spotted a large lone California Oak on a hillside on the left. I was amazed that it was located right where I was to make my turn to go into Menlo Park. The previous fall, I had done a women's empowerment workshop, and we were asked to do a visualization of something we wanted to accomplish. In my imagination I saw THAT tree on THAT hill and understood that there was some underground activity. I related the concept to Alice in Wonderland for lack of better understanding! So here I was at THAT very place! "Curioser and curioser!"

Philip Priska and I had a marvelous evening at "Chins" on Santa Cruz Avenue in Menlo Park. We talked and talked and talked about many things. We had a variety of interests in common, particularly our love of art and antiques. He worked at Stanford Linear Accelerator which was just beyond THAT TREE! It was a two mile long underground tunnel in which particles were shot at the speed of light to smash atoms. Philip worked there on a rotating shift.

Philip worked 7 days on night shift, then he got a day off, and then he worked 7 days on swing shift, and he got a day off, and then he worked 7 days on day shift, and then he had 4 days off. Then the shifts started all over again. He was a guard at the inner gate, and everyone entering that secure area housing the accelerator was required to show the guard their updated dosimeter badge which was to be turned in every three months to check for a person's possible radiation exposure.

Since the next weekend was his long weekend off, Philip invited me to attend a large antique show the following Saturday in San Francisco. I accepted and we parted ways. I returned to my trailer and he to his small carriage house on the back of a property nearby in Menlo Park. I wrote him a note, thanking him for our nice evening. On Saturday afternoon, he appeared at my doorstep holding a red rose and calla lily that he had picked in his garden. That was the first time anyone had brought me flowers!

We enjoyed browsing around all the booths at the large antique show. Philip had promised himself that he would buy me something first in case he later found something he wanted. I picked out an old yellow glass bowl with corn impressed on the outsides of it because I was very interested in ears of corn in those days! He never did find anything for himself. Afterwards, I suggested we go to my favorite place in South San Francisco called "Pipes and Pizza." The company had purchased an old pipe organ and built a restaurant around it. A musician played fun jazzy tunes while we ate pizza. We had a great time.

The next day, Philip helped me set up and sell at the Cherry Chase outdoor antique show in Cupertino. We enjoyed the opportunity to be together. He had bought and sold old and antique items that he liked in the past and had been collecting older things since 1974. He asked me when he could see me again and I suggested he join me as a guest at my health spa on Tuesday evening.

There we sat in the sauna and talked some more. Finally, Philp asked me to come and live with him. Then he had to go to work on the night shift, and I went home to think about it. The next morning, he called me early and woke me up. He had been concentrating on me all night! I told him I had lived with my first husband for two years before we got married and I did not want to do that again. We both agreed that the most important thing in our relationship was commitment to each other. So, I said YES!

Just before Mother's Day, I introduced Philip to my mother in Pacifica where my parents had been living up on the hill overlooking the Pacific Ocean for a few years. She was very gracious.

Next, we drove up to Petaluma to see my father who was serving as an interim pastor for the Presbyterian Church there while the congregation searched for a new pastor. We met my father at an ice cream parlor in the older part of Petaluma. We were seated around a small round table on old white wire chairs. After ordering, suddenly Philip stood up and went around to my father's chair and got down on one knee and asked him for my hand in marriage! That was a total surprise to me! My father rather curtly remarked: "She has a bad track record." Philip replied that he did not have a good one either and had been divorced several years before. PHEW. We enjoyed our ice cream in peace and got dad's blessing as well!

Philip meets Winnie and I gave her a small shoe I painted for her for Mother's Day.

Earlier that year, both of my parents had participated in a "Cursillo." It was a non-denominational Christian renewal retreat. I was so impressed by the spiritual effect it had on each one of them that I also chose to do the weekend retreat in San Francisco late in May. It was an all-volunteer program that outlined the basic tenants of Christianity.

During one session on "confession," I begrudgingly confessed that I was a sinner. That was a turning point in my life back to Jesus and away from my futile search in the 1970's for spiritual fulfillment in the "New Age" movement.

The programs were delightful and after each course, we 30 ladies returned to our cots in a large hall and discovered all manner of wonderful gifts on our beds - flowers, cards, and even stuffed animals from people we never even knew. The cards assured us that they were praying for each of us all weekend, day and night, bed by bed! By Saturday evening, we were overflowing with love and joy! It was as if heaven came down and blessed us all abundantly! It was an experience that carried my family all the rest of our lives, giving love generously to all we met!

The Daughters of the American Revolution chapter asked me to be their next regent (as they called their president) that September. I became a member in 1977 but had not held an office. I agreed with their assurance that they would guide me through all the details. One day the secretary called me and said that they wanted to have my new married name in their Schedule of events for the next fall and the new list of officers.

So, I needed to get married to get my name changed for their publication deadline the end of July! I called Philip and we arranged to have our wedding on July 5th which was the next long weekend in his work cycle.

A few weeks before I had attended the wedding of my Hastings College friend Lori and Carl Cordini. They had printed up their wedding vows in a bulletin. Philip and I sat down and read those vows to each other. We married each other with great joy!

My dear friend Shirley from the San Francisco State Registrars offered me her white satin wedding dress that she wore when she was married in back in 1949! It fit! There were tiny satin covered buttons going all the way down my back and the sides of my arms. I felt truly glamorous with the long satin train flowing behind me!

Shirley's wedding dress. Note my "Family History Quilt" that I made for my parents.

My parents planned a small wedding in their garden. My mother picked flowers and made me a fabulous bouquet. The 5th was a foggy July day as usual along the coast, however the sun broke through the clouds just as my father read our vows to us in the center of their garden in the small gazebo. Then mom prepared a lovely wedding dinner for a few close friends and my brother John's family.

After that, we drove up the California coast to the Mendocino area for our short honeymoon and stayed at Jughandle Creek Farm. I visited there at the pioneer farmhouse in February with a friend for a women's retreat. It was very quaint. Philip and I had a marvelous time exploring the Pygmy Forest nearby and viewing the ocean all up and down the coast. Philip liked to recall that when he held my hand as we were saying our vows, he realized that he was now responsible for me. He was indeed a good husband all the rest of our lives.

Because the wedding was done on such short notice Philip's family in Michigan and Atlanta, Georgia could not attend. We planned a reception later when both of our families and friends could come. Stern Grove is a large valley of Redwood trees in the heart of San Francisco. We booked the picnic area for our reception there for August 30th. Philip's brother Marty and his wife and daughter flew up from Atlanta to Detroit and picked up his mother, Julia, and her sister Reggie. They all flew out to the San Francisco Airport where Philip met them and drove them in to the reception. However, Philip got a bit lost on the way getting off the freeway, but eventually they did arrive. I meanwhile went with my parents and greeted many friends.

Carl and Lori with the stained glass window I commissioned Carl to make for us in trade for my red glass collection!

My dress that day was reminiscent of an Austrian outfit. When I met Julia she was delighted. Mom wrote a song to the tune of "Edelweiss" as a salute to our marriage. I was amazed to learn that Julia's family was from what is now Romania in the area near where I had been when I stayed in Yugoslavia in 1969! Small world!

Philip's father was from Vienna where I had also stayed for a month! Joseph and Julia had both emigrated to America in the 1910's and finally met and married in Detroit. Julia Folding's father worked for the Ford Motor Company and Joseph Priska was a machinist in the plant. He was invited to the Folding home for dinner one evening. He met Julia and eventually they married and had three children. Marty and Julie were the older son and daughter, and Philp was born five years later.

Eventually Joseph divorced Julia and then she worked as a housekeeper living with Philp in "well to do" people's homes in Detroit. Both older children had joined the armed services as soon as they graduated from High School, and so did Philip at the age of 17! After his 3 years in the Army, much of it in France, he chose not to live in Detroit. He stayed briefly in Las Vegas and then got various jobs in the San Francisco Bay area.

When he was growing up, Philip's family loved to play poker. As an adult he tried his hand at gambling in Las Vegas and went broke. Later he played "Lowball poker" at gambling joints on the San Francisco Peninsula where it was legal. He did so well that he quit his job and gambled full time until the owners of the club asked him to leave because he was so successful that they were losing money!

He got a job with Ideal Cement as a chemist and helped to mix the batches used to construct the nearby San Mateo Bridge. Then he went to work for Stanford University at Stanford Linear Accelerator Center in 1971 as a guard at the inner gate and lived in a small apartment on Harvard Avenue in Menlo Park.

In 1974, Philip became very interested in the Menlo Park watercolor artist, Rachel Bently and started purchasing her watercolor paintings from her whenever she would sell them to him. She liked to keep the original painting that she had done and would paint a copy when asked for it. Philip purchased at least 50 of her miniature paintings at a local bookstore.

By the time we met, he had about 75 of her larger paintings, some of them were "one of a kind" when Rachel would let him have one. Philip became her major collector and admirer. Rachel never exhibited her paintings in a gallery although she did hang 120 of her paintings of one room schoolhouses which she had done in Northern California and Nevada at the California State Fair in 1952. This exhibit put her on the map so to speak and her work was always in demand and her paintings often went to collections around the world.

Rachel Bentley with some of her Watercolors.

Ms. Bentley was one of Menlo Park's best-known figures in its very rich history. Born in 1894, a resident of Menlo Park since 1937, she had a very rich and full life until her passing in 1991. After having devoted her life to home and family, Rachel, at the age of 56 found a new talent painting in watercolor. In the beginning she said, "I struggled. I wasn't any good." But she took her teacher's advice: art is one-tenth talent, and nine-tenths hard work and perseverance, and it worked.

She prowled California back roads doing on-the-spot sketches and watercolors of rural schoolhouses, ghost towns, and churches that had been there since the 1800's and were showing their age. By using photography and interviewing the locals, Rachel was able to make her paintings come alive by capturing the mood and meaning of these structures and landmarks as they reflected the past. She usually made a pencil sketch at each site with notes as to colors, then produced the painting in her home studio on Cotton Street.

Normally she kept the originals and painted copies when requested. During one of her early shows at Menlo Park Presbyterian Church (now, Menlo Church) she met Susan Gale, Menlo Park's librarian and first historian. Ms. Gale gave Rachel some photographs of early Menlo Park and commissioned her to paint the scenes. Eventually Rachel painted more than 50 early Menlo Park scenes, 25 of which Susan willed to the City of Menlo Park, many of which are now displayed in the city library. Her work can also be found in the State Capitol Building in Sacramento, in many private homes, in public buildings and all over the world. Rachel's interest was in bringing to life the vanishing rural past. Why the past? As Rachel said, "Like many people in this fast-moving and complex world, I feel a fond nostalgia for the things we're leaving behind forever."

Philip arranged to take a month off that fall in September so we could make a honeymoon drive around the country! We loaded up my brown Ford Pinto station wagon with a bed in the back so we could sleep in it and save money. He put a "Boot" on top to carry our "stuff" and off we went. Philip's favorite author, John Steinbeck, wrote "*A journey is a person in itself, no two are alike.*" Our first stop was Yosemite National Park. My grandparents had honeymooned there, and my parents often went there as well. We camped in the station wagon up near the top of the pass. I stepped out in the middle of the night and gazed up at the dark sky and distinctly heard celestial music from the myriads of stars!

My cousin Val lived in Prescott, Arizona, so that was our first destination. She worked as the city manager, and I often told her over the years that she was not responsible for the traffic congestion downtown that occurred as the town developed into a major city!

We drove to the South Rim of the Grand Canyon to marvel at its expanse and grandeur.

Then as we headed east, Philip brought out his copy of Steinbeck's "Travels with Charley" written in 1962. I read the story aloud of Steinbeck's 10,000-mile trip around the United States with his large standard poodle, named Charlie. As we crossed the great plains, we recalled our own travels and youth filled adventures of living in the mid-west. We finally got to know each other and learn about our childhoods and the places where we grew up. Whenever I saw a town named Washburn on the map, we drove over to see it. We found three including one in Arkansas. They were all humble villages, often located along the railroad tracks, sometimes only with a grain silo to mark the spot!

Our target was Atlanta, Georgia where Philip's older brother Marty lived with his family. I was charmed by the southern antebellum homes. Philip and Marty enjoyed seeing a locomotive and passenger car painted red, white, and blue for the recent Bicentennial.

After a pleasant visit we headed north to Detroit to see Philip's family. His mother scurried about purchasing all her favorite European sausages for the family get together. Philip's sister, Julie, and family came from Battle Creek and then aunts, uncles, and cousins arrived. They gave me a warm welcome and after lunch, they sat down around the large round oak table in the kitchen and proceeded to play penny ante poker for the rest of the afternoon. It was their way of socializing! Because of his long gambling experience Philip carefully allowed the younger folks to win without them realizing it!

Heading west as we crossed the border from South Dakota into Wyoming, much to Philip's amazement, I burst out singing the University of Wyoming theme song "Rooten Tooten, son of a gun from old Wyoming, Rag Time Cowboy Joe" with much gusto! Our goal that day we to stay with friends in Sheridan where I had gone to High School. However, as we came to Buffalo on the freeway, it was snowing heavily, and we watched semi tricks going up the hills sideways. I spotted an off ramp and suggested that we turn there

Immediately we had more traction and as we came to the stop sign at the bottom of the hill, we noticed a farmhouse on the opposite side of the road, so we drove over to it. We were greeted by a large baking dog, followed shortly by a friendly man who invited us into his home. We discovered that there were more stranded travelers In the warm kitchen. Two hunters from out of state and two young girls just out on a drive. The family graciously made room for us to sleep in the children's beds that night.

In the morning, the travelers pulled out food to share. We contributed homemade bread and cheese that we had gotten at the Amish Flea market in Shipshewana, Indiana. It was an unforgettable experience and has served to reminded me ever since: *"To be a house by the side of the road and be a friend to man!"*

After visiting my dear friends in Sheridan, we traveled west and marveled at all the sights at Yellowstone National Park. We learned that Henry Washburn from Vermont had been the Surveyor General in Montana and explored the area in 1870.He was instrumental in helping to create Yellowstone into a National Park in 1872. Perhaps he was a distant relative to my father's Washburn family in New York.

Then heading further west into the state of Washington, we saw grey ash everywhere from the recent volcanic eruption of Mt. St. Helens on May 18th. 1980. The ash covered 11 states and several Canadian Provinces. Philp and I were at Jughandle Creek Farm at that time of the eruption on a date and were too preoccupied with each other to know that had happened!

We arrived in the Seattle area to visit my brother George and his wife and two young children, then drove down the coast to Pacifica to pick up Pepe from my friend Shirley and say hi to my parents. And finally, home. After a month of driving we called ourselves "the mad traveler" and the "driving fool!' We had gone 4,000 miles!

Shirley Biby took care of Pepe for us while we traveled. Note our brown Pinto wagon with the "boot" on top on the left.

Harvard Avenue, in Menlo Park, was a lovely older part of town with large trees arching over the street. Philip lived in the carriage house behind an older home built in 1915. In the summer of 1980, Drummond and Teddi McCunn purchased a large home across the street a few doors down and were busy remodeling it so that they could eventually move in. Drummond was an Estate Lawyer with a practice in Redwood City 15 miles to the north and spent evenings and weekends doing as much of the work as he could by himself. I took food over to him or invited him over for a meal when he could take a break. He was preparing additional rooms for both of their elderly parents to live with them.

Eventually, I met Teddi, and we discovered that we had the same birthdate. She was one year older than me. When it was finally finished, Teddi invited me to her home for a Stonecroft Bible Study that she led for several ladies from Menlo Park Presbyterian Church.

About two years along, my marriage seamed idyllic, yet I knew something was missing, I got down on my knees in front of our blue velvet chair up in our bedroom, and prayed: "Lord what do you want me to do?" The Lord said, "read the Bible." So, I was happy to join the fellowship at Teddi's house each week. She had some booklets in the middle of the dining table.

I took one titled: "My Heart, Christ's Home" by Bob Munger. It was a story of a young person who had invited Christ to visit his inner life. As Christ went from room to room, Christ asked, "Am I the center of this place? Was the living room welcoming to Him? Were the things done in the kitchen honoring Him?" As I read it, I thought that Christ was already in my life, But when Christ came to a small closet underneath the stairs, the person paused. Did they want Christ to know about the secrets hidden under there? I reflected and sensed a small black box about two inches square in my heart, and I cried out *"Lord come into my heart!"* **And HE DID!!!** *The Holy Spirit filled me! I was literally High for a day and a half!!! Praise the Lord!*

I attended Teddi's Bible studies with new eyes and ears and heart. She eventually led a study on Genesis, and I became convicted that I had to let go of all the evolutionary teaching that had permeated my whole life until then! It was a gradual process, first I let go of all my "New Age" books that I had accumulated in the 1970's at various workshops in San Francisco.

Later, she introduced me to the Institute of Creation Research. I was totally converted when I read their recent findings starting in 1982 called "RATE = Radioisotopes and the Age of the Earth." They proved that the half-life of radioactive Zircon crystals, common in granitic rock formed in cooling magma, was 6000 years. These careful measurements were done by independent labs to avoid any bias. Teddi told me about the "Study Bible" edited by the "Father of Modern Creationism, Henry Morris." I have been reading and praying with it ever since.

Psalm 40: 1-5 I waited patiently for the Lord; and he inclined unto me and heard my cry. He brought me up also up out of a horrible pit, out of the miry clay, and set my feet upon a rock, and established my goings. And he had put a new song in my mouth, even praise unto our God: many shall see it, and fear, and trust in the Lord. Blessed is the man that maketh the Lord his trust, and respecteth not the proud, nor such as turn aside to lies. Many, O Lord my God, are thy wonderful works which thou has done, and thy thoughts which are to us-ward: they cannot be reckoned up in order unto thee: if I would declare and speak of them, they are more than can be numbered.

Chapter 23 – Pandora's Box

My parents, Harry, and Winnie Washburn celebrated their 40th wedding anniversary on July 27, 1981. Inspired by dad's parents, who sailed around the world in 1923 on their 40th anniversary, mom and dad planned a trip around the world mostly in the southern hemisphere. It was my turn to be their support at home while they traveled and manage their affairs. Their airline ticket was nine feet long!

They had contacted Christian churches and missions to visit all along their route. They departed early in September, flying first to Christchurch, New Zealand where my father served a church as their pastor for a couple of months. After sightseeing in New Zealand, they flew to Sydney, Australia and visited with our friends Ian and Carol Cameron and his parents. Then they flew to the Far East, India, Africa, South America and finally home eight months later! Meanwhile, there was heavy rain that winter in Pacifica and the hillside opposite their home had a mudslide that blocked their road for a time trapping their house sitter. All was cleared up by the time they returned in May.

Philip knew that steam locomotives were developed in Europe and the Unted States in the 1850's and toy trains were invented for young children by 1859 in France and Germany. In 1901, Lional Cowan started making metal toy trains that ran on three tracks that he later electrified. "O" gauge was the most practical size and Lionel Trains became very popular in the United States. A. C. Gilbert also started producing more accurate models of locomotives in 1907 and his Standard Gauge American Flyer ran on slightly narrower two rail tracks.

Both companies stopped production during World War Two and produced metal items for the war effort. When they returned to producing toy trains in 1946, they also printed wonderful catalogues showing young boys playing with their new toy trains and illustrated inventive accessories such a log loader, talking railroad stations, water towers and Plasticville buildings.

A Catalogue that many children studied to see what they might have.

Boys who had been born in the late 1930's like Marty, older Philip's brother, and boys born in the war years like Philip were old enough to drool over the wonderful color pictures inside these 12 - 24 page paper catalogues. Marty purchased a set of Lional trains complete with a ring of track and a transformer with the money he had saved from doing odd jobs. As a young boy Philip mowed lawns for 25 cents and was only able to save enough money to buy one passenger car for eight dollars. That lighted Lionel car was a great wonder to him.

Such was the situation with many young boys in the 1940's and 1950's in America. I had already ridden two different trains to California by the time I was five years old, and I received a Lionel set to go around our Christmas tree in 1948. The toy train market waned in the late 1950's as slot cars became more popular with the younger "Baby Boomers" and Television and the "Space Race" drew children's attention to other venues.

However, those boys that drooled over the post war catalogues grew up. Philip was working in San Francisco in the early 1960's and discovered some toy trains for sale in an ad in the newspaper. Now he had the funds to buy them, and he was off and running with his dreams! A. C. Gilbert also made Erector sets.

Philip found an Erector set that he could make into "Hudson" which was a large locomotive with a tender that was three feet. The catch was there were NO instructions with it when he got the kit, they had been lost. He tirelessly assembled the train in his spare time screwing it together with almost impossible angles inside for his large hands!

Later Philip sold the large locomotive and tender to a toy train dealer along with the rest of his collection and turned to his interest in buying Rachel Bentley watercolors and then to collecting American Art Pottery from the early 1900's.

In the fall of 1981, Philip came home from work one afternoon after his day shift. We stood in the driveway as he began to inform me that he had an opportunity that he described as "Opening Pandora's Box" which really meant that IF he did this, he would not be able to stop. He had a disease called "collecting toy trains!" A man at work knew that Philip liked trains and had just offered him his own boyhood American Flyer collection for $200.

I took a deep breath, and the Lord gave me the grace to say "If you put the money back into our savings account" you can buy them.: My friend Leslie at the trailer park in South San Francisco, had sent us a check for $1000 for a wedding gift and that was the beginning of our savings account which we had been adding to whenever we could. Philip was elated and immediately drove off to buy the trains and bring them home to examine the treasures that made his heart sing!

To fund his hobby, Philip decided to sell hit 75 pieces of art pottery at our antique shows. This proved to be a wise move because interest in Arts and Crafts items was high at that time and then waned a few years later.

After we married Philip joined me at all the one day outdoor antique shows and we used his larger green 1970 Ford station wagon to transport our boxes and tables. It was nice for me to have help setting it up and so forth. We continued to do two or three shows a month.

I found a one day sale that fall in the East Bay, so we drove over the San Mateo Bridge to that shopping center. Philip set out his trains and began to figure out what they were worth and what he could sell them for. Several toy train collectors came along and soon they were having great conversations. We learned that these men had a lifelong passion for toy train collecting and in some cases were building model railroad layouts in their homes

The power of nostalgia was almost overwhelming and in some cases the wives, like me, were caught up in something they did not totally understand. Over the course of time we saw some divorces happen because of this addiction!

Late in the fall of 1981, I made our first Christmas card. I drew a feather in pen and ink free hand. We invited friends, neighbors, and my family to come to our home for an Open House at Christmas time. I did all the baking, including my mother's Pillsbury Cook off Prizewinning Pumpkin cookies with almond icing! We had a great time in our cozy carriage house of 400 square feet downstairs in the living room, dining room and kitchen.

1982

and you shall soar . . .

Happy Holidays!

Philip & Harriet Prisk

By 1982, I had been studying porcelain painting with my Swiss teacher, Elizabeth Uttinger, in San Francisco every week for five years. My mother gave me her small electric kiln and then I was able to do my own firing and felt that I could paint on my own after that.

I was walking Pepe one day when I met a neighbor three houses down from me and he remarked that he wondered who would take care of his wife after he passed. Shortly thereafter, he died unexpectedly. I went to visit Ruth Davis and she invited me to come and use a spare room in her home as my studio. This was wonderful because I had no real work area in our home. I was a good companion for her, and she always welcomed me warmly. I continued to paint flowers on old pieces of porcelain I found in garage sales.

Columbine done in 1992

Philip actively pursued any opportunity to buy trains. He got a badge to put on his grey Stetson hat that read "I BUY TRAINS" and he had many chances to buy collections, always replacing whatever money he spent back into our savings as soon as he could. He started to make a collection of American Flyer Trains of his own. We put trains out at Christmas, but mostly he stored them in specially made boxes under our high old fashioned cast iron bedstead.

I was a Rail Fan myself and created ways for us to go visit his family in Michigan on Amtrak. We would get a Sleeper roomette and enjoy a glass of wine which was furnished right after we boarded. The first time this happened, Philip said, "How long has this been going on" He loved to travel on the train, too. I would route us to Chicago, traveling first to Seattle then through Glacier Park. Another time to Los Angeles and New Orleans and north to Chicago and on to Detroit, Michigan.

We always returned passing over the Mississippi river, then while sleeping we crossed the Great Plains and awoke the next morning to see the Colorado Rockies. Then on the other side of the mountains we rode along the Colorado River Gorge where we observed Interstate 70 being constructed on the north side of the river. Utah was next and I recall seeing the La Sal Mountains to the south and being struck by their beauty and finally across Nevada at night and through the Sierras in California looking down on my dear Donner Lake as we ascended the summit.

In the fall of 1982, I found a black and white photo taken at Chicago's Union Station by well-known railroad photographer, Don Ball Jr. For our second Christmas card I made a scratchboard drawing of it. Scratchboard is a thick piece of cardboard covered first with white chalk and then painted with a layer of black ink. Using a thin Exacto knife, you scratch through the ink and uncover the white below. This image was a very challenging subject of a locomotive in a snowstorm.

Scratchboard done from photo by Don Ball, Jr.

That Christmas, I got smart when I invited people to our Open House. I suggested that they bring a dozen cookies. That was brilliant and we got several very fun things including giant macaroons!

One day in the summer of 1983, I saw a large blimp tethered to the ground advertising a government automobile auction. In those days the government sold their vehicles after being driven for six years. We went to look at what was available and discovered a white 1977 Dodge panel van. The auction was by silent bid, you turned in your bid and the highest bid won. We wrote down $3300 and were delighted to be awarded the van.

Philip was thrilled, because now he could buy MORE TRAINS!!! He put big letters on each side of the van: “I BUY TRAINS” with our telephone number. One day we drove over to the East Bay, where he studied an entire collection very carefully. Philip had to figure out what he wanted to keep and what he could sell the rest of it for to return the funds to our savings account. He spent $8000 and loaded many banana boxes into the van and came home on cloud nine.

By that time, I knew that he had a mistress, trains, and I had to adjust to his desires. He would sit at work and write lists after each purchase, first of what was now in his collection under the bed and second pricing what he had to sell. There were two large reference books for both Lional and American Flyer and he memorized them. If anyone came to him with a screw missing in a locomotive or car, he could tell them exactly what was needed and often had the item necessary. His true love was American Flyer, but he would deal with Lionel if he had the opportunity!

That fall, I found photo by Don Ball Jr. and did another scratchboard for our Christmas card of Amtrak descending along the Truckee River east of Donner Pass near where I lived in the 1960’s! We invited people to our Open House and suggested they bring a dozen cookies. The house got crowded, but we all had a great time.

Harvard Avenue was only two blocks long and we had many older women in our neighborhood, known as "Allied Arts" named for the establishment a few blocks away which had lovely gardens and shops in the mission style.

One day, I was alarmed to learn that an older lady had fallen in her bathroom and lay there for several days unable to move until a neighbor went to check on her. On another block a man fell between his car and the wall in his garage and lay there for four days before someone found him! I created our "Neighborhood Watch" for the residents. We had a program on how to turn off the gas line to your house in the event of an earthquake. We enjoyed potluck dinners in someone's driveway on summer evenings. "Those were the Days my friend, we thought they would never end!"

My next door neighbor, Helen, adored Pepe and would ask me if she could take him to a nearby rest home for a visit. He was a real ambassador and people loved him.

Helen told me about the wonderful music at Menlo Park Presbyterian church and I attended whenever I could. Most of our antique shows were on Sundays. Eventually the church did have a Saturday evening service and I got to go more often. I attended Ladies Bible Studies and learned a lot more about Christ and his work for mankind. When I could I went an Adult Bible Study on Sundays. My heart ached for Philip to know the Lord, I prayed for him a lot.

That summer we drove up to see my brother in Seattle and on the way back we stopped in Ashland, Oregon to visit my Aunt Marion who was working on her clay model for a bronze sculpture there in a large storeroom owned by the Shakespearian Festival. She had already completed "Street Scene," a bronze "bas relief" which stood over twelve feet high featuring the various stages of life. Some actors at the festival had served as her models. It was placed at the bottom of the hill just below the entrance to the theatre.

Street Scene in Ashland, Oregon. Bronze Sculpture by Marion Young.

In the evening, Philip and I saw Shakespear's "Taming of the Shrew." It had a marked impact on me. I had been an independent woman for so long and self-employed and self-motivated, that the thought of submitting to my husband was very difficult for me. I wanted to die rather than say to him as the Shrew, said:" The sun is the moon!" That night I put my pillow over my head and held my breath! It is not possible to commit suicide that way!!! Your body will not let you! Finally, I prayed and said, "I cannot do this, Lord, please help me!" I really worked in it over the next few months.

One day nine months later Philip said to me, "I have decided to love you just the way you are!" (That is Unconditional Love! Thank you, Lord!)

My next Christmas card in the fall of 1984 reflected my increasing interest in in the Bible. We had another Open House and I rejoiced in the Lord's hand in my life.

In February of 1985 the National Society of the Daughters of the American Revolution presented their "National Radio and Television Award" to Carleton E. Morse. "One Man's Family" ran for 27 years on the radio starting in 1932 and then for five years on Television. I was delighted to wear a lovely, crocheted top recently made for me by my dear friend Lori Cordini and it is my DAR uniform to this day!

Thursday, February 28,

DAR meeting convenes in San Jos

The California Society, Daughters of the American Revolution, will hold its 77th state conference today through Sunday at the Red Lion Inn, San Jose.

Mrs. Raymond Fleck, recording secretary general of the DAR, will speak at the opening session tonight at 7:30. Dr. Helmut Schmitz, president of Evangelistic Outreach, will speak at a national defense banquet Saturday and Alfred Ginkel, president of Bacone College in Oklahoma, a school for Ame Indians, will address a brea meeting Sunday. The DAR a ly furnishes financial aid t cone.

Other convention highlight include a debutante present Saturday evening and a lun on Sunday at which an awar be given to Carleton E. Mor Woodside, the creator of the serial "One Man's Family."

Our lives continued with me painting on porcelain and Philip buying and selling toy trains. Once when we came back from a trip, Philip was quite tired because he had done all the driving, however, there was a message on the answering machine from a man in Redwood City saying that he had some trains to sell. Immediately Philip was revitalized and drove up there at once to buy them! He was known by collectors at "Mister American Flyer."

Mister American Flyer

Philip had quite a range of buyers from very experienced collectors to ones who were new to the whole thing, like Max Mizuhara. Max was a Japanese American who had been interred in Delta, Utah, in World War II as a child. He became successful businessman in Silicon Valley but was unsure if "the guys" would accept him at the toy train club meetings. Philip assured Max that he would fit right in, and sure enough he did. Max became one of Philip's major collectors and a very dear friend.

Another customer was Doug Hardy who had been collecting for some time and lived near us in Menlo Park. One day he sold his property there and decided to move up to the Gold Rush country. We wondered why anyone would ever leave paradise??

Ephesians 5:22-24 Wives, submit yourselves unto your own husbands, as unto the Lord. For the husband is the head of the wife, even as Christ is the head of the church: and he is the Savior of the body. Therefore, as the church is subject unto Christ, so let the wives be to their own husbands in everything.

Chapter 24 – 324 – D

I continued to paint on anything that interested me. This is a fun gravy pitcher I did in September of 1986, here seen are both sides. The pink day lilies grew by the side of Harvard Avenue near our home. I enjoyed painting scenes that extend all the way around the object.

Marmie Spay, was a dear friend of mine in my Ladies Bible Study. In the summer of 1986, she moved to Taos, New Mexico. She called me and said that she had left a few boxes of her craft materials in Menlo Park. Philip agreed that we could take our vacation to visit her. He constructed a wooden frame to place our double mattress in the rear of the Dodge van and put Marmie's craft materials under it. I asked the AAA Travel agent to plan a route so that we could drive through Zion National Park, which I missed seeing when we were children in the mid 1950's.

We departed early in October and first drove to see Doug Hardy, Philip's train collecting friend who had recently moved to the Gold Rush Country. We learned interesting things about the rural life he found there and enjoyed all his tales about the local people.

Then we headed over the Sierra Mountains and across the barren desert of southern Nevada, stopping for the night in Rachel, a very tiny wayside stop on the road. We slept beside a small restaurant and were intrigued to learn about the couple who had recently moved there from California to run the business located about one and a half hours north of Las Vegas. In the morning, they gladly gave us directions to drive up into the hills and explore an old mine.

Then we went on our way to see my heart's desire, Zion National Park in Utah. We arrived in nearby in Hurricane that afternoon and drove down into the Virgin River canyon to camp at "Pah Tempe," a hot springs resort. We were amazed to learn that the new owners had recently moved from their home in Menlo Park near where Philip worked! The thermally heated water caused by volcanic activity came from deep under the ground. It bubbled up in the middle of the river. There were pools constructed for people to soak on the side of the cliff! It was delightful to feel the hot water coming up between our toes when we walked in the river!

In the morning, I pulled out my pastel chalks and did a drawing of the rock precipice looming above us on the other side of the river. I saw Utah Rocks as an artist for the first time! The drive through Zion was awe inspiring with fantastic views at every turn! I was transformed by the concept of wrap around scenery!

Traveling on up to Bryce Canyon National Park, on Highway 89, we noticed the pink cliffs of Bryce on our right and soon were driving through in the scenery on Highway 12 proceeding up Red Canyon under two tunnels in the red rocks and on to the top of the plateau to explore Bryce Canyon. It was as wonderful an experience for me as it had been the first time I saw it as a child.

The tunnels on Highway 12 in Red Canyon. I did this painting in 2022.

Later in the day we headed east as directed by the AAA lady on Highway 12. We came to a steep grade in grey clay hills and suddenly the van started making a shrill high pitched whine which continued all the way up the seven tight curves to the 7600 foot summit. I Prayed *"Lord please help us*!!" The alarming sound did not stop as we continued down the next fifteen miles to Escalante. Unfortunately, the service station at the edge of town was already closed for the evening so we camped at the Escalante Petrified Forest State Park just east of town.

The next morning, we drove to Midnight Auto and Walley Woolsey greased the speedometer cable in the van for two bucks! Philip always said, "Diogenes should come through here with his lamp, I have found an honest man!" We would have been willing to pay anything to make that horrible noise stop!

While the repair was in process, I chatted with the kid at the gas pump and asked about the dark ominous clouds to the east over the mountains where we were to travel next. He assured me that it was wonderful scenery and since it was it was the first day of hunting season, the roads would be fine because the local men had been driving up the highway over the 9600 foot pass to their favorite hunting grounds.

We ascended a large hill and at the top rain started to beat down fiercely on the van that we understood erosion for the first time in our lives as water poured down over the slickrock. The highway was a very windy narrow two lane road. We saw nothing of the scenery because of the snow at the higher elevations. Philip drove with the storm all the way to our destination in New Mexico over five hundred miles away.

It was so cold in Taos that we could not stay in our uninsulated panel van, it was like sleeping in a refrigerator! We slept on Marmie's couch for a couple of nights. Returning home, we vowed to make better studies of the weather before venturing out again.

As the holidays approached, Philip advised me that he did not want to have another Christmas Open House in our home because he felt it was too focused on our possessions. I was extremely disappointed by the thought of not having a celebration.

Finally, I suggested, what if we give the party away? He eagerly agreed saying that he had always wanted to do something at a hospital. He urged me to go to the Veterans Hospital there in Menlo Park where I was a representative for the Daughters of the American Revolution for our Bay area chapters.

I contacted Frank Schleifer, the Chief of Voluntary Services, and went to his office. He said "Yes, there is one section that is in dire need of adoption, 324 - D, the Schizophrenia Ward. Would you like to walk over and see it?"

My blood froze. Memories of my dad taking me to the VA hospital in Sheridan, Wyoming sprang to my mind. As a teenager I saw men huddled up against radiator heaters in the hallways. The memory was so painful, and I felt totally helpless in such sad conditions I quickly replied, "No thank you" and walked out the door.

In the next few days, the Lord began to work on my heart, and I returned to "have a look at the ward nobody wanted." After interviewing Philip and I, Renata, the Director of the ward arranged for us to give a Tree Decorating Party mid-December and a Holiday Buffet luncheon for the men and the staff on the 24th.

However, a day later Frank called me and asked if we would also give the ward a Thanksgiving party two days hence! My blessed mother quickly agreed to bake three turkeys and eight pumpkin pies. With several friends we prepared a Thanksgiving feast for fifty patients and thirty staff. The meal was an enormous success and showed us there was a great need for love and concern not only for the patients, but also for the staff.

I mailed out our Christmas card advising friends of the change in venue for our party. We received an amazing response in donations from the community and from all around the country. We soon learned that there is a great love for veterans and a real desire to reach out to them in a meaningful way! One lady donated new Christmas ornaments for the tree trimming party. We presented gifts for every patient and staff member at the Christmas Buffet which was bountifully supplied by numerous people.

After Christmas, there was money left over. Frank asked us to give the ward a New Years Eve party. Our neighbors cooked fifteen pizzas in their ovens, and we enjoyed drinking sparkling cider and munching on popcorn with the men while watching movies in the locked down ward until midnight. It was the best New Years Eve party we had ever attended!

After the holidays, I realized that there was a greater need for ongoing service to the men. We still had three hundred dollars. We asked what the men needed. Frank told us that "Purple Heart" organization would donate two gallons of Ice Cream every month, so we committed to giving a monthly Ice Cream Social.

Over time people from our church and my DAR chapter volunteered to help when they could. This outreach continued for 5 years! We purchased various hygiene items not furnished by the VA and created a fund to supply those needs as time went on. When the funds we had received were running low, a lady who was housebound chose to support the work for three years and then another widow stepped in when the first lady passed away!

I also worked with a substance abuse recovery ward, teaching a Bible Study with Teddi McCunn one afternoon a week and helped to offer a class for literacy. We found funds for art therapy for children of fathers who had PTSD and collected clothing for homeless veterans. The needs were unending!

I the summer of 1987, I heard from my friend Luanne who was born with cerebral palsy. She was still living in Laramie, Wyoming, and had graduated from the University with a BA. She had a job working at Coe Library on campus. Even though her mobility was limited, she decided to come to visit us and flew to San Francisco. I was so proud of her as she slowly made her way down the stairs as she got off the plane. I drove her around to see the sights in San Francisco. She had a smile on her face that was as wide as a mile! She had never been out of the state before!

She told us that her boss at the library would not teach her how to use a computer, so I introduced her to my neighbor across the street who taught her how to use a laptop! She could already type and even played a small keyboard organ in her home. She learned the process easily and when she went back to the Library, she was able to advance into the digital world!

I took her to my physical therapist, who adjusted her spine as best he could, which helped her to walk better. When she departed, she got back on the plane, and she had a much better gait climbing up the stairs!

Ian and Carol Cameron flew into San Francisco from Australia to visit us for a briefly that summer. We drove them up to the Napa Sonoma Wine Country because we knew that they were wine aficionados in Sydney. I remembered that Ian had played a large church organ when he studied in London in the late 1960's, so I was delighted for him to see and hear the wonderful pipe organ at

Menlo Park Presbyterian Church. Carol came to visit us several more times with her work and Ian's parents even came once on their way through.

Teddi and Drummond McCunn our dear neighbors across the street invited us to join them with their friends on a trip to Mexico early in October 1987. We flew to La Paz, on the Baja Peninsula and the men had a wonderful time deep sea fishing and bringing in their catch which was prepared at a restaurant for dinner that night.

Then we flew to the mainland and took the train up through Copper Canyon which is three times larger than the Grand Canyon! Our friends, Al, and Val had alerted us to take art supplies to a school for the Tarahumara children who lived in the canyon. I had a friend who worked for an art supply company, and she had given us twelve boxes of wonderful crayons and other things which we were glad to drop off when we visited their village.

We traveled on to Chihuahua. The group saw an Amish Farm and we were interested to learn that years ago the local government had asked them to come to Mexico and teach framing techniques to the people there. Our last day was October 19th. While waiting for the bus to go to the airport, Philip saw a newspaper in the window of the hotel He was terribly upset to learn about the Stock Market Crash, later to be known as Black Monday. Although we did not have any money in the market, he was very alarmed and eager to learn more when we got back home.

THE COPPER CANYON - BARRANCA DEL COBRE

Later in the fall of 1987, I woke up one morning and knew that something was different in my life, but I did not know what it was until Philip came home and told me that he had accepted Christ as his Savior the night before at work while watching the Billy Graham crusade on TV! We had a wonderful life ahead of us as we began our walk of faith together!

Luke 14: 12 – 14 Then said he also to him that bade him, When thou make a dinner or a supper, call not thy friends, nor thy brethren, neither thy kinsmen, nor thy rich neighbors; lest they also bid thee again, and a recompence be made thee. But when thou make a feast, call the poor, the maimed, the lame, the blind. And thou shalt be blessed; for they cannot recompense thee: for thou shalt be recompensed at the resurrection of the just.

Matthew 25: 40 And the King shall answer and say unto them, Verily I say unto you, In as much as ye have done it unto one of the least of these my brethren, ye have done it unto me.

Chapter 25 – "Lord, why can't I go back to sleep?"

By 1987, Ruth Davis began to decline and eventually she was moved to a senior care facility in Menlo Park. I took my art studio equipment out of her home. When I shared my need for a studio with my neighbor Jim Hewlett, who lived across the street on Harvard, Jim graciously offered me the opportunity to set up in his storage room on the side of his garage. After major scrubbing and painting, I moved into my new studio.

My experience of Zion National Park weighed heavily on my mind. How does one express scenery that surrounds you? I studied photos of the park and began to paint the dramatic scenery around a twelve inch classic style vase. The challenge was to make the scenery appear correctly from every angle. I needed to create a skyline going all the way around the top of the vase and paint the Virgin River flowing around the lower part of the scene. Another element was the marvelous blue Utah sky! I had to fire the vase five times to totally get the depth of the colors. And I had to be careful not to get my fingers in the paint while I held it as I continued working!

In May of 1988, we decided to return to Escalante, to see what we had missed due to the heavy snowstorm in October of 1986. Again, we parked our van in the same spot at the Petrified Forest State Park campground. The wind blew extremely hard that night making the van go back and forth. Since I was a light sleeper, I finally cried out in desperation: "*Lord, why I can't I go back to sleep?*" **AND the LORD said to me**: "***I want you to live here***." I then lay awake for some time contemplating what the Lord had said to me and what it could mean for us. In the morning, I told Philip, and he said' "***OK.***" We looked around town a bit, but could not find a real estate agent, so we went on our way, still pondering what we were to do.

This is the road, Highway 12, we first drove over in the pouring rain!

I did this painting in 2023.

In May of 1989 we retraced our original trip to Utah, visiting Doug Hardy again in the California Gold Rush country and connecting with the couple we enjoyed in Rachel, Nevada. Again, we explored the Tungsten mine and ghost town up in the hills. Arriving in Utah, we drove down to the hot springs at Pah Tempe in the Virgin River gorge for a nice soak. However, when we arrived in Escalante, the real estate agent was out of town, so we returned home.

The Hogs Back on Highway 12. From a Photo taken by a Drone.

I did this painting in 2022.

While we again visited Bryce Canyon, I took over a dozen photos, and when we got home, I painted another vase featuring the Natural Bridge on the rim of the canyon facing east.

Philip soon realized that for us to afford our move, he needed to sell his precious train collection stored in many boxes under our bed. It was really a trial for him. He went back and forth for a couple of months before he became resolved that it was the right thing to do.

What spurred him on was an article in his Toy Train magazine stating that the demand for these toys was ending and the market would become less active as the younger generation of collectors was more interested in other things like slot cars just as it had been when he was growing up

There was quite an uproar among the readers, however, Philip took it to heart and began to present his collection at the Toy Train Shows. One day he sold $5000 worth of trains and that broke the ice for him Eventually he netted $15,000 just from the trains under our bed!

On October 17, 1989, the World Series between the San Francisco Giants and the Oakland Raders was beginning that day at Candlestick Park south of San Francisco. Philip was home in front room watching TV as were many other Bay area residents. I was walking my dog, LP, and chatting with a friend down the street. At 5:04 PM a **6.9** Earthquake hit the Bay Area!

The Loma Prieta Earthquake was later named after its epicenter in the Santa Cruz Mountains 50 miles south of us. The surface vibration was 7.1! I grabbed the Power pole beside me as the shock rippled under our feet in the sidewalk for 20 seconds! I quickly went home to see our station wagon rocking back and forth in the driveway and heard the neighbor's Doughboy pool sloshing wildly on the other side of their fence!

Our 1915 carriage house had lathe and plaster ceilings and I often worried if it would come down in such an event. Chunks of the ceiling did fall into the kitchen sink but that was all the damage we had except for a few pieces of my precious red glass that fell down from the windowsill and broke. There was a 5.2 aftershock later that week. We were all extremely nervous for a while as we learned about damage to the Oakland Bay Bridge and a collapsed freeway on the Oakland side as well as major damage downtown in Santa Cruz and liquefaction of the earth in the Marina area of San Francisco that caused several buildings to collapse. One does not soon forget that kind of experience!

Philip standing in front of our 1915 Carriage House.

In May of 1990, we drove the van north through California to a train show in Portland, Oregon. As we came into Oregon, Philip spotted a garage sale sign just off the freeway, so he pulled over. Philip casually bought two oil paintings for three dollars each. As soon as he had driven about a block away, he jumped out of the van, ran and opened the back and began to exclaim about the original paintings by Hanson Puttoff a preeminent California impressionist painter from the early 1900's.

Eventually we sold them to an art dealer for three thousand dollars each! The Lord was blessing us and preparing for our future! After an extraordinarily successful train show, we drove down to Escalante and met Dawn Griffin in her real estate office just off Main street. She showed us an older house that had been remodeled. I liked it, but Philip said: " We will have to pray about it overnight." We had indeed been praying for the Lord to guide us for a long time.

Then Dawn said, "Well there is some property out by the airport." My immediate response was, augh, noise! Philip's favorite pastime we to go up to the San Francisco Airport and watch the jets take off. However, we agreed to look at it and drove east out of Escalante on Highway 12 about two miles and took the road off to the right to the small airport and then almost immediately turned left on a dirt road. We drove through a gate in the barbed wire fence and along it to another opening in that fence to see the sagebrush covered hillside.

Philip said that the moment he put his feet on the ground, he knew that we were to purchase it. Now he had to convince me that this was what the Lord wanted. I agreed because the view was stunning. We went to Dawn's house and over a glass of lemonade we signed the papers to buy fourteen and a third acres for fifteen thousand dollars.

The view of the cliffs from our new property.

Dawn suggested that we meet Bill and Carolyn Bowmar who had moved to Escalante from Southern California ten years before. Bill ran a machine shop beside his home and had manufactured parts for live steam miniature trains. Carolyn reminded me of my grandmother making preserves on the stove while we talked. We enjoyed meeting them and were thankful to make friends and have a connection in town. They took us to see Devil's Garden out in the desert south of Escalante and showed us other sights in the vicinity.

While we were driving home, Philip kept saying "We should buy a motorhome like Fred's Motorhome." And when we got home, we bought Fred's 1984 Class C Dodge Brougham for the same amount of money that we got for our white van plus we traded him a toy train set that Fred really wanted! We named the motorhome "Sweet Thursday" in honor of one of Steinbeck's books that Philip was very fond of.

It was extremely hard for me to think of leaving my neighbors on Harvard Avenue, especially Teddi, my church friends, and my parents who lived nearby. I was particularly concerned about who would take over the work with Ward 324- C at the VA. I had to learn to surrender to the Lord's will and trust His timing in all things.

Bill Bowmar wrote that he was concerned that we did not have a "right of way" to the acreage we had just purchased. We then learned that the owner of the land we drove over did not want to give us the right to travel on his property. We traveled back to Escalante in November and worked with Dawn to purchase another thirteen and a third acres to give us access out to the dirt road we had originally turned on from the airport road.

Dawn called her cousin to make sure we could get the needed power connection brought from the main line across the highway. The city water hookup was eight hundred feet down the hill by the runway. We were going to pioneer the land! No one had ever lived on it!

Early in 1991, Stanford University announced that they would give "Golden Handshakes" to employees who would retire, and their positions did not need to be refilled. Since his position as a guard at the inner gate at SLAC was still needed, that offer did not work for him, but it got Philip thinking and he realized that by September our rental agreement was up for the year, and he would then be vested in his retirement fund after working for Stanford University for twenty years.

Inhale, exhale…pray!

That spring someone agreed to take over the volunteer work at the VA and I began to see that while we did not know what we were to do, it was like train tracks spurring off the main line, I could see the Lord's hand at work for that ministry.

In May, we bought a 1984 Ford Bronco because we figured we would need four wheel drive out there in the "Wild West!" We gave our Pontiac station wagon to my niece Eilzabeth as her first car.

Philip with the Bronco and Motorhome.

In June of 1991, we learned that Philip's mother's health was failing. We planned to drive to Battle Creek, Michigan, to be with her and the family. On the way east we stopped for the night in the parking lot at the Peppermill Casino in Mesquite, Nevada. After dinner we were browsing through a "Thrifty Nickel," the local want ad newspaper, and saw the notice again for a Double Wide Modular home for sale in Bunkerville, seven miles away. We had seen the ad before but had dismissed it as being too far away to have the two units towed to Escalante five hours north and east from there.

We made a phone call and Terry Nevil invited us to come and see it. At 9:30 at night we were wandering around in the field beside their home. The remodeled unit had recently been painted white with lovely blue trim around the spacious windows. I was really delighted when I saw the two sinks in the master bathroom. Our bathroom at home only had one sink and it was always a challenge for both of us to use in our very small home. We put down a deposit and arranged for the Nevils to transport the two units and set them on four cement runners on our property by September 15th.

We talked with Dawn when we got to Escalante, and she asked Lincoln Lyman to go out with his large tractor and cut the road on the property. We paced out the place with him where the house would be located beside half a dozen small Juniper trees and nearby where the waterline would be trenched up eight hundred feet from the main line beside the airport runway. We joined the water co-op that had paid to bring city water south to those nearby residents in the valley.

Lincoln Lyman plowing the road to our homesite.

That Sunday, I stood up in the small Baptist congregation in Escalante that we had been attending and said that the promise in Isaiah that the Lord had given us three years before had been fulfilled! **PRAISE THE LORD!**

Isaiah 43: 18 – 19 Remember ye not the former things, neither consider the things of old. Behold, I will do a new thing; now it shall spring forth; shall ye not know it? I will even make a way in the wilderness, and rivers in the desert.

Chapter 26 – HOME OF OUR OWN

In May of 1991, Rachel Bentley passed away at the age of ninety six and a half. She had painted watercolors since she was in her early fifties and produced a great volume of work inspite having the use of only one eye! She was very highly thought of the San Francisco Bay area where she lived and there was always a lot of interest in her art. Rachel had requested that Philip not sell any of his collection of her original art until after she was gone

. By that time Philip owned over one hundred and twenty five of her paintings in various sizes from miniatures to half sheets to full sheets. She had never been represented in a gallery and sold directly to her clients from all over the world. We respected her wishes and waited a for few months until we advertised the availability of her paintings.

We drove to Utah in June to settle things with our property, bought the double wide and planned for the water, power, septic, cement foundations to be poured for the units, and the gravel road to be completed before we would move there mid-September. Then we went on our vacation to Battle Creek, Michigan.

Philip with the motorhome in Red Canyon on Highway 12. Our Dog L.P. is at his feet.

It was a good reunion for Philip visiting with his aunt and her children and his mother and his brother and sister as they all sat around on the grass outside of the care facility where his mother was living. She passed away two weeks after we returned to California.

Back in Menlo Park, our task was to downsize, let go of what we did not want to bring with us and sell it at a garage sale. Philip found a medium sized trailer that he could pull behind the motorhome to transport furniture and things we needed to bring. We stored some larger items to pick up on return trips.

Early in the morning on September 15th, we pulled out of our driveway with dear neighbors waving goodbye as the mini caravan of Philip driving the motorhome pulling the trailer and me coming behind driving the Bronco, edged away from our familiar life. The route was an easy one, down Highway 101, and then we turned east on Highway 152 to drive over the hills to Highway 99.

As we drove up the grade about 100 miles from Menlo Park, I suddenly felt the hand of the Lord under us. It was firm and very certain. We were stepping out in faith and His hand has been under our feet ever since! We had left virtually everything we knew behind, friends, family, jobs, yet we had been obedient to the Lord's call and were ready to seek His will for our lives in all things.

We met with the Nevils in Mesquite, Nevada to finish paying for the doublewide. Terry told us that the ad want we had seen in the paper had been running for some time and was done gratis by the newspaper owner. The Nevils had not paid for it for a couple of months! Thank you, Lord!

We arrived at the property late on September 17th and asked Glen and Sherwood Wilson at the service station in town to come out and help us unload our mattress so we could sleep in the house!

This was the first Home that we had ever owned. Over time we had saved $125,000 which we used to buy the land, trailer, and get situated. The telephone line still needed to be brought over from the airport. Everything else was ready for our new beginning. My mother got a bit frantic because it still took three weeks to get the phone line trenched up to the house. One day she called Dawn who came out and told me to "go call you mom!" I had to go down to the airport office to make the call.

Our first home near Escalante.

For the next five months, we ran ads about Rachel's paintings in the Menlo Park area newspaper with my mother's phone number for contact. We returned and set up at the Valco Village Antique Show the last Sunday of each month and then sold paintings to people who were interested in them.

In January of 1992, Philip sold three paintings to a Real Estate Agent in Woodside for $5000. However, we felt that the commute had to end, so we sold out of most of our antique inventory that Sunday.

We had heard about a Flea Market in Quartzite, Arizona so we drove down and were able to rent a small space for one day. Philip sold a train set for $600. He said he went fishing in a mud puddle and caught a Marlin!

For the next year we decompressed from city life and learned what it was like to live 125 miles from a stop light. A man in church said, tell me what you need, and I will teach you how to live without it!

I had moved a lot of cactus plants out of the way of the path of the construction equipment and made a cactus garden along the driveway in front of our home. I was very interested to see all the wildflowers that bloomed on our land in the spring. The desert was a whole new world for me. My garden that summer in the red dirt was not very successful. I was determined to raise Indian blue corn; however, the wasps really liked the ears when they developed and they won!

A cactus blooming on our desert landscape!

Philip spent a lot of time laying a cinder block foundation around the edge of the house and then built a back porch and later a 700 sq ft redwood deck around the front sides which faced our marvelous view. We would sit out on the deck in the evening and just take in the beauty of a sunset over the hills to the west, reveling in the silence and serenity of our new Home.

Psalm 19: 1 – 4 The heavens declare the glory of God; the skies proclaim the work of his hands.

Day after day they pour forth speech; night after night they reveal knowledge.

They have no speech, they use no words; no sound is heard from them.

Yet their voice[b] goes out into all the earth, their words to the ends of the world.

CHAPTER 27 – SERENIDAD GALLERY begins.

Philip celebrated his 50th birthday in August just before we moved to Utah. We came to understand that 50 was a Biblical Jubilee year for him. In Leviticus, Moses wrote about the Lord's commandment to the Israelites to set aside a year every 50 years as a Jubilee year.

It was a time of new beginnings! Philip had been suffering some heart issues in Menlo Park and we often said that moving to Utah saved his life! In the evenings, he enjoyed his leisure time in the company of LP, our dog and Greyling the tabby cat who just showed up on our doorstep one day.

We later learned that was the day our cat in California had died. Dyna was a tortoise shell Manx given to us after she had been abandoned in 1988. She was a bit wild. I always wanted to hold her, but she only lasted about fifteen seconds in my arms! Hence, we did not think we could bring her with us. I cried out to the Lord for a cat I could hold! Philip had kept some of his special trains that he really loved and displayed them in the front room on bookcases so that we both could enjoy them.

Philip with L.P. and Greyling.

On September 17th, 1991, as we drove into Panguitch, Utah, we stopped at the office of the Garfield County News. I met the editor, Katie Thomas and told her we were moving to Escalante and needed to change our mailing address. We had been subscribing to the paper for three years to keep informed about the happenings in the area. I noted that Faye Alvey, who had been writing the Escalante column for many years was no longer doing so. I asked Katie if she would like me to write the weekly Escalante column for her and she immediately said yes. I was hired for 30 cents an inch! This ultimately helped me to get acquainted with many people in Escalante that I might never met otherwise because we were living outside of town. Katie wanted "Gossip" about the goings on in the community, family reunions and whatever else I could find to write about. Gossip is what sold her paper!

In California, I had been painting porcelain buttons for various members of the National Button Society at the recommendation of Lucille Weingarten who was a past president. I joined the organization and advertised in their monthly magazine. I received commissions from around the country to paint specialty themes for the members for their cards for various competitions. Ultimately, I was listed in a book published featuring Studio Button Artists.

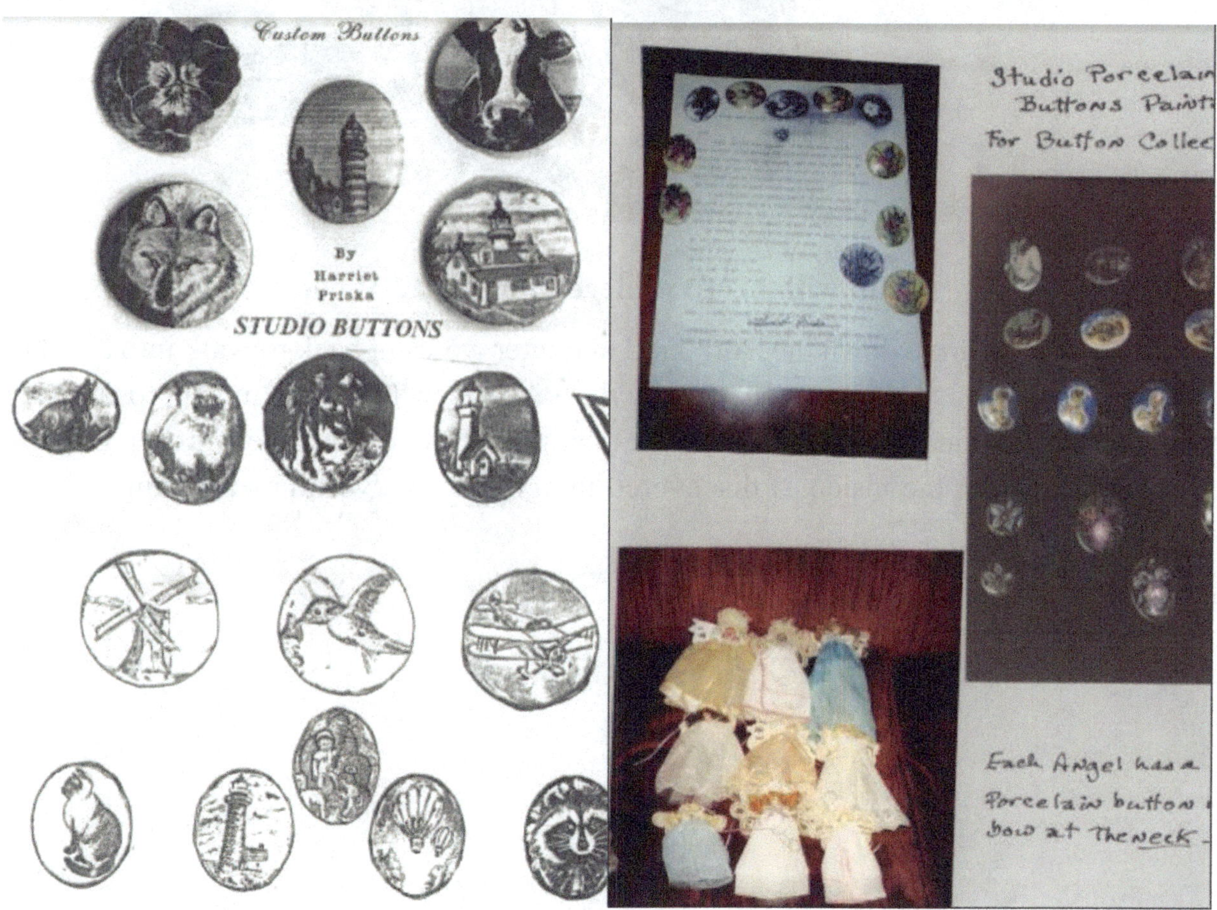

A variety of the buttons I painted for collectors and craft projects.

After very heavy snow that winter, we were ready to go out to explore the countryside in the spring of 1992. We joined the local rock club. On our first trip we drove 60 miles east to the base of the volcanic formation named the Henry Mountains. The members knew where they could collect some petrified wood on public land. I stayed behind and looked at many large volcanic boulders laying all over the ground near where we parked. Philip hiked with the rest of the group to see what they could find. Finally, after quite a bit of effort, he returned with a large piece of Petrified wood on his shoulder! This was the first of many large rocks that Philip would collect to bring home!

Philip with his first piece of Petrified Wood!

On that trip we had to drive down the Burr Trail and later we went back to walk into a slot canyon that was just off the road. I was so enchanted by the experience that I used my photos for reference and painted another wraparound vase. One part looking in from the outside and then going around it and looking out from the inside. I discovered the gift of my dyslexia was being able to think from the inside out!

Vase with views of the Slot canyon from outside looking in and then from in the inside looking out!

My father was a Presbyterian minister. In 1943 he baptized me as an infant in both of his first two churches in Idaho. However, when we started attending the Baptist Church in Escalante, I came to realize that I wanted to be baptized by immersion. My parents and my brother John drove from California that summer and our pastor, Jim Dagget, baptized me in Wide Hollow Reservoir at the Petrified Forest State Park just east of Escalante. It was a joyous occasion for us all as I came to understand that I was baptized into Christ's death and then risen again with Him into eternal life.

On order for us to buy redwood for the back porch and the front deck that Philip was constructing beside the double wide, we had to go out of town to purchase our supplies. The nearest hardware stores were at the Garfield County seat in Panguitch, 75 miles west. We hauled the wood back in the motorhome and supplies the Bronco.

On one occasion, I was carrying a large load of cinderblock pilings in the Bronco. As we drove slowly up the "Blues" as the locals called that very windy road in the grey clay hills, I remembered the first time we came up it when the speedometer cable went dry. I was praying this time that I had enough gears to make it to the top.

One day, we drove all the way to Cedar City 125 miles west to do some shopping and met a man in his secondhand store. We got into conversation about where we lived, and he mentioned that he wanted to advertise his business in Escalante. Highway 12 had already been recognized as a very scenic road and there was an ordinance against any advertising signs all the way along the 120 miles from Highway 89 before Bryce Canyon National Park to Highway 24 near Capitol Reef National Park. He asked us if we would start a business in our home so that he could have the right to put a sign near our business on Highway 12 to advertise his business. We finally agreed and I went home and began to think about a business name.

I had done quite a lot of recovery work in California regarding the effect of my father's war experiences and learned how Secondary Post Traumatic Stress Disorder affected all our family. I had the opportunity do some Christian work at my church studying Bible references to help me in my healing process in a group for Adult Children of Dysfunctional Parents. Part of my work was to repeat the Serenity Prayer.

I continued to pray with it for wisdom daily as we faced many challenges and unknown circumstances in Utah. Finally, Philip and I agreed on the name "*Serenidad Gallery*." I filled out the paperwork and we became a business although all I was dealing with at the time was my porcelain buttons through the mail. We contacted the man in Cedar City to tell him what we accomplished. His wife answered the phone and told us that her husband had just died unexpectedly! So, we had a business name anyway!

All this activity brought us to the awareness that "Hmm, maybe we should be making money!" We called our Real Estate friend Dawn Griffin, and she showed us three different properties on Main Street that were for sale, none of which were actual business locations. One was a small old brick home built in 1896, that had been abandoned for many years and needed a lot of work. The other was a building that had been used as a garage in times past, and it was not very useful for our needs either. We prayed and finally made an offer on the old Forest Service office building.

In 1965, a group of 5 local men built this log building using a kit with old original growth Canadian Red Cedar for the purpose of renting it to the government. In 1974 they added two more large rooms and bathrooms onto the back for more office space. At that time the men covered the logs with aluminum siding and after adding more electrical wiring placed wood paneling on the walls inside. Eventually one widow ended up as the sole owner of the building and then the Forest Service built a new office building west of town and moved out. The building had been vacant for a year. Many people had looked at it, but it was still on sale for $52,000. Later that fall, we took a leap of faith and offered to put half down and asked Mrs. Leland Haws living in Boulder, Utah to carry the rest and we would pay her monthly. She agreed! Praise the Lord!

The Serenity Prayer

God grant me the serenity
to accept the things I cannot change;
courage to change the things I can;
and wisdom to know the difference.

Chapter 28 – 360 West Main Street

February 1, 1993, Escalante received over two feet of snow the day we took possession of 360 West Main! We had to shovel our way in to the front door! Neither of us had ever owned a business building, so we were very excited to begin Serenidad Gallery! It was a real leap of faith!

The only other building on the block was the Escalante Outfitters. A large log cabin just east of us down Main street. It was built by Barry and Celeste Bernards, who retired from their careers with law enforcement and moved to Escalante some years before.

Serenidad Gallery with the Escalante Outfitters just east of us.

The Old Forest Service Office (as it was commonly referred to) was a 2000 square foot building with 8 rooms, two bathrooms, a long hallway, and a furnace room. It was situated on .39th of an acre. The back of the property had been a parking lot for the Forest Service vehicles and was covered with gravel.

Escalante was founded in 1876 by Mormon pioneers who discovered that the weather was better in the Escalante River valley at 5800 feet, than in Panguitch at 6200 feet, seventy five miles to the west where they had been sent by Brigham Young to settle a second time despite the poor growing season.

The new settlers in Escalante used chains to divide the town into five acre blocks according to the Zion Plat system. Then each block was subdivided into four 1 ½ acre parcels. The pioneers drew numbers out a of hat to determine who got each of the parcels on the thirty seven blocks. Eventually more parcels were added around the edges of the town. Each family were given 2 acres of alfalfa land on the north side of the Escalante River which flowed east into the Escalante Canyon. Additionally, each family was assigned twenty or more acres of farmland south of town.

Originally, the business buildings were mostly located on Center Street which ran north to south crossing the river at the north end of town. However, when Highway 12 was paved in Escalante in 1956, Main Street going east and west became the location for the business district. Highway 12 was gradually constructed in portions over the years and in 1984 the last sixty miles was finally paved over Boulder Mountain between Boulder Town and Torrey at the end of Highway 12 on Highway 24. Before that people only came to this part of the world because they wanted to, not because they were on their way to somewhere else!

Painting I did of Center Street from 1940 Photograph by Dorothea Lang.

Painting I did of Main Street in 1940 from Photograph by Dorothea Lang.

Local woodcraftsman, Vergean Porter, kindly constructed and routed out two large signs for the front of the gallery from a single piece of lumber which he got from an old sawmill west of town. Philip painted them brown with white lettering and installed the posts deep into the ground on either side of the front of the property. The land on Main street just to the west of us was vacant at that time, however as you can see by the yellow machinery in the background of the photo below, the ground was being leveled and the next year, we would see the two-story brick Prospector Inn arise next to our parking lot! We were ready to open on March 22, 1993.

WE OPEN – March 22, 1993

Our dear friends Bill and Carolyn Bowmar with their daughter in law, Jackie Novotny, were some of our first guests for our Grand Opening on April 3rd. When we met the Bowmars in 1998, I was amazed to learn that Carolyn, like my grandmother, Olivia Young, was a skilled Black and White Photographer. She had won many prizes when they lived in Los Angeles years before. Carolyn took wonderful photographs of the Escalante area, developed her negatives in one of her bathrooms, and printed her own photographs. We were delighted to have her be our first featured artist in a small room in the heart of the building.

GRAND OPENING -
April 3rd - 1993

Bill and Carolyn Bowmar and Daughter-in-law Jackie Novotny

Early in March we discovered two glass display cases for sale in Richfield, 125 miles north of Escalante. Philip carefully loaded them both into the motorhome and then when we got to Escalante he maneuvered them safely into the lobby of the Gallery. In the beginning, we did not have any inventory, so Philip put in all his precious toy train collection to fill one case, and I put my art glass collection and other small treasures we had brought along with us in the other one. I printed up some of my color photographs of the Escalante area and made them into greeting cards to sell from a spinning card rack we found. That was the start of my greeting card production which continues to this day!

Our opening – a Leap of Faith.

One of the front rooms was dedicated to showing Rachel Bentley's Watercolors. We brought along Philip's favorite red crushed velvet sofa from California, and over the years he would spend many hours sitting there waiting for customers! On the other two walls he exhibited more of Rachel's paintings. We have owned one hundred and fifty of her works.

Philip in the 'Bentley Room."

Early in January, after a deep snow, after the road was plowed out, we drove up ten miles east on Highway 12 to what the local's call "The Head of the Rocks." From that vantage overlook you can see the vast expanse of the Escalante Canyon lands with the Henry Mountains in the far distance. Standing on three feet of snow, I took photographs to capture the overwhelming experience of it all.

I studied the photos and with the help of local artist, Ruthanne Oliver, we placed thirty white ceramic four-inch tiles in an interesting arrangement. Then I sketched the view on them and proceeded to recreate the panorama with my porcelain paints. I must confess, I got lost a time or two as I worked my way across the vista. I fired the tiles several times and finally arranged them on a sheet of plywood as seen in the upper photo. Philip carefully cut the board to fit them and glued them down. Then he put hangers on the back and displayed the tiles on the lobby wall in the gallery. The tiles became a tourist information opportunity to show people who had just driven east on Highway 12 from Bryce Canyon why they must drive another ten miles to see what was on the other side of the hill!

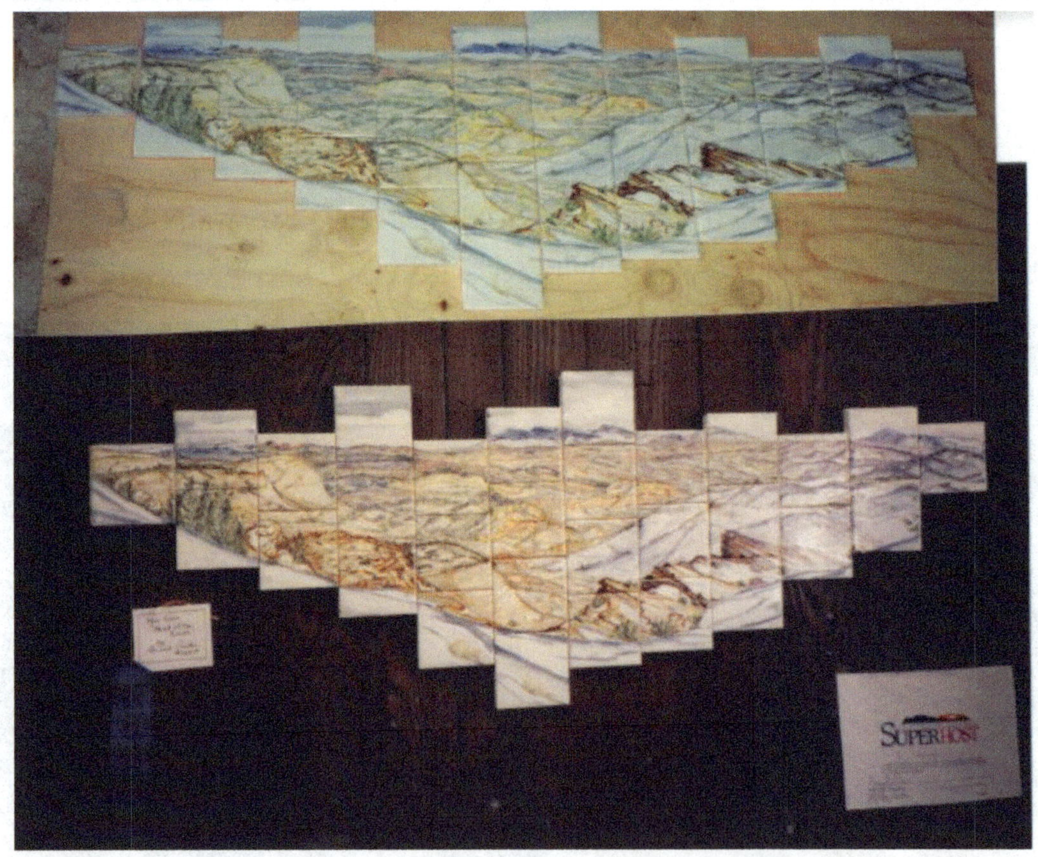

Tile painting done from "The Head of the Rocks."

Philippians 4:13 I can do all things through Christ who strengthens me.

Chapter 29 – The Long Trailer

Almost as soon as we signed the paperwork at the Security Title Company in Panguitch in November of 1992 to buy the building on 360 West Main Street, we realized that we had to sell our property outside of town! This was a real heartbreaker for us both. We had poured our hearts, time, and energy into making it Home. We loved the silence and as recent city dwellers scenery was so precious to our souls.

That November day when we got back to Escalante, we immediately went to see Dawn at her Realty Office. Jay Belbe was sitting there asking her about places to buy. His daughter has recently graduated from Turn About Ranch, and he fell in love with the area when he came to take her home. We had many conversations with Jay over the years, but he never bought the property outside of town from us.

Early in August 1993, our dear neighbors, the McCunn's, from Menlo Park came to visit us and celebrate our birthdays. Philip was going to turn 53 soon, Drummond was already 52, Teddi was 51 and I was 50 on the same day, July 28! Our friends the Bostics came with them. We had a grand visit and recalled the ten years we had celebrated our "stairstep birthdays" in California together.

Harriet and Philip, Shirley and Dave Bostic, Teddi and Drummond McCunn.

That fall I put an ad in the newspaper for the property and we got a phone call from Dr. Ron Hardy, an optometrist in Denver who had been hiking the Escalante Canyons for many years and always wanted to have a vacation home here. We eventually sold them the property and carried the loan. They put some money down and their monthly payments helped us pay our payments on the building.

Ron and Rose Hardy hired Philip to complete the seven hundred square foot redwood deck around the front two sides of the double wide. They came a few times whenever they could get away from his practice.

I mentioned our need for a place to live to Katie Thomas, the Editor of the Garfield County News, and she told me of a trailer for sale in Tropic, We purchased it for $5000 and had it placed behind the building on the gravel parking lot in November. It was an older model, but sufficient for our needs. It had a nice open kitchen and living room area with a wood burning stove, one and a half bathrooms, one master bedroom and two smaller bedrooms on the other end, one I used for an office.

The Trailer arrives from Tropic and is placeced on our back parking lot.

By January of 1994, we had pioneered our newest home, putting in power, water, connecting to the sewer and telephone. Philip attached a wooden skirting all the way around it and eventually built a nice porch on the front. Philp loved to work with wood and was very skilled with whatever he constructed.

Philip built all the skirting around the trailer and then later a front porch.

Philippians 4:19 My God shall supply all your needs according to His riches in Glory by Christ Jesus.

Chapter 30 – Learning curves in Business and Art

In the summer of 1993, Escalante Mayor, Wade Barney, invited all the town's business owners to come to the City Hall. About a dozen of us sat in a circle and the Mayor advised us to form the Escalante Chamber of Commerce. As we went around the room telling what office we could hold, Philip and I agreed to answer the Chamber phone because we were in the gallery all day long. As things progressed, I became the manager. We published a trifold brochure listing the businesses along Main Street hoping to attract tourists to our town.

Escalante is in the information shadow of Bryce Canyon National Park, and we were not recognized as a tourist destination. Some travelers came here from Bryce out of curiosity and others on their way to Capitol Reef National Park at the east end of Highway 12. Whenever anyone came in the gallery, I pointed to my tile painting to explain to people that driving another ten miles east on the highway would give them a vast panorama of the Escalante Canyon lands.

I still must give that talk today!

One tourist brochure after another was produced. We designed a logo saying that Escalante is on the "Heart of Highway 12"because we are halfway between Highway 89 to the west and Highway 24 in the northeast. I learned how to write grants from Garfield Travel Council and Utah Travel Council to print colorful informative travel information.

One of our bright ideas to attract people to the area was to put on a Mountain Man Rendezvous reenacting the early trapping days in the west. Several men in town had participated in them in other locations. In the fall of 1994, Philip and I drove up Cedar Mountain and turned off Highway 14 to visit a Rendezvous being re-enacted among the tall pine trees. My friend, Lance Jagger, i.e. "Horsehair" (his mountain man name) and others assured me that they would act as lead men, so we began to look for land to hold the event on, raise funds, and get donations for prizes.

Lance Jagger, in this photo is on the left listening to a Mountain Man describing his hand made leather pouch.

When we bought the building on Main Street, Philip was not fond of its government pea green color. So, he spent quite a bit of time painting the entire gallery white with brown trim. Then he painted the trailer the same colors after he built a nice wooden porch on the front. He carefully painted white letters advertising our business on the upper part of the front of the gallery on both sides. The Prospector Inn was built next to us in 1993, adding an additional business presence to our side of the street. Our sales doubled once they opened! Thank you, Lord. Additionally, the Escalante Outfitter built small log cabins for overnight rentals just east of us and put up a nice pole fence along the street. We all looked much more businesslike!

Serenidad Gallery and the new Log cabins beside the Escalante Outfitters.

Serenidad Gallery and the new Prospector Inn.

A man came in one day and sold us some large sandstone rocks that he had carved to look like ancient dwellings and slabs he had painted with native symbols. Over time we sold them all. Philip even packed one large stone very carefully and shipped it!

Sandstone art and a brown pitcher that I painted with an ear of corn in California.

A Navajo lady who lived on the Navajo Reservation south of us in Arizona came in selling her rugs. We wanted Navajo art were glad to purchase some of her weavings and paintings. However, we soon learned that the Navajos live in the same economic world that we do, and she asked fair prices for her work. We bought seven small rugs and discovered that they were difficult to sell because of the prices we had paid for them.

Navajo Rugs and art work.

Since we are in the southwest, customers expected us to have Native American jewelry. By April of 1994 we were able to offer turquoise, coral, and hand-crafted sterling silver earrings, necklaces, and rings that we bought at Quartzite!

Seen in the photo above in the first display case are two of my China paintings I had done by that time. On the shelf in the middle is a pitcher I made of a desert trumpet flower, called Sacred Datura, with a sandstone background. On the lower left is the narrow-necked vase of a Slot Canyon on the Burr Trail.

In the display case above on the bottom left is my first Zion Vase I painted in 1988. On the bottom right is the vase I also painted in California of Bryce Canyon National Park featuring the Natural Bridge. The three photos below show all the sides.

My Bryce Canyon Vase with the Natural Bridge and Thor's Hammer.

I offered Art lessons to the local children, starting with some of Karen and Reed Munson's family. They learned "how to see" as I gave them drawing exercises using the material from the book "Drawing from the Right Side of the Brain." I have continued to teach from that book for many years.

I started collecting sewing buttons again and invited the Girl Scouts in Escalante to come and learn about the different styles of buttons. They put several types on a card and had a great time playing in the button boxes.

While we did feature a couple artists in the early years, the most important person was local cowboy artist, Lynn Griffin, who came into the gallery in January of 1995 and sold us several of his paintings illustrating the life and times in the Escalante area. He was already a well-known artist, and we were very pleased to represent him and eventually we bought and sold 40 of his works. Lynn and Philip were just a few months apart in age and enjoyed each other's company over the years.

Local cowboy artist, Lynn Griffin.

In the spring of 1995, City Council member, Marilyn Jackson realized that Escalante's Brick Homes and Log Barns built in the late 1800's and early 1900's were disappearing or falling into disrepair. She got funds from Escalante City Council to print 500 copies of a map and tour of the remaining buildings with a short explanation for each of them. Local artist Shiela Wooley helped to do the first inventory. The publication was very popular, and they soon ran out of the brochure.

The two ladies in conjunction with the Daughters of the Utah Pioneers then asked the Escalante Chamber of Commerce to sponsor a bigger pamphlet. I wrote a grant in the fall, and we printed the first "Walking Tour of Pioneer Homes and Barns" complete with a map of Escalante showing 96 brick homes, buildings, and barns. The bifold, trifold brochure was compiled by local historian Marilyn Jackson and illustrated by Sheila Wooley. It was very popular with tourists, and locals who wanted to know more about their ancestor's homes.

In July in 1995 we held our first Mountain Man Rendezvous in a field west of Escalante. We recruited men from Mountain Man clubs in the area who came to help us run the competitions and sell their wares. It was a great success and enjoyed by all.

The Barsh twins demonstrate how to pack a mule.

The Rendezvous site east of Escalante off Highway 12.

Psalm 1211 – 8 I will lift up my eyes unto the hills, from whence cometh my help.

My help cometh from the LORD, which made heaven and earth.

He will not suffer thy foot to be moved: he that keeps thee will not slumber.

Behold, he that keeps Israel shall neither slumber nor sleep.

The LORD is thy keeper: the LORD is thy shade upon thy right hand.

The sun shall not smite thee by day, nor the moon by night.

The LORD shall preserve thee from all evil: he shall preserve thy soul.

The LORD shall preserve thy going out and thy coming in from this time forth, and even for evermore.

Chapter 31 – Grand Staircase Escalante National Monument

Philip and I met Sandy Larsen. in 1986 when we camped at the Escalante Petrified Forest State Park where he was the ranger and we met him there again in 1988, We connected immediately because he was also an antique dealer at his winter home in Yucca Valley, California.

After we bought the Gallery, we traveled south each winter to buy merchandise. We visited Sandy in Southern California, and went "garage sailing" with him near Twenty-Nine Palms. One day in January of 1994, we were out shopping with him, and he picked up a large slab of pink petrified wood and told us we should buy it and advised us to sell Petrified Wood in the Gallery. We paid the fifty-dollar price tag and wondered at his advice.

When we got home, we visited a couple who were selling rocks at the local RV park across the street and asked them what they thought of our purchase. They liked it immediately and suggested that we could ask two hundred and fifty dollars for it! Then they told us that a lady in town had recently offered them her petrified wood collection from her parents, but they could not afford to buy the collection.

We called Marjie Spencer and were invited to come over and look at all the cut and polished petrified wood that her father, who was blind at the time, had produced many years before! We asked how much her family wanted and agreed on a price for the whole lot and come home with an amazing collection of marvelous pieces.

Philip built shelving in one room to accommodate all the various sizes of Petrified Wood and bins for the small, tumbled rocks. Little do we know that they would be our "Bread and Butter" money so to speak, for many years!

My art project that winter was to paint the amazing rock formation just beside our favorite slot canyon on the Burr Trail on a 6" by 8" tile.

Burr Trail Tile.

Our other major sales discovery at that time was, of all things, automobile license plates! One winter day we visited the antique dealer in Hatch, located south on Highway 89 and asked him how things were going. He said he had just sold one hundred dollars' worth of license plates to tourists that day! We were stunned and amazed but began to buy them and sell them in the Gallery.

Soon we were saying "it is like printing money! " Our prices were reasonable and the tourists, many of whom were from Europe, liked the fact that the plates were lightweight, easy to pack, and gave them good memories of the states they visited.

In the photo below, you can see how Philip hung various license plates on the walls. Please note in the lower right-hand corner of the first display case there is my vase that I painted of the Escalante River Canyon. It was four sided and I liked to say that the "River ran through it" because on the other side of the vase I showed the far side of the canyon where the Escalante River came out at Highway 12 fifteen miles away. In the second display case you can barely see my first Zion vase toward the front and in the far side my Bryce vase. In addition to my tile painting on the wall, you can see the cowboy hats and fishing lures that Philip enjoyed accumulating. We were diverse in our antique collecting. (Note the wood paneling still on the walls!)

Front room in Serenidad Gallery.

Late in the morning of September 18,1996, I happened to notice a camera man and a reporter from Channel Five Television in Salt Lake City, taking videos of the Escalante River Canyon standing on the back of our driveway. I stepped over to chat with the reporter, John Hollenhorst, whom I recognized from the Evening News. I asked what they were doing, and he informed me that the New York Times had broken the story early that morning that President Bill Clinton had just designated 1.7 million acres around Escalante as the new "Grand Staircase Escalante National Monument!"

The declaration had taken place on the South Rim of the Grand Canyon in Arizona earlier in the morning, and no one from Utah had been invited! Not the Governor, no one!

John had been attempting to reach the Mayor of Escalante, and Garfield Country Commissioners for comments to no avail. When he found out that I managed the Escalante/Boulder Chamber of Commerce, he asked me if I would be willing to be interviewed on the 5 P.M. Evening News if he was unable to reach anyone else!

I agreed and immediately began to pray, 'Lord please show me what to do!"

I called the head ranger at Capitol Reef National Park northeast of us because I knew that that area had been first designated a National Monument and then a National Park. He explained that a Monument designation allows grazing on public lands, but no grazing was allowed on National Park lands.

I was most concerned for the local pioneer families in Escalante and Boulder who had made their living running cattle on the land for many years. Most of Garfield and Kane County to the south of us was managed by the Bureau of Land Management.

The outline for this Monument had been in the Federal books since 1934 but was just now being implemented during President Clinton's Democratic bid for re-election. At that time, Utah was still mostly a Republican state which is possibly why no one was notified.

John Hollenhorst called me later in the afternoon and asked me if I would be willing to be interviewed live at 5 P.M. I met him outside town by the Escalante cemetery where there was a good view of the Escalante River Canyon in the background. I do not remember exactly what I said, however the basis of my remarks was that "we must learn how to live with it." The man listening back in the studio in Salt Lake City, said to John in his earphone, "Well, that was refreshing."

In the late 1800's, the concept of the name of this land formation originated when an explorer was standing in the southern part of the area looking up toward the north and he said the rock layers looked like a "Grand Staircase" speaking about what is now Zion and Bryce National Parks.

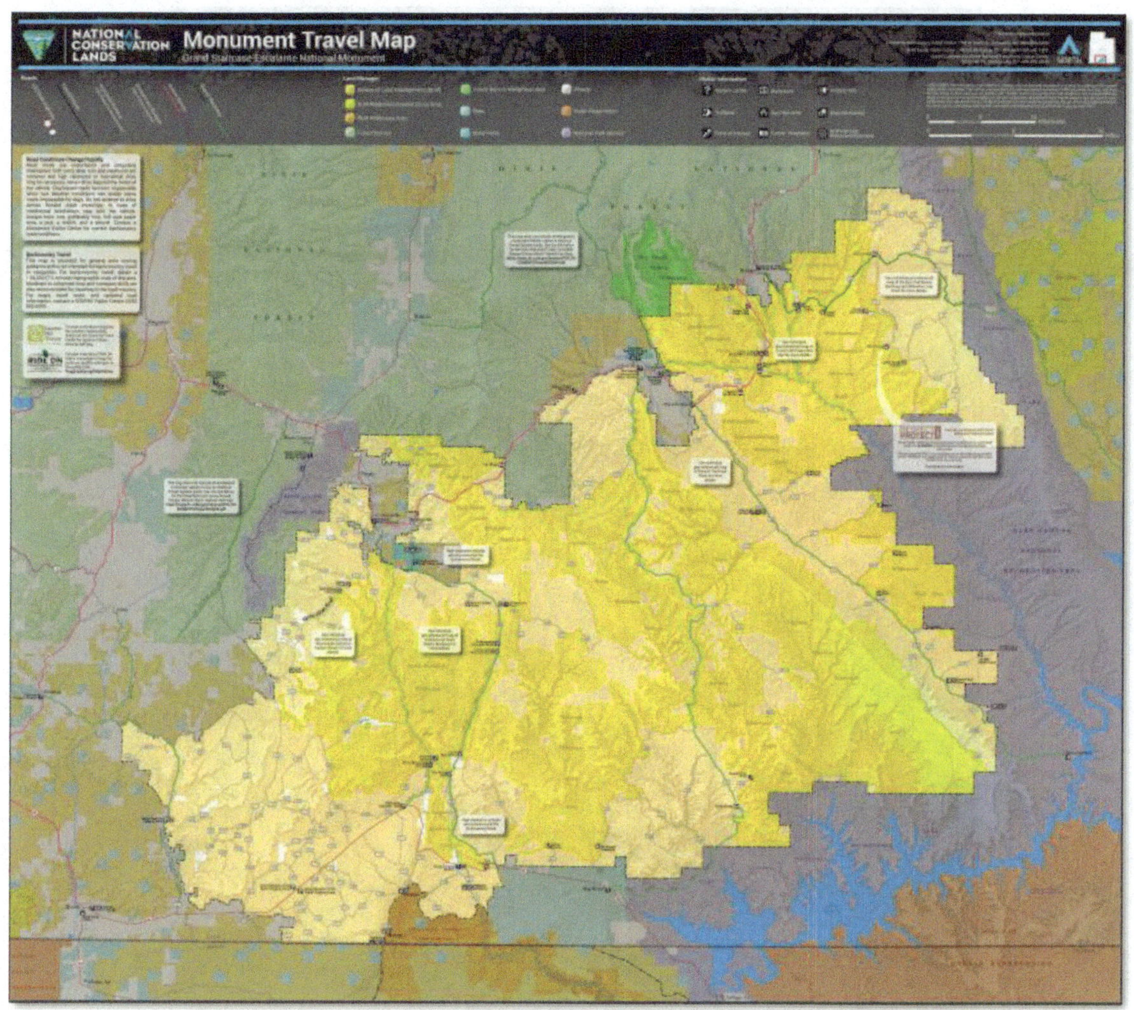

The Grand Staircase Escalante National Monument is shown in orange and yellow on the map. 1.9 million acres.

There was quite an uproar throughout the state, and I got a bit of flack for my remarks from a local resident. However, the designation put Escalante on the map in a way that no amount of advertising could ever pay for! Regardless of which was the contributor, our new petrified wood collection or the Monument designation, our sales in the Gallery doubled almost immediately!

On behalf of the businesses and the Chamber earlier in the summer of 1996, I contacted Great Mountain West Supply, a postcard company in Salt Lake City. The owner came down and took forty-five rolls of film in the area just before the Monument designation. So, they were able to produce a line of postcards with many scenes of the new Monument later in the fall. The company needed a local sales representative, so I agreed to cover the territory, and I sold postcards for them for the next twenty years.

Early in January of 1997 we received over two feet of snow in one storm! Philip quickly got up and shoveled the heavy snow off the roof of our trailer. Some people didn't bother, and the roofs of their trailers caved in over the doorways which had weaker construction!

Two feet of snow!!!

Philip always said he wanted a log building and finally one day we looked at the walls in the furnace room, and we realized that indeed entire the front building was constructed of original growth Canadian Red Cedar logs. Philip began to carefully remove the dark wood paneling from all the walls. It was like Cinderella every day as he exposed more and more of the lovely logs that had been covered up since 1974! However, there was also agony as he discovered that in order for the men to install more electrical wiring, some of the logs had been chopped rather brutally then covered up with the paneling. This photo below shows the worst of the repairs that Philip had to replace to make the log wall uniform again. The best part of it all was that the logs did not have to be treated in any way and they glistened in the light.

Philip carefully repairing the walls!

I enlarged some of my best-selling photos of the area and sold matted prints.

By April of 1997 Philip had transformed the other front room into what we fondly called "The Rock Room." There he carefully displayed many of the pieces we had purchased from our local collection, and we continued to acquire Petrified Wood bookends when we traveled to Quartzite, Arizona each January to the big rock show and sale.

The "Rock Room" with Philip's shelving of display Petrified Wood.

Exodus 31: 3

I have filled him with the Spirit of God, with wisdom, with understanding, with knowledge and with all kinds of skills.

Chapter 32 – Serenidad Retreat

Early in June of 1996. the second Mountain Man Rendezvous was held near Escalante. We offered a lot of activities for local kids to participate in and mountain men came again from other areas to help us run the competitions.

Kids learning Mountain skills.

Discussing fire starting techniques.

However, the big event was a microburst wind that blew a tent down on my head and about a million board feet trees up on the mountains! I survived, but the trees did not! My neighbor at the Prospector Inn carried down several large logs down to put around his property. The one seen here is a 45-foot Ponderosa log weighing 2 tons, which was what his forklift would carry. It was set on large rounds of itself at the back of our driveway!

The Ponderosa Pine tree that got blown down in June.

When I attended the University of Wyoming in Laramie in the 1960's I taught a Sunday School class at the Presbyterian Church. Brad Howard was the supervisor for the Elementary section. In the mid 1990's he saw my name in the Alumni News and contacted me in Escalante. He was still in Laramie and had many life challenges. I thought I should introduce him to someone who faced even more difficulty in life to get his mind off himself! I told him about Luanne Davis who I had assisted with her Cerebral Palsy encumbrances in the 1960's and 1970's. Eventually they met and married! Brad took Luanne out into the wilderness on grand adventures like carrying her into an ice cave in Wyoming. In September 1997, Brad drove Luanne down to visit us! We had a marvelous time together and Brad pushed Luanne in her wheelchair to the rim of Bryce Canyon, much to her delight.

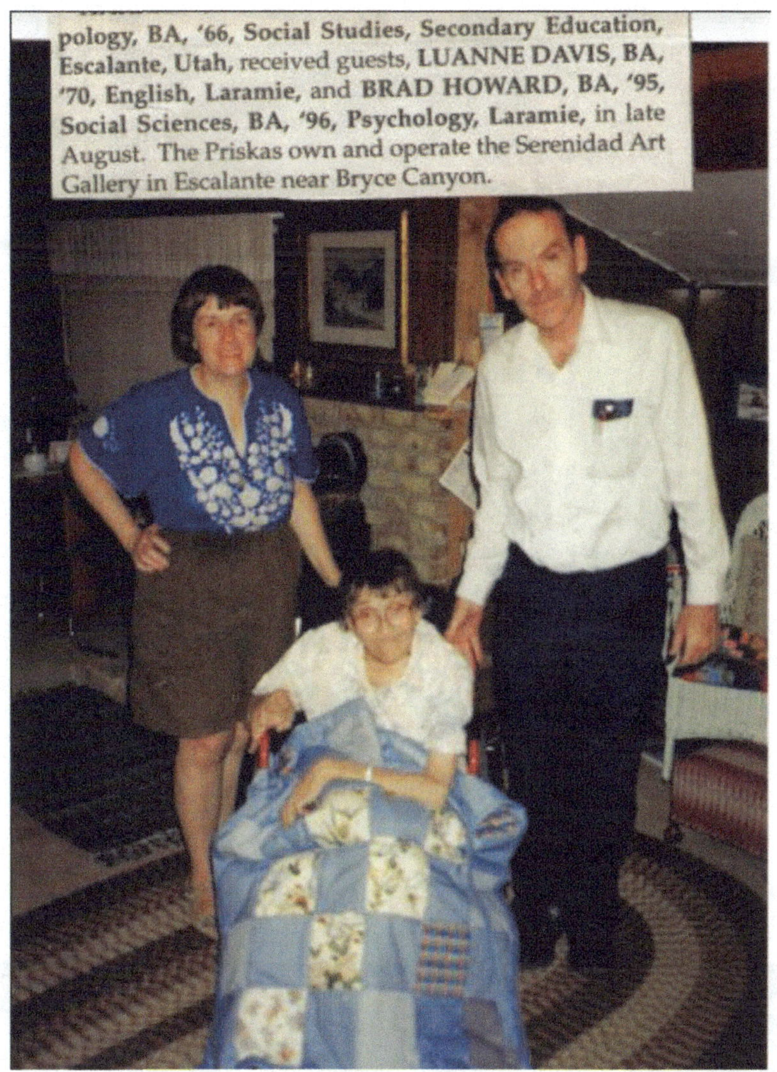
pology, BA, '66, Social Studies, Secondary Education, Escalante, Utah, received guests, LUANNE DAVIS, BA, '70, English, Laramie, and BRAD HOWARD, BA, '95, Social Sciences, BA, '96, Psychology, Laramie, in late August. The Priskas own and operate the Serenidad Art Gallery in Escalante near Bryce Canyon.

Brad and Luanne come for a visit!

Each fall, Philip was very industrious about gathering fire wood up on the mountain and cutting it to size for our small woodburning stove in our living room in the trailer. The stove provided enough warmth for the whole unit, although I had to get up in the night to put more wood on the fire to keep it burning.

When we went up the mountain, I would drag trees over to Philip and after he cut them up with his trusty chainsaw, we loaded the logs into our small trailer. The snow photo was taken in November of 1996. We learned to go up earlier to get wood after that. You can see how he stacked the logs beside the trailer by October of 1997.

Philip with a chainsaw in the snow.

Philip with our wood supply for the coming winter.

My desire to capture the wonderful rock formations here led me to paint this ten-inch pitcher of Allan Canyon near Escalante. The first pioneers came into this area late in 1875 and left some cattle to overwinter at the base of these cliffs. In the spring of 1876, Philo Allen returned and found his heard thriving and decided to move from Panguitch to this area. Other hardy pioneers soon followed eager to find better pasture for their cattle and sheep along the river. That spring, they met the survey crew sent there by John Wesley Powell, and the crew advised the settlers to call the town Escalante because they had just named the river after Friar Silvestre Escalante who explored Utah a hundred years before.

Allen Canyon and my wrap around vase of the red rocks there.

One day in 1997, while walking my dog, LP, I met Ricki and Sandy Brown who had recently come from Colorado and built a solar vacation home southeast of town, which he called "La Luz," which means "The Light" in Spanish. I learned that Ricki wanted to rent out the home when they were not in Escalante as a nightly rental. I agreed to be his manager, and we presented the concept to the city planning and zoning committee and worked out the details to their satisfaction.

This was the first vacation rental home in Escalante. We designed a website and people made reservations online. I also had Ricki's phone line in my home and took calls for him from his clients. At first, I cleaned the house after every stay, but eventually we hired someone else to do that.

I enjoyed going into La Luz at any time of the year because the temperature was always about 65 degrees! The solar design was very well done with the house facing the sun at just the right angle all year round. Ricki had laid heating elements in the cement floor so that it was always had very even temperature. I blocked out the days that the Browns wanted to be in Escalante and booked the rest. La Luz was a popular destination for hikers and travelers from around the world. Ricki was an award-winning kitchen designer, and all the furnishings were very high end.

I met Jake at the Rendezvous in 1996, and he started visiting us whenever he came through the area on his motorcycle. He taught me a lot about the native plants that grew well in the desert. He was over six feet tall, and, in this photo below, Jake is standing by native sunflowers growing near La Luz. Note that the flowers were even taller than he could reach!

Jake with native sunflowers beside La Luz.

Dr. Ron and Rose Hardy bought our property outside of Escalante in the fall of 1993 and came here to hike and eventually had their wedding on the deck in the summer of 1994. They enjoyed their visits, which unfortunately because of Ron's health issues then came less and less as time went on. To help them with their utility bills we offered to rent the house out to tourists and even a schoolteacher for a semester.

The Turn About Ranch father, Jay Belby, who originally wanted to purchase the property arranged with the Hardys to pay to live in the house and leave whenever they came to town. That worked out for several years. Unfortunately, Ron's health declined. First, he had heart surgery and then brain surgery and they finally had to give up the idea of coming back again.

By January of 1999, Philip and I began to think about purchasing the property again. We agreed to pay what they asked and applied what they owed to the principal. We took out a loan and got it back fully furnished early in April. We notified Jay and he agreed to come to live there permanently at that time, however three days before he was scheduled to arrive, he called to say that his mother was dying of cancer, and he could not come!

What were we to do? We had a $700 a month mortgage to pay! Within a few hours, Ricki's phone rang. Someone was looking for a place to rent during the Easter Break. La Luz was already fully booked, and since we had a furnished house, we immediately rented ours to them. We rented it eight of the first ten days we owned the house that Easter Break! Then we decided to create Serenidad Retreat!

I designed a website to take reservations. Sometimes we got reservations from La Luz when it was full and other times we gave La Luz the business when we were booked! It worked out well for both of us! We were able to pay the mortgage and even pay ahead because Philip hated being in debt!

I painted some four-inch ceramic tiles and fired them with the name and address of Serenidad Retreat. Philip made a nice sign with them, and we put it up on our property near Highway 12 with a big dead Juniper tree to attract attention.

Tile sign I painted for Serenidad Retreat.

By the following spring the lovely old-fashioned yellow roses I had planted years before were flourishing by the front deck.

Serenidad Retreat with local yellow roses flourishing beside the 700 Sq ft. Redwood deck.

Isaiah 30: 15 **For** thus saith the Lord GOD, the Holy One of Israel; In returning and rest shall ye be saved; in quietness and in confidence shall be your strength:

Chapter 33 – "Y2K"

As the year 2000 AD approached, we realized that we were not only turning into a new century but also another millennium! Many celebrations were prepared around the world. Also, there was some angst in the internet community about whether the computers which managed many things, were programed to handle the change in the digits from 1999 to 2000. This was "much ado about nothing" as it turned out! I just read about it in Wikipedia and in general there were few problems worldwide and some countries like Russia did not even do anything about the transition at all!

For me the best part was watching all the daybreak celebrations around the world on TV. Late in the afternoon of December 31st. 1999, while watching the sun go down here in the west, I was also viewing the same sun rise over the Pacific Ocean on the TV broadcast where January 1st, 2000, had begun! That was particularly meaningful to me as my friends Ian and Carol Cameron lived in Australia. I realized that I was seeing the same sun on TV as they were looking at in their own sky! I enjoyed the concept of triangulating the sun with them!

Meanwhile back on the home front…my parents had finally retired from their various ministries in the San Francisco Bay Area, sold their home in Pacifica, and moved to be near my brother John in a nice, manufactured house in a lovely mobile home park in Salinas, California. On one visit, i presented them with a Certificate of Appreciation from the Daughters of the American Revolution for all the work they had done over the years for the American flag especially with the large 48 stars flag my dad had brought home with him from World War II! They were active in the American Legion in Salinas and participated in many flag ceremonies there, such as placing American Flags in cemeteries on Memorial Day and Verterans Day.

I presented a DAR Flag Appreciation Certificate to Mom and Dad.

Harry and Winnie celebrated their 60th wedding anniversary on July 27th, 2001. And then as was so often the case those days, my brother John moved away from them to Fresno, California to be near his three children who had gone to Fresno State University, married and started their families in Fresno! However, my parents enjoyed being near the ocean and were active in the Presbyterian Church in Salinas as well as keeping up friendships with the congregation at the Presbyterian Church in Burlingame where mom had served as a lay pastor.

In the summer of 2000, I was in the Gallery and Philip was in the trailer doing some chores. A nice French man walked in the front door with his wife and showed me a book he had just published in black and white about hiking in southern Utah. I was not very interested in selling it. Then he asked me if I would like to see his original color photography. I agreed and Laurant brought in a large folio of his work and laid it on the counter. I was stunned! My knees were weak with amazement at the beauty of his images as he showed them to me one by one.

I stopped him and called Philip on the phone and told him to come to the gallery right away! Together we continued to view his marvelous and vibrant images of our desertscapes. We discussed the possibility of representing Laurant Martres' photography in the gallery. This opportunity had not yet occurred to him, so we had to talk about it at length over time until we came up with a plan for us to sell his images, some framed and others matted in various sizes. Eventually we learned which images were most popular with the public. As you can see by the photos below, we exhibited a wide variety his work, and we sold them for the next 15 years.

Laurent then began to exhibit his images in other galleries and locations here in Utah. He eventually went on to sell his work at outdoor art shows in Southern California. His images and photo guidebooks are available on his website today. He can be reached on: Photo Trip USA Publishing - Travel photography guidebooks

Laurent and Patricia Martres, Philip and me holding Charlie.

Some of Laurent's marvelous photography.

When I was answering the phone for the Chamber In the mid 1990's, I got calls looking for a company called "Escalante Rugs." I contacted the owner, Robert Weed, and suggested that he join the Escalante Chamber of Commerce so that we could connect him with those customers. He sent a sale representative in to see. We really liked their fine handwoven wool rugs that they imported from a village in the Oaxaca Valley south of Mexico City. We began purchasing rugs and coasters and I still handle them to this day. There is one the wall in the photo below of our western room.

An Escalante Rug in our Western Room.

On a trip to the Quartzite flea market one winter, Philip found a very complex wooden model of an early steam tugboat called the "Seguin." After a much discussion with me about what it would entail in terms of time and energy on his part, he purchased it and worked on it for over ten years. The photo below shows Philp with the model in the later stages after many hours of painstakingly laying each board by hand sometimes with me holding one in place until the glue dried!

Philip laboring on his model of the Seguin, a 1890 steam tugboat.

One morning in September of 2001, as was his usual practice, Philip walked down to have a mid-morning cup of coffee with his friend Tom at the Grand Staircase Bed and Breakfast a block away, and I was in the Gallery. He called me on the phone and excitedly told me to turn on the small TV we had on the counter. I got reception just in time to see the second jet plane crash into the Twin Towers! The rest of 9/11 is history, individual to each person!

For us, it was a phone call from a group who was planning to fly students to Europe for two weeks at that time. Instead, asked to come and stay at the retreat. Some of the kids slept on the deck in their sleeping bags! There were about 20 in all, and they had a great time hiking here.

On a morning in August of 2002, Philip decided to move a couple of very heavy rocks to protect the sewer upright behind the gallery in the driveway. Then he went to have a cup of coffee with Tom. Tom was a volunteer Emergency Medical Technician and drove the Ambulance. Tom was quite alarmed at Philip's color and immediately called me and 9/11.

I got down to the B & B just as they were loading Philip into the ambulance. His skin was orange! Tom told me that Philip was having a heart attack! It was a seventy-five-mile drive to the nearest hospital in Panguitch. I followed behind in my car. By the time I got there, Philip had just received a very expensive injection to stabilize him until they "life flighted" him to a hospital in Salt Lake City. There they put a stent in one of his arteries. Some friends brought him home a couple of days later.

Thus began the process of learning what medications he needed, going to various doctors, and the Veteran's Administration clinics in St. George and Las Vegas for the next several years.

In early October of 2002, my father had a stroke, was paralyzed on right side and hospitalized in Monterey, California. Both my brothers and I got to his bedside as quickly as possible. The family was advised that dad had no chance of recovery and mom made the painful decision to have him removed from life support and be transported to a hospice facility nearby.

My brothers had to return to work. I stayed with mom and supported her until dad passed on October 16th. Then I assisted her with memorial services in Salinas at the American Legion and at the Burlingame Presbyterian Church. Both were well attended by many friends and family members.

At the age of 85, my mom moved to Escalante in 2003 and purchased a two story, 6-bedroom, 3-bathroom home on two acres of land with 2 shares of irrigation water just south of Escalante. There she lived out her dream of having a "prayer garden." She planted 100 trees, put in drip irrigation, and built numerous raised beds for her flower garden. I fondly referred to her as the "Energizer Bunny" as she drove around the property on her green riding lawnmower!

Winnie's new dream house!

Winnie in her garden.

Romans 12:12 **Rejoicing in hope; patient in tribulation; continuing instant in prayer**.

Chapter 34 – "WE'RE GOING TO HAVE AN ART FESITVAL"

Early in 2003, longtime resident and historian, Jerry Roundy, approached several citizens in Escalante and Boulder suggesting that we get together and talk about creating a memorial for Veterans who were born and raised in these two communities. He recommended that we ask Escalante City for space in the City Park to erect it.

The committee members talked at length and made lists of the men and women who graduated from Escalante High School and then served in the military. I became the secretary-treasurer and recorded the funds as families donated in honor of their veterans. Leslie Venuti contacted sculptress, L. Dean Trueblood, in St. George, Utah. She had designed three life sized bronze sculptures of two veterans which she wanted to be in Veterans Memorials. L. Dean sold one of them to us at her cost of $25,000!

The total expense for the entire memorial was $50,000 when it was completed.

In the photos below, you can see the ground breaking on Memorial Day in 2004 with Jerry and me dedicating the land at the City Park. The second photo is Jerry observing the installation of the Bronze sculpture in July. We had the formal dedication on Veteran's Day on November 11th. Over time more names have been engraved on the lists of the third the marble pillar and additional bricks have been placed in the walkway with names engraved for anyone who wanted to honor a veteran. It is a very wonderful memorial for all who visit it.

Memorial Day 2004, Dedicating the Veterans Memorial.

Installing the Bronze Sculpture at the Veterans Memorial.

The Veterans Memorial at Escalante City Park.

In March of 2004, Philip and I invited local artist, Valerie Orlemann, to exhibit her work at Serenidad Gallery. We were her first gallery, and she has gone on to be a very successful artist with her wonderful landscape paintings capturing the essence of the desert. We were glad to encourage Valerie and sell her work until she moved away a few years later.

Valerie Orlemann displays her work at Serenidad Gallery.

In June of 2004, I went with the Elementary School kids on their "Art Day" to Calf Creek Campground. I did a porcelain painting for them on a plate. Below you can see me in the photos discussing what I was painting. I had them raise their hands and trace the outline of the cliffs to help them "see" the edges by pointing at the rocks with their fingers.

Demonstrating seeing edges of the rock walls to the students.

Students trace the edges of the rock walls with their hands to feel the shapes.

Late In the summer of 2003, I was walking down the to the Post Office when my neighbor, Steve Roberts, the new owner of the Escalante Outfitters, stepped out of his business and pointed his finger, almost touching me and said: "*We're going to have an Arti Festival!"*

At that moment, I had not been to an art festival, nor did I have a clue about how to organize one! Steve told me that he and his girlfriend had been sitting on the shore of Lake Powell recently reading "Vagabond for Beauty" a biography of Everett Ruess, by W. L. Rusho. At the age of 20, artist and explorer Everett Ruess had hiked into the pioneer town of Escalante in October of 1934. A few days later, he ventured on south into the Escalante desert with his two mules and was never seen again. Steve's girlfriend noted the date and said "that was almost 70 years ago. You should have an Art Festival in his honor!'

As I learned his reasoning, I immediately reminded Steve that there was a lot of animosity in the community about Everett's disappearance and we would be going upstream against many people's feelings and opinions in town. Ever since we moved to Escalante in 1991, I had heard various rumors and comments about the young 20 year old artist and traveler who had arrived here with his two pack animals. But the general undertone about the mystery of his disappearance was always negative. Unabashed, Steve insisted that we proceed.

Our first step was to invite various local people to come and sit on the tall stools in the restaurant area of the Escalante Outfitters one evening and have people present their thoughts. Among those attending was a long time rancher, Arnold Alvey; local artist, Lynn Griffin; another "move in", Rick Howell; my husband, Philip, and me; Steve Roberts; Gibbs Smith; and several other residents. Steve explained his concept of having an art festival to honor the 70th Anniversary of Everett's disappearance in 1934. Everett's story, block prints and watercolors had been preserved by Gibbs Smtih who was given Everett's journal in the 1960's. After reading it, he engaged W.

L. Rusho to write "Vagabond for Beauty." Gibbs published the first edition 1973 by his company, "Gibbs Smith Publisher".

People made various suggestions about what the festival could look like. The concept of a Plein Air competition was presented to encourage artists to come paint in our very scenic desert scape. Rick Howell suggested that we would need several different events to keep people engaged.

Arnold Alvey sat silently with his arms folded listening to all that was being said. Finally, he unfolded his arms and told us that he had seen Everett in 1934 when Arnold was seven years old and recalled that he and his friends went with Everett to Star Hall to watch the movie "Death Takes a Holiday." Arnold's remembrances turned the corner on the atmosphere. Lynn Griffin agreed that an Art Festival would be a great way for the community to get involved. Gibbs Smith said he would donate $1000 to start the fund raising. Steve Roberts also made a substantial donation. We were off and running so to speak.

Garth Noyes, Steve Roberts, and I presented a request for funds to the Five County Association of Governments and received a grant. Later Garfield Travel Council and Utah Travel Council awarded us funds. Mark Austin and his family also made a sizable donation.

I traveled with my mother north to Helper, Utah in August to observe their Plein Air Competition and take notes. Local artist, Susan Bellew, had been kind enough to explain to me that Plein Air meant "painting outside on location!" I acquired the brochure for the Helper event, came home and studied a photo of their large group of volunteers to deduce what types of committees we needed to have to make our festival work.

We sent out invitations to artists throughout the state. I contacted Steven German in Salt Lake City who had gotten permission to produce copies of Everett's prints. Steven kindly volunteered to create a website for the festival. We spent many hours on the phone and online using his expertise to make that happen.

"Battlements" Block Print by Everet Ruess

By the time the festival began on September 30th, 2004, we had raised about $10,000. My mother, Winnie Washburn, kindly agreed to act as treasurer and receive the 39 Plein Air entries. The committee hired renowned Utah artist, Doug Snow, to be our judge for the competition. Our first place winner was Doug Braitwaite from Sunset, Utah.

The cash prize was a "purchase award" and the committee then owned the painting. It is currently hanging at the Kazan Clinic east of Escalante along with other first place winners that the committee has purchased over the years. There were second and third place winners as well.

Doug Braitwaite, first place winner in the Plein Air Competition.

Cyndi Jaeger from Henriville suggested that we tie dye 3' x 2' flags torn from bed sheets to present to "Sharing Place" a recovery facility for young children with cancer in Salt Lake City. Cyndi furnished all the materials, and everyone had a great time learning how to tie dye and the activity even shifted over to include dyeing our festival tee shirts. We used a block print on the tee shirts designed by Sheila Wooley which resembled Evertt's work. The tie dying activity was done on the Community Center lawn and the flags were hung on the fence to dry. We made 200 flags and were much appreciated by the children.

The children of Waldo Ruess had fun doing tie dye flags.

Perhaps the most important part of the event was the opportunity to invite Everett's older brother and his family to attend the celebration. Waldo Ruess was then 95 years old and he, his wife and 3 of his 4 adult children joined us as we began the festivities on Thursday afternoon, September 30th, at the Boulder Mountain Lodge, in Boulder, Utah. Gibbs Simth, Steve Roberts and I were privileged to introduce the family to members of the community in attendance, some of whom had seen Everett in 1934. There were people who had family members that searched for Everett when alerted by the Ruess family late in 1934 that they had not heard from him for some time.

Renon Peterson – Boulder: Arnold Alvey spoke to Everett in 1934

Deon Alvey: Herb Allen's father led a search party in early 1935.

Seated, Waldo Ruess, and standing his wife Conchita and three of their children and a guest who happened to come also named Ruess!

I invited musician, Dana Robinson, who sang his ballad about Everett Ruess which he wrote after reading "Vagabond for Beauty" in 2002. Dana was our featured musician for the Festival on Friday and Saturday in Escalante. We asked the City if we could block off 100 West and then we set up a stage for the music and presentations. Several vendors sold their wares, some demonstrating knapping knives and weaving rugs to accompany the theme of it being a "Working Art Festival." The whole event was a great success and historic in nature.

The following August, in 2005 Steve and I traveled again to the Helper Plein Art Festival and met with a few artists who had participated in our festival the year before. Their comments were cogent. They argued that Doug Braitwaite would probably always win the competition because he did superior work. They also complained that the range of media entries was very limited.

We discussed our findings all the way home and arrived at the conclusion that two solutions were needed . First, that the winner of the current competition would not be allowed to enter again for three years, thus assuring a better chance for other artists to win. Second, we created two parallel competitions with first place prizes and so forth for both contests. One classification was for oil and acrylic paintings and the second for watercolor, pastel, and mixed media paintings. It was a learning process for us all.

We had begun another round of fundraising and got many of the same supporters to donate, including the Ruess family. Kent Cottam, born in Escalante and then a successful businessman in St. George agreed give us $2000 to purchase the tee shirts if we would clean up some of the properties on Main Street to make the town look more presentable. Howard Hutchison and I worked long hours on three different properties getting old dead trees cleared away. Escalante City workers hauled large piles of branches to the dump!

The second year our judge was Jeff Dunn, an art professor from the University of Hawaii. He had called me about the festival. I invited him to be our judge. Many artists and local people volunteered to make the festival happen. Howard Hutchison was the silent energy in the background, creating signs and designing the brochure, and doing many other unnamed tasks.

The third year, I asked Karin Simmons to be the treasurer because my mother had moved to Cedar City, Utah. Karin has very faithfully served in that capacity ever since.

Just after the third festival was over In the fall of 2006, a couple from New Mexico walked in the door of our gallery and after some conversation, they signed papers putting $2000 down to buy the building from us! Suddenly we were without a home, and we started looking for some place to live but we did not find anything in Escalante that spoke to us. I wrote up all the various committee descriptions and by the end of December I turned them over to the festival committee and resigned.

Our communications with the buyers in New Mexico were very unsatisfactory. For example, they did not answer my questions about what inventory in the gallery they wanted to buy. So early in January of 2007, Philip and I drove down to New Mexico to see them. We met them in a very tiny town just north of the Mexican border. They were remodeling an old schoolhouse and planned to make it into nightly rental. After dinner they admitted that they were overextended and had to withdraw their offer. So, we came home and went on with our lives.

That spring of 2007 Steve and I discussed the need for the festival to have a 501 C 3 nonprofit status, so he hired me to write the application. It was a complicated process and took me some time. We chose the name "Envision Escalante" to be an umbrella organization for any activity in the community that would need to have a nonprofit designation. Eventually, the thrift store, Skyhoopie, was formed by Envision Escalante, and some other entities have also used the non-profit status over the years as well as what is now called Escalante Canyons Art Festival.

In the festival's third year, Allysia Angus had come on the committee and took photos of the events. I did that the first two years and made an album of them. The fourth year Sandy Larsen agreed to manage the festival for several years. Then Allysia managed if after him and currently Lisa Hartman is the manager.

Runing the Festival was a very heavy burden for me in many ways. I even dreamed about Everett and the festival. After each event, I had to take a month off, and just not think about it. Then I could begin again, starting to raise funds and organizing events for the following year. I am very grateful to the many volunteers who have grown the festival since then. I have great empathy for all of them as they strive each year to make it a wonderful event. They have received many compliments from participating artists over the years about how friendly and welcoming the community and committee have been to them. Now in their 20th year, I am very gratified for all the work that has been done to make Escalante Canyons Art Festival a preeminent and renowned Plein Air competition and festival.

Psalm 139: 17 – 18 How precious also are thy thought unto me, O God! How great is the sum of them! If I should count them, they are more in number than the sand. When I awake, I am still with thee.

CHAPTER 35 – Serenidad, too

In July 2005, my mother gave Philip and me a reception in her home for our 25th Wedding Anniversary. She had a lovely cake made and put a photo on top of us cutting our wedding cake at her home in Pacifica, California in 1980. We had rededicated our vows earlier that year at church with two other couples with Mom playing the wedding march on the piano as we walked down the aisle! Very fun.

Our 25th Wedding Anniversary in Mom's home.

However soon after that, Winnie realized that the 2 story house with 6 bedrooms and 3 baths on 2 acres of land were too much of her. Plus the dust and bugs had become intolerable, so she found a small house in Cedar City to rent. We packed her up and moved her into "Apple Cottage" built in 1895. That winter was very hard on her as the icy winds sliced through the thin walls.

In the spring of 2006, I suggested that she write a list of things she desired in a home. She took that list to a realtor who had just the right thing for her, so she bought it that afternoon, and we moved her again to a much newer home west of Cedar City. While she lived here in Escalante, Winnie started a Native Plant Society and when she moved to Cedar City, she started a Native Plant Society there as well! She was very active in the Cedar City Presbyterian Church and thrived in her new environment, gardening and making new friends. Winnie even went on a cruise to Alaska in her mid-80's!

Winnie.

One day in the spring of 2006, Jim Poteet stopped to chat with Philip out in front of the gallery. Jim suggested to Philip that we could sell the property outside of town for a good profit. Philip decided to list it and we got a buyer who paid us cash by October of that year. Then Philip could really look for something to buy! In the spring of 2007, he called me as I was returning from a visit to mom in Cedar City and said "I found it! It has good bones!"

120 West 200 South

The first time we walked into 120 West 200 South we were shocked to see that the front room had pink walls and green shag carpet! Undaunted, Philip made an offer, and we purchased the home. We could not even see into the garage at first because Glen Wilson, the son of the original builder took six weeks to clean out all manner of farm and automotive things from the double car garage! The back of the .6 acre lot was a mess with fallen down farm buildings, overgrown dead trees and weeds everywhere.

Lots of fallen down barn structures in the back!

Philip figured that it would cost $25,000 to fix the house up. Well as it turned out, that is what the new roof and 27 new windows for both the upstairs and basement cost before we even went inside. We called it "Serenidad, too!" Philip dedicated his heart and soul to bringing new life to every inch upstairs, the basement had to be dealt with later.

First things first, a new roof!

Our new life schedule was - Philip working in the house full time and me being in the gallery full time. I would not move into the house until we had a new bathroom and a new kitchen. The upstairs took 27 months to complete.

Meanwhile I participated in the art festival again in September of 2007, entering in the Watercolor, Pastel and Mixed Media competition painting on a vase "en plein air" 25 miles west of Escalante along Highway 12. First, I painted four tiles to give me a sense of the tremendous rock formation I called "Sinking Ship." Then for the competition, I set up for 3 days beside Highway 12 and came home each afternoon and fired the 12-inch vase with wrap around scenery from that vantage point. I had finally figured out how to capture the entire landscape.

My tile of "The Sinking Ship" and my Vase for the festival all painted alongside the road!

Earlier that summer had I visited Zion with my mom. We hiked up to Weeping Rock which was an amazing rock wall with springs dripping out all over it. We enjoyed standing behind the waterfalls pouring out over us from the winter run off. I took a lot of photos and came home and painted the amazing views on a 12 inch vase from under the falls.

Zion Vase painted from the Seep.

Philip and I always enjoyed wheeling and dealing In our business. In the mid 1990's when Philip still had American Flyer trains for sale in the gallery, a man walked in and really wanted three of the locomotives. He offered us six antique pocket watches in trade for those trains. Philip was satisfied with the trade. We put the watches on the top shelf in the glass display case and people immediately saw them as soon as they walked in the front door. I said that old pocket watches made us look like antique dealers!

One day Clay and Rebecca Wagstaff came in to see the gallery. He immediately wanted one of the watches and offered us his handmade soap that they had been making since 1996 in trade for his purchase. So that is how we came to sell Pioneer Soap, which I still carry to this day! The Wagstaffs are very fine artists. Clay won first prize in the Plein Air Competition in 2005! We were delighted to have the opportunity to feature Clay's work in the gallery. They both have gone on to very successful art careers exhibiting their work from coast to coast!

Oil Paintings by Clay Wagstaff.

Matthew 7:24 Therefore whosoever heareth these sayings of mine, and doeth them, I will liken him unto a wise man, which built his house upon a rock: 25 And the rain descended, and the floods came, and the winds blew, and beat upon that house; and it fell not: for it was founded upon a rock.

CHAPTER 36 – RETRO TO 1910

I started writing a daily prayer journal when we began the process of purchasing Leo Wilson's house "as is" on **.6** acres from his son Glen whom we met when we first moved to Escalante. I prayed over my concerns and poured out my thoughts about all the things that seemed unsurmountable. I continued to write in my journal throughout the entire remodel of the house into the Arts and Crafts style until all was accomplished in the basement several years later. I still cast my burdens upon the Lord and am so very grateful for His provisions and guidance one day at a time!

The Arts and Crafts movement was an international trend in the decorative and fine arts that developed earliest and most fully in the British Isles and subsequently spread across the British Empire, to the rest of Europe and America. The movement was a reaction against the perceived impoverishment of the decorative arts and the conditions in which they were produced. The movement flourished in Europe and North America between about 1880 and 1920.

In the fall of 2007, I drove mom across Nevada, over the Sierra Mountains to Yosemite National Park on our way to visit my brother John in Fresno. California. We stopped at the Ahwahnee Hotel in Yosemite Valley for lunch in the Grand Dining Room. I was immediately awe struck by the looming architecture and the wonderful use of wood in the Arts and Crafts Style.

Over lunch, Mom and I reminisced about her parents, George and Olivia Young riding in a horse drawn open buggy on dirt roads to Yosemite for their honeymoon in May of 1913 before this hotel was built. I recalled that Grandpa taught wood shop classes in those years and constructed all his own furniture for their first home in the Arts and Crafts style in his High School shop.

Later in 1920 when grandpa bult their home on the Oakland hills he laid a huge rock fireplace and the living room was enclosed with wooden walls, and I recall benches made from logs on each side of the hearth. The warmth of wood was the atmosphere I grew up in as an infant while my father was in World War II.

That afternoon at the Ahwahnee I came to understand my subconscious affinity with wood because of my childhood experience. I realized that when Philip introduced me to his love for Arts and Crafts pottery and hand crafted wood furniture, it was natural for me to resonate with it.

I returned home with this new awareness. We went shopping for furniture and bought a reproduction Arts and Crafts dining room table and chairs. Slowly we began to retro the 1948 "Early Ranch" brick house on the inside to the Arts and Crafts style!

We studied every book we could find about that movement. Many of the books were printed by Gibbs Simth Publishing! We learned of the philosophy of bringing nature into the home. Thankfully we had big south facing windows which allowed sunlight to come in the front room and dining room year round. These windows faced the property directly across the street from us that had a broad sweeping green lawn which was surrounded by many tall trees providing us a park like view.

Perhaps our greatest blessing was the fact that in 2007, contractor Jacob Croft moved into town across the street from us on another corner. Up to that time there had been no one in Escalante who was willing to take on a project of this magnitude. Jacob brought many carpentry skills with him, and a strong desire to remodel older homes in Escalante! *Thank you, Lord!* Jacob came and discussed what was possible and became our general contractor for all that needed to be done, and that Philip could not do.

One of the major renovations was the removal of two doorways into the dining area and constructing arches in both walls to open up the front room and kitchen to reflect the Arts and Crafts or Mission Style. Matching colors from an old Persian Carpet that we had bought several years earlier, Philip painted the walls a strong red/orange and he then painted the ceiling a lighter yellow called " Daisy Mae." The use of two colors in a room was a practice he observed from photos of the rooms of that time. He painted all the ceilings in the rest of the house that yellow except the bathroom, the bedroom and my study. You can see our dog Charlie in the photo. He always seemed to know when I was taking a picture with my camera and posed just right!

Charlie posing beneath the new Arches in the Dining room.

Sandy Larsen, whom we met at the Petrified Forest State Park when he was a Ranger in 1986 and 1988, who later suggested that we sell Petrified wood in the Gallery, had gone on to a very interesting art adventure. He took broken pieces of cast off glass and soldered them into old window frames. We had two of these windows by the time we purchased the house. Philip realized that he could insert them in our front doors which already had two small horizontal glass windows in each of them. The stunning windows are a surprise to all who see them and a delight as the afternoon sun shines through them.

Stained glass style window by Sandy Larsen in our front door.

Both stained glass windows by Sandy Larsen in both of our front doors.

Philip purchased Asian hardwood flooring and laboriously covered all the floors upstairs except the two bedrooms which we were amazed to discover had white pine floors under linoleum tiles. He spent a month in each of those rooms on his knees removing the tiles! We were delighted to find that he did not have to do anything to the floors once they were uncovered!

We made a concerted effort to select reproduction Arts and Crafts lighting for all the rooms. The fixtures were made by Rejuvenation, a company in Portland, Oregon. In the photo below, you can see the dining room as it is today with the table and chairs that started our theme. We loved the stained glass chandelier over the table called "Pasadena" and matching sconces on three walls which went well with the window in the door that Sandy made.

Arts and Crafts dining set and light fixtures in the Dining room.

When we got to the kitchen, we asked Jacob to design the cabinetry using the style of the dining room chairs. The cabinet doors on the far wall have glass behind the design. We chose Arts and Crafts metal drawer pulls and cabinet handles from Rejuvenation. Note the avocado green electric stove on the left - “Custom Crafted by Hotpoint.” It is a real workhorse with two stoves and a wonderful work area in the middle between the burners.

Arts and Craft style cabinetry in the kitchen.

The bathroom was another challenge. We were in contact with Pastor John Innis in Marysvale, 100 miles west of Escalante. He had founded "Christian Vocational Ministries," a recovery program for young men who had come to Jesus as their Savior and needed a professional skill. He taught carpentry and gave them Bible Study lessons each day. In 2000 they had built the kitchen cabinets, office shelving, pulpit and cross in the sanctuary for our new Baptist Church in Escalante.

Jacob sent John the cabinet schematics, and the men constructed the mirrors and bathroom cabinet, then brought them over and installed them. They said it was a real pleasure to do something different for a change! The cabinets were of the same Arts and Crafts design like the cabinets that Jacob built in the kitchen. You can see the original turquoise green tile of the back splash that was in the bathroom when it was built in 1948. Jacob constructed a shower area and tiled it above the tub, and he then used that same grey green tile to cover the floor. The glass brick windows were installed as the house was built and they add a lovely touch allowing the light to come in the bathroom.

Arts and Craft Style cabinetry in the bathroom.

Philip was at the art festival one day in 2008 and found a colorful stained glass window. He bought it and installed it in the bathroom door. It is a lovely addition to what I call my Library-Laundry because I also have bookshelves in this room. We had Jacob remove the lower drawers in that area and plumbed the two spaces for a washer and dryer. Truly a brilliant solution so I do not have to go to the basement to do the laundry.

Stained Glass window on the bathroom door.

Philip scrutinized every inch of the house as he laid the flooring. The transition in width from the hallway to the Library-Laundry was a masterpiece all by itself. He spent hours doing the math and came up with a very inventive herringbone pattern!

Herringbone pattern to resolve the turn in the hallway.

The Front room is 18 feet long. One day we realized that the other Persian carpet we had purchased from an Estate sale here some years before was 17 feet long! It fit perfectly and this is a view of the room today. We had Jacob design the fireplace to match the style of the Arts and Crafts furniture we purchased to go with the dining room set. He placed the slate tiles around the fire insert that was already there and built the mantle and designed the wood framing around it. In the far left you can see the back hallway which is a bright yellow with green trim on the doorways. Philip painted everything in the entire house with great care!

Arts and Craft style furniture in the front room and repeated in the fireplace surround.

At last, we moved in 27 months after we purchased the house and enjoyed our first Thanksgiving dinner with my mother who came from Cedar City and my brother John and his wife Marjie who drove up from Fresno, California to celebrate with us! Thank you, Lord!

Psalm 92: 1- 5 It is a good thing to give thanks unto the Lord, and to sing praises unto thy name, O Most High: To shew forth thy lovingkindness in the morning, and thy faithfulness every night, for thou, Lord, hast made me glad through thy work: I will triumph in the works of thy hands. O Lord, how great are thy works! and thy thoughts are very deep.

CHAPTER 37 – "WRAP AROUND SCENERY"

During all the years of construction and activity on the new house, I continued to paint on various porcelain shapes to portray our wrap around scenery. I always said that it was just hard to point the camera in one direction because the scenery was all around us!

Gibbs Smith became an active buyer of these works and owned seven pieces by the time all was said and done! He asked me to paint Zion National Park. I went with Philip to the overlook above Zion at the top of the canyon by the tunnels on Highway 9 and took several photos. Here is the view from that vista point.

View from overlook above Zion Canyon National Park.

The real challenge was to include the 3000' escarpment on our left where the tunnels for Highway 9 were drilled through the rocks from 1927 – 1930, and then show the switchbacks below. Finally, I had to paint the rocks behind where we were standing!

At that time, I was taking my vases across the street to a friend's house to have them fired in her kiln. I had been quite energetic in painting the deep blue sky. When I went to get the vase after it was fired, I was dismayed to see that the blue paint had dripped! What was I to do? I mused over the dilemma as I walked back across the street to the Gallery where I had my studio in one of the back rooms! I could not erase or remove the strong blue lines, so I came up with the thought of painting gold over the drips and making Native American symbols on them such as the image for clouds that had lines hanging down! I successfully redesigned the sky and it looked quite nice.

I never told Gibbs what had happened and finally confessed it to his wife several years after he passed away! Happy Accident!

Zion Canyon Vase with view from the overlook and the rocks behind where I stood.

Gibbs commissioned me to paint seven 1" round buttons with various scenes of the area around Boulder and later asked me to do something about Boulder itself. I knew he wanted a vase, but Boulder is in a valley, so I decided to paint it in a bowl! I included the original pioneer road descending into the valley.

Boulder Bowl overlooking the valley below.

Gibbs also purchased the pitcher I had done of Allen Canyon and the Rectangle vase of the Escalante Canyon with the River going through the vase. These two vases and the buttons are in this photo below. Then the next photo is of the Rectangle vase with reflections in the mirror so you can see all four sides.

Buttons of Boulder, Escalante rectangle vase and Allen Canyon Vase.

Occasionally I still painted on plates. I was attending our Daughters of the American Revolution meeting at an historic home in Beaver, Utah, so I did a portrait of the house for the owner.

Historic home in Beaver, Utah.

One of the most important historical scenes in this area was the "Hole in the Rock." It is located at the end of a very long bumpy road southeast of Escalante. In 1994, Philip and I both drove down 60 miles on "Hole in the Rock Road" to deliver a vehicle for a hiker who floated down the Escalante River with his friend in their small boat and then planned to climb up the Hole in the Rock from Lake Powell a week later to their vehicle. Philip and I had to get out of the cars several times and tell each other how to turn our wheels to get the vehicles around the large rocks in the road. I am glad I went then, I have not been back since! I had taken photos, so I had good reference information to paint from.

In 1879, Mormon colonists carved a road down this narrow opening on their way to the area they were sent to settle southeast in what is now known at the Four Corners area. I have deep respect for the mammoth efforts they made to get down the rocky chasm to cross the Colorado River and then continue over the slick rock to establish an outpost many weeks later. Travelers never went that way again! In my painting I included the bronze plaque on the rock there dedicated to the pioneers.

The" Hole In the Rock" with like Powell below.

On another part of the vase, I painted the famous "Dance Hall Rock" where those pioneers stopped and rested and had a dance on the flat surface beside the looming rock.

Finally, I included a section of the road in what the early ranchers called "Carcas Wash" perhaps because it was a steep grade and difficult to ascend. The very large Hydroelectric Dam at Page, Arizona in Glen Canyon was completed in 1966. The Colorado River behind it became Lake Powell. A Boy Scout Troup from northern Utah traveled down to explore the area before the water covered the canyons. They came to Escalante on June 10th, 1963, and hired a large farm truck to transport 46 men and boys with their equipment down the last part of the road. Unfortunately, when the truck got to Carcas Wash, the gears slipped, and the truck toppled over. 7 boy scouts and 6 adults were killed! There is a monument for them by the side of the road that I included in the painting. Gibbs Smith purchased the vase.

'Hole in the Rock": the Plaque dedicated to the Pioneers: Dance Hall Rock and the Boy Scout Memorial at the lower left.

One of my very favorite places on Highway 12 is the view of Powell Point. This 10,000-foot precipice can be seen for many miles around. Explorer John Wesley Powell used it as a reference for surveying the area when he came here in the early 1870's. As I took on the project I was frustrated because I had to show parts of the "pink cliffs" as the locals called it, that were not visible from the location where I chose to start. Ultimately, I had to give myself permission to paint what I could not see! After I finished painting the vase, my brain ached so much that I told myself to stop painting wrap around scenery for a while! Gibbs bought the vase!

Powell Point seen at the Overlook on Highway 12.

Powell Point and the formation continues around the vase, and back again!

A project I had in my mind for many years was to paint the view of the Escalante Canyon as we can see the opening here in town and portray it from inside a barn! I really did not know how to paint the roof of the barn looking up from the inside at the top of the vase. I used photos I had taken inside of some barns that were still standing and eventually worked my way around the vase, depicting these old structures from the inside and the view looking out at the Canyon and surrounding scenery.

Views out of a barn looking at the Escalante Canyon

In 2008, I signed up to paint in the Plein Air Competition for the Escalante Canyons Art Festival. I went out to Pine Creek Road north of Escalante and worked on four – 6" x 8" tiles to get the sense of what I wanted to do. Below is the photo of that work in progress. Later for the competition itself, I checked in with my last 12" vase and set up along the road again.

As I was painting, some tourists came by and asked me for directions. As we were chatting a gust of wind blew my vase over and it shattered on the rocks! Since that was the last vase I had on hand, I checked in again with a plate and went out to the Petrified Forest State Park and sat at a picnic table and did a painting of the colorful cliffs there. My friend Doug Braithwaite, winner of the first festival, purchased the plate!

My practice Tile in progress on Pine Creek road..

Hebrews 11: 1 – 3 Now faith is the substance of things hoped for, the evidence of things not seen. For by it the elders obtained a good report. Through faith we understand that the worlds were framed by the word of God, so that things which are seen were not made of things which do appear.

CHAPTER 38 – "I DON'T LIKE IT"

In May of 2009, the Saturday before Mother's day, we had our monthly meeting of the Bald Eagle Chapter Daughter's of the American Revolution in Cedar City. My mom's younger brother Bill had done the Young family genealogy research all the way back to the American Revolution, and she became a member of the DAR in California and then transferred to Bald Eagle Chapter when she moved to Utah, That April, she served as the State Chaplain at the Utah State DAR Conference in Salt Lake City. After our chapter meeting in May, I went to visit her before returning home. We had a lovely time as always.

Then Sunday, after church, mom's friend Amarante encouraged her to consider moving to a Senior Living Facility. Winnie was then 91. Her pastor had also been suggesting this thought to her the previous three Sundays. Amarante said, "Winnie, you should go and live where my parents are at Monte Vista Grove in Pasadena, California!" Winnie responded that she had applied there just after dad passed away in 2002, and the admissions office told her that she was over their age limit of 80 at that time!

Amarante told her that he thought they had changed that policy and advised her to apply again. Monte Vista Grove was built in 1924 by the Synod of California of the Presbyterian Church for retired ministers, missionaries and their wives, They purchased an orange grove in Pasadena and built duplex homes for the residents, and eventually a long term care facility and a nursing home. Mom applied online on Monday to the Presbyterian Church USA in Philadelphia, Pennsylvania. On Wednesday she was accepted by their board and on Thursday she was accepted by the board at Monte Vista Grove.

Then she called me and informed me she was moving to Pasadena! I turned to Philip and said, "we are on the train!" I drove her down to look at the duplex she was assigned to, and she told them that she wanted sea green walls in most of the rooms, and discussed how to redo the kitchen, etc. We came home and arranged for her furniture to be transported to Pasadena when the remodel was complete. This was the fifth time I had moved her since 2003!

Moving Winnie included a large volume of books, a grandfather clock which she dearly loved and had to be very carefully packed, a China hutch, plus various pieces of furniture, kitchen wares and a dish washer which did not fit in our kitchen, so we gave it to her new in the box!

My mom was from Oakland and my father was from Pasadena. There has always been tension between people from the northern and southern parts of California. So now here she was moving to that "Other" part. As we drove into the Los Angeles Basin on moving day, the sky was thick with smog. As we descended into it, she murmured, "I think I made a mistake!" I groaned. Fortunately, the ambiance of Monte Vista Grove overcame her trepidations, and she was welcomed warmly by many retired ministers and their wives, some of whom she had known over the years.

That fall of 2009, I signed up to paint in the Plein Air competition again. My friend, Sandy Larsen suggested that I paint on four 6" X 8" tiles as he liked what I had done in the past. Philip made a holder for them. I sat beside the Kiva Koffee House and proceeded to paint the large Kiva windows with the reflection on the glass of the canyon walls across the way and the Escalante River Canyon below.

After three firings I handed the tiles to Philip to frame. He was always very gracious about framing my work. When he had mounted them , he handed them to me and said: *"I do not like it."*

I was stunned and said nothing! I had become a biblically submissive wife many years before and did not question his judgement. I truly respected his opinions about all artwork, he was very well informed about many things in the Art world. I made no response.

On the last day of the festival, we had a buffet breakfast at the Kiva. I sat with Brad Holt who had won first place in the festival several years before. I poured out my heart to him and said: "What shall I do?" Brad answered, "Change medium." I thought for a bit and recalled how much I had enjoyed painting with watercolors in years past, so I realized that I could do that again. My mother later graciously funded the supplies I needed to begin.

Kiva Koffee House – note the reflection of the rocks across the canyon on the windows.

View of the Escalante River Canyon south from the Kiva Koffee House.

Our dear friend Marjorie Davies lived in Panguitch 75 miles west of Escalante. I had become friends with her through the fund raiser for the Garfield County Memorial Hospital and often stayed in her basement while doing things like participating in the County Fair. Pretty soon the room was named "Harriet's room!'

Her husband Cal had suddenly passed away that fall, and Philip and I immediately drove over to help her as best we could. On one of our visits Marjorie offered us the opportunity to stay in her thirty foot Park Model at the Happy Trails Resort in Surprise, Arizona on the west side of Pheonix. She was nearly blind and since Cal had done all the driving, she would not be going down there for the winter anymore. We gladly accepted her generous offer and made plans to stay there for a couple of months.

My friend Sheila needed a place to live. She had been house sitting for Toby and Wanda, our church friends, and they were coming back just about the time we wanted to leave, so Sheila agreed to come and take care of our cat. I had visited Shiela once at Toby and Wanda's place and was stunned to see how full the refrigerator was! Shiela could sleep in the basement but would have to use our kitchen.

As we were driving out of town to begin our vacation, I remarked to Philip, that I could not live in the same refrigerator with Sheila when we got home! That remark launched us onto the next step of remodeling the basement. We had already redone the two bedrooms and the bathroom downstairs, so now it was time to think about how to design the kitchen area. That absorbed a lot of our time in Arizona.

When we arrived at Happy Trails, I bought watercolor supplies and literally began to teach myself how to paint. I studied books to become familiar with the techniques and did some paintings of things nearby like palm trees and cacti. I painted my neighbor Ginny's cactus that was beyond our driveway

Ginny's cactus.

Then I rode around on the golf cart in the park and found a Barrel Cactus. I did a painting of it while sitting in the cart. Later we went shopping and when I glanced down at something on the lower shelf, my eyes locked in place for a moment because I had been looking down in that direction a lot to do the cactus painting! Lesson learned. Take care of your eyes!

Fishhook Cactus"

On Superbowl Sunday of 2010, Philip finally asked me to take him to the ER. He had been suffering with abdominal pains for a week without relief. He was diagnosed with appendicitis and had the surgery right away. However, it was so badly infected that he had to stay in the hospital for 10 days until they released him!

That gave me time to attend the Arizona Button Society Convention. I had always wanted to know more about button collecting and had attended the local chapter monthly meetings while we were there that winter. I was pleased to see Lucille Weingarten there who launched me on my button painting career in 1980!

When we returned to Escalante, I visited my dear friend Jacke Withers who was dying of cancer. She gave me a good piece of advice. "If you want to be an artist, do something about it every day!" I took her suggestion and walked around town with my sketchbook drawing whatever interested me. I discovered that my real love was the old homes and barns in Escalante!

I contacted Cory Jensen at the Utah Division of State History. He offered us his services free of charge to do the necessary architectural survey of Escalante to get the town listed on the National Historic Register. We worked on this project for four years. First getting the town listed on the Utah Historic Register and then on the National Historic Register in 2013! This was a huge effort on both of our parts. He and a staff member came and photographed every building in the city limits and then I had to check the printout for accuracy of information including who built the structure, when, and noted the correct architectural style. Cory's office then accumulated all the statistics which stated that 42% of the town looked like it had 50 years prior to that.

I have often said that Escalante was a Brigadoon, and was stuck in time which was a blessing and a curse because so many of the brick houses were not being lived in. In this case it was a blessing! I went to the mayor and city council and helped them understand that the designation had no restrictions on what the owners could do with the structures. The designation was simply a statement of the statistic. I won their approval and got signs put up on Highway 12 of either side of town stating that it is a "National Historic District."

We also republished the "Walking Tour" for the 4th time: "Escalante, Utah – Historic District Guide - Homes, Back Houses and Barns in 2013". I have just updated the brochure and published it again in 2024. Here is the QR code.

In the fall of 2010, I decided to paint my friend Steve Roberts' pioneer home for the Plein Air Competition. He had just removed the siding that had covered the bricks for many years. I did a study of part of his house to help me get a focus on it. This painting now hangs in Cory Jensen's office in Salt Lake City.

Steve Robert's home. Built in 1896.

In the fall of 2011, I walked down the street from my home to the next block and did several studies of the house which I wanted to paint for the Plein Air that year. I noticed that the decoration at the roof line had the date of 1911. I took a photo of it with nice shadows and painted its Centennial portrait "The Shadows of 1911." This image took me a couple of months to complete, and I learned a lot about painting with watercolors in the process! I came to realize that I was painting portraits of these older homes and people have told me that I had captured the soul of their homes.

Shadows of 1911.

My doctor in Cedar City challenged me to do a painting for him. He said, "Paint me looking in a mirror at something I cannot see!" Well, that was a real mind twister! I thought about it for some time and finally came up with the idea of painting him sitting inside a car and looking out at some scenery in front of him and then painting a reflection of some other scenery in the rear-view mirror! On our trip to Michigan in the late 1990's to visit Philip's family we got to ride in a brand-new Prius. I had taken a photo from the back seat that night. I used that image and painted Allen Canyon out the front windshield and a reflection of the Escalante Canyon in the rear view mirror. And I painted a tour guide on the dashboard. When I took the painting into the office, his nurse immediately said he always had a travel book on his dashboard. The doctor was very pleased with the painting!

Then my mother wanted one like it! So, I sat in the back seat of my friend's 1927 Model T and took photos of them in the front seat and the dashboard. Then I painted them in old fashioned clothes with the Pacific Ocean out the front windshield and a suggestion of a figure in the rear-view mirror which was supposed to be me! I gave the painting to my mother when we visited her at Christmas in 2012. She was delighted. Her parents may well have parked beside the ocean in the late 1920's in their Model T, and mom and dad sat in their car by the ocean many times in their lives. Happy memories!

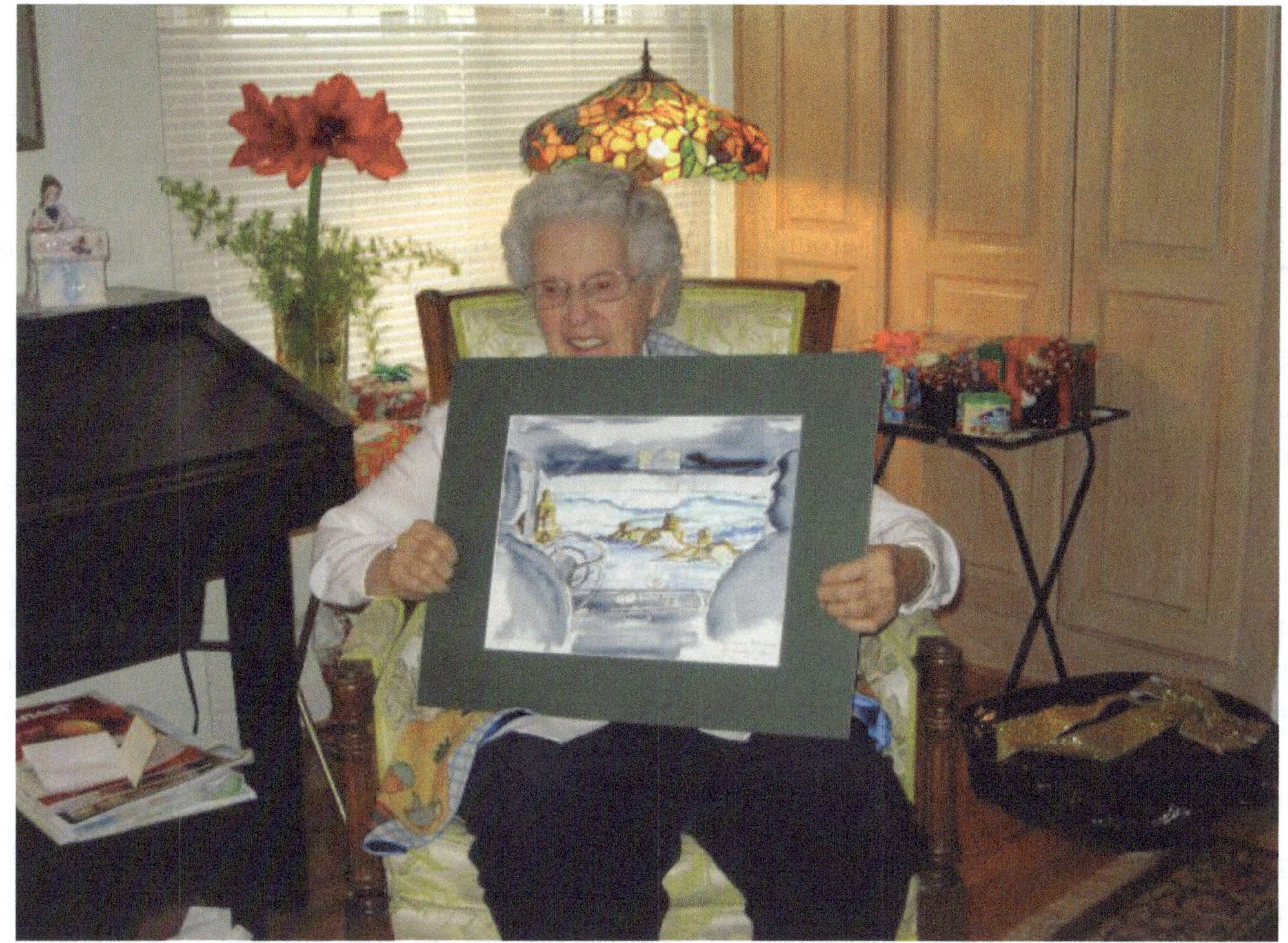

Winnie with her Painting from inside a Model T"

Ephesians 5: 22- 25 Wives, submit yourselves unto your own husbands, as unto the Lord. For the husband is the head of the wife, even as Christ is the head of the church: and he is the Savior of the body. Therefore, as the church is subject unto Christ, so let the wives be to their own husbands in everything. Husbands, love your wives, even as Christ also loved the church, and gave himself for it.

CHAPTER 39 "FALLS"

For many years my mother struggled with issues with her feet eventually having both of her big toes removed. She told me she had to walk pidgin toed to keep her balance. At the age of 94 mom was very active and walked all around the Monte Vista Grove campus and drove her van in Pasadena and in the surrounding areas attending church, going shopping and visiting with friends.

Monday afternoon February 11th, 2013, I got a call from her friend Donna telling me that mom had been vacuuming in her bedroom, tripped over the cord, fell against the dresser and broke her upper left arm. She was in the hospital in Pasadena awaiting surgery. I immediately threw a few things into the car and headed south.

I got to the hospital Tuesday afternoon where Donna greeted me outside the entrance and told me that the surgery was successful, and mom was recovering. I stayed in mom's duplex and went in Wednesday morning to see her and received instructions on ordering a hospital bed and having railings placed in the hallway to assist her when she got home again. Thursday morning, I was by her bedside again and learning more about the hospital routine. She had little handmade crosses which she had me give to every nurse and doctor who came into her room.

Thursday afternoon, my cell phone rang, and it was Philip. He said: "I am ok, I am going to the ER!" Apparently, he had just been eating pizza since my sudden departure and had given himself a bad case of indigestion. Since his heart attack in 2002, we were always concerned about the condition of his heart. So, the EMT's took him to the hospital in Panguitch 75 miles away for observation.

I immediately drove back home, arriving on Friday evening to find him doing well. Thus began the tension for me between the two of them over the next several years.

Mom was taken back to her home and had physical therapy on her arm. Apparently, the therapist encouraged her to stretch her arm more than she was comfortable, and it became quite painful. She went to her surgeon, and he took an X-Ray straight on and said he could see the screws and the plate, and all was fine, but she was in more and more pain.

I drove down right away. We went to a different surgeon. He had an X-Ray taken from the top and immediately saw that the screws had come out of the plate! He was a Sports Doctor for the Los Angeles Angels baseball team. He said that he could do a new procedure of reverse shoulder surgery but that he could only do it once! We made the appointment for the operation early in June. I flew down and took her to a different hospital and was there with her the whole time until she was able to return home. Then I drove her van home to Escalante, because friends and family felt that she should not drive again.

Finally, I was able to continue with my artwork. I was preparing for the Plein Air competition that fall. I had been given permission to work in and around a wonderful barn owned by Arnold Alvey which was built by his family. The horse barn was larger than any other barn in town. I called it a "Cathedral in the Desert!" I sat inside and drew the high timbers of a two story loft above me. Finally, my artistic life was back, I drew the light bulb hanging down from the rafters and titled it: "The light is on!"

"The Light is on"

Mom flew out for the Art Festival that fall and was doing very well. However, because her 95th birthday was approaching on November 11th, my brothers and I asked her not to renew her driver's license. She reluctantly agreed. I put her on the plane in Cedar City and she flew back to Pasadena where her friend picked her up at the Bob Hope Airport nearby.

However, early in November, she went back on her word and asked that friend to take her to the Department of Motor Vehicles to get her license renewed. She got out of his car and walked toward the entrance. I am not sure what happened, but he later showed me where she tripped on the curb and fell forward smashing in her face on the sidewalk, breaking three teeth, and her jaw, and her left wrist. She was rushed to the hospital, and I got the call from Donna.

Philip and I had already been planning to go to Arizona again for the winter, and quickly revised our arrangements and drove to Pasadena instead to stay in her duplex. Cynthia, a dear friend from the DAR, went to be with mom until we arrived. In Cynthia's words, "Winnie looked like a train wreck!" Her jaw was wired shut for seven weeks and she had a feeding tube. She was transferred to the Nursing Care unit at Monte Vista Grove, and I was able to walk over and be with her every day. We arranged to have her 95th birthday party there in her room and many friends came to sing to her and wish her well.

I did some painting with the art club there and enjoyed a break from my daily routine of getting instructions from mom which she wrote on her yellow legal note pad. Sometimes I had to pray my way through the morning to get prepared to be with her and occasionally I just sent Philip over when the stress was too much for me.

People were encouraging me to have mom admitted to the long term care facility that was located across the street from her duplex. I knew that there was a waiting list to get in and I doubted that it could happen. I prayed a lot and finally went to the admissions officer and learned that since Winnie was a resident she would be first on the list, should a vacancy become available.

Amazingly it did happen, and we began to prepare to move her into a much smaller living space of 300 square feet. We gave her precious Grandfather Clock to John's daughter, Susan. At that time in Fresno, a friend of John's home burned down and so we sent John home with several household items for him that we thought that mom would no longer need.

By the time she was released by the doctor, the room in the long term care facility in was ready for her.

Philip and I drove home and recovered from the three month ordeal. However, after mom had lived in her small long term care room for about two months, she called and said that she wanted to come and live with us in our basement apartment! Sigh.

We said we would pray about it and call her the next day. After much thought and prayer, we advised her that there were two things she would have to abide with. First, we had three cats, and she was not fond of cats in general. Second, the apartment was seven steps down from the entrance to the basement and she was not to fall again! She agreed and we immediately hired a contractor to complete the last basement room for her study and TV area with new laundry machines.

John loaded up mom's books, china cabinet, and other furniture and drove her here early in April. The day she left Pasadena there was an earthquake in the LA area and when they arrived to Escalante there was a microburst wind which blew parts of an old city building across Main Street, that landed just short of our gallery! Winnie had arrived with a bang!

Mom became active in the community and walked down to town with her walker. She recovered well from all her injuries. She attended church each Sunday and warmly greeted any visitors. In the fall a Mennonite couple from Ontario, Canada, visited the church and she took their address and wrote to them several times.

At Christmas she received a two page letter from them describing what each of their children had been doing. At the last half of the second page, they wrote about their son Leon. They told how Leon had been going to the hospital to visit David who was now quadriplegic. David had been riding his bicycle in a charity event on July 29th, 2014, when he suddenly had a flat tire. David was trained to fall to the right and unfortunately, just then there was a car passing and he hit his head on their side mirror and was paralyzed from the neck down!

I was stunned and very disturbed by his condition. Mom and I had entertained cyclists for "4 K Ride for Cancer" and "Habitat For Humanity" while she lived in Escalante before. I continued hosting "4 K Ride for Cancer" students for many years and was always concerned for their safety as they rode their bicycles from coast to coast. I contacted Leon and learned that David had been given a laptop with a program on it called "Dragon Speak" so he could talk on the telephone.

We began to communicate, and he told me because of the injury, his wife had left him and none of his three children communicated with him. He lost his high paying jobs as an accountant and college instructor. He was all by himself in a bed that faced a widow looking out at a brick wall of another part of the hospital. It was a very gloomy and lonely existence for him. I often prayed for him and with him. He said that he had Jesus in one hand and God in the other. That is how he got through the loss of everything that he owned and almost everyone he had ever known. I was challenged to *"Live for David"* who had been a very active athlete and traveler. I emailed him sunrise and sunset photos and pictures of whatever was going on in my life. I was challenged to live my life to the fullest!

In May of 2015, my cousin Robyn drove out from Oregon with some of my aunt Marion's bronze Sculptures. Marion was my mother's youngest sister and a very talented artist, who had done amazing work for many years, however her mental health was failing, and Robyn had finally committed her to a care facility in Ashland, Oregon. She brought seven of Marion's bronze sculptures which Philip and I agreed to exhibit in the gallery. Robyn made two trips to bring them to us. This photo is the bust of Vincent van Gogh that Marion did after studying the bronze sculptures of Aguste Rhodin at Stanford University, near where we had lived.

Vincent Van Gogh – Life sized Bronze Sculpture by Marion Young.

I took mom on several trips including driving to Thanksgiving Point near Salt Lake City to see the Tulips and springtime flowers; to Moab, Utah for a ladies' church conference; and finally, back to California to see her dear friend Dr. Waltermuller retire from Burlingame Presbyterian Church. There she was greeted by many friends.

However, when I returned home in August of 2015, Philip told me: *"Do not leave me alone again."* He was more and more short of breath and found it hard just to walk the block down to the Post Office and back. He was waiting for an appointment to be made for him to go to the Veteran's clinic in St. George to find out what was going on with him. But they never called. We finally went to our clinic in town and got an appointment in Cedar City to have an MRI taken in October.

The Art Festival began late in September. We always set up a booth together. That year I had wanted to take a watercolor workshop, but Philip told me that I had to stay and sell with him the whole time, so I did not get to attend, However, I did meet the instructor, and she said to me: *"Use fresh paint!"* I had just been reusing the same paint that I had in the last painting because you can do that with watercolors. I must admit that my paintings lacked contrast because of that habit. The old brick house I painted for the Plein Air competition was quite challenging, and I had done several paintings from various angles to practice. One day as I was returning home, I stopped to chat with my friend David Heaton who had his photography studio in an old brick building. He challenged me to paint it, so after the festival, I did, and I used fresh paint!

Heaton's Studio on the old Seminary Building.

I was quite pleased with the results when I finished the painting and took it to show him. Since my mother's 98th birthday was coming soon on November 11th, I asked him if he would trade my painting for a Photo session with her as a gift for her birthday. He agreed and she came in and sat for her portrait. While he was working, she said that she would like to pay him to also do a portrait of Philip and me! He said that he would have to do it in our gallery as he was giving up the studio the next day. He came to take our photos on November 4th, 2015.

That day, we had a good session with Dave and the next day we headed to St. George to finally see a doctor about Philip's report on the MRI he had gotten done in October. As we departed on the 5th, and I recall mentioning that it was" Guy Fawkes Day," when a plot was discovered to blow up the British Parliament in 1605! We sadly had to bring our cat, Cinco, with us because her health was failing.

As we rounded a corner on Highway 12 in Red Canyon, a very large rock had just fallen on the road and Philip came to a slow stop right in front of the rock so as not to upset the cat in her cage. The boulder was the size of a delivery truck and blocked our entire lane! I later realized that our whole life was to come to a stop that day! First, we had to have Cinco put to sleep in Cedar City and then the Doctor in St. George, said: "I wish I could have seen you sooner, there is nothing I can do for you." Philip in his typical gambling mode, said: "You have just dealt me a death sentence." The oncologist agreed that Philip's lung cancer had spread beyond repair.

Mom's 98th Birthday party was held as soon as we got back, so many people learned about Philip's condition there. Twenty or so of her friends came over from Cedar City to greet Winnie. It was a very fun yet bittersweet time.

After I drove us home from the doctor's office, we began to liquidate the inventory in the Gallery. We had no idea how long he had to live. Philip was losing weight and his pants had even fallen off because he had gotten so thin. After a couple of weeks, he told me that he could no longer work in the gallery, so it was up to me to sell off the fixtures and the remainder of the inventory. I finished doing that by the first of January 2016.

Mom and Philip both started eating less and less at each meal. We learned that cancer gets the nourishment anyway, so Philip had little desire to eat. Mom was having digestion challenges. I had an identity crisis because I did not know who I was when I was not preparing meals!

One day, Philip got up from a nap in the bedroom to go watch the evening news in the front room. I usually had been holding on to Philip's belt loops of his trousers to steady him, but this moment I was not around. He lunged forward in the hallway and hit his head on a square metal knob on the cabinet door above the dryer. He had a bad gash on his forehead. I quickly gave him a compress to stop the bleeding while the Physician's Assistant from clinic came to the house. He put nine stiches on Philip's scalp! It was then that I finally realized that we had to shove over all the furniture in the front room and make a place for a hospital bed for Philip.

Early in the month, I had received a phone call from Juliete who lived in front of us in Menlo Park. Then she called her son and told him about the situation. Luke called me. We had not spoken for twenty-five years! It was a delightful conversation as we remembered all the times I had helped him learn how to paint on plates. At the end of our two-hour visit, he asked if he could pray for us. In his prayer, Luke said, "I see Harriet bringing Philip a wildflower every day!"

I mused over that comment and recalled that my dear friend, El Ray, up the street had recently given me a photo montage of nine wildflowers from this area. I used a piece of watercolor paper on which I had painted clouds during the art festival and then began to paint a wildflower for Philip every day and eventually 4 birds which he really enjoyed. Finally, I sat next to his hospital bed in the front room on January 19th and painted a butterfly with its wing tip off the top middle of the paper and when I was finished, I told Philip that this was him going to be with the Lord. He died at 12:05 AM the next morning as I lay beside him with my arm around him listening to his last breath.

In the last week of Philip's life, I came to him as he lay on the hospital bed every day and told him that I loved him. There was simply nothing else to be said. Finally, he replied: "Love is all there is." Those were his last words.

Philip holding the painting as I began to "Bring Philip a wildflower every day."

Note El Ray's flower photo beside his arm.

Wildflowers for Philip with the butterfly leaving the page in the top middle.

We had the memorial service the following week, and both my brothers, and his brother, Rich Priska spoke fondly about Philip's life. John sang the song that summed up Philip's life: "He knew how to hold them, and he knew how to fold them." Our friend Tony, who had received Philip's ship model the Seguin some time before brought it with him for people to see. At the end of the service Tony read this poem by Henry Van Dyke.

Gone From My Sight

I am standing upon the seashore. A ship, at my side,
spreads her white sails to the moving breeze and starts
for the blue ocean. She is an object of beauty and strength.
I stand and watch her until, at length, she hangs like a speck
of white cloud just where the sea and sky come to mingle with each other.

Then, someone at my side says, "There, she is gone."

Gone where?

Gone from my sight. That is all. She is just as large in mast,
hull and spar as she was when she left my side.
And, she is just as able to bear her load of living freight to her destined port.

Her diminished size is in me -- not in her.

And, just at the moment when someone says, "There, she is gone,"
there are other eyes watching her coming, and other voices
ready to take up the glad shout, "Here she comes!"

Chapter 40 – Waltzing into Heaven

Winnie Washburn got her Utah driver's license before her 98th birthday in Cedar City. When Philip passed the 20th of January, 2016, she asked me for her van. I willingly signed it over to her. She drove it around Escalante and was very pleased to have it back.

After we liquidated the inventory in the gallery in early January 2016, I realized that I would like to build a small gallery beside our home and Philip supported the idea. I spoke with our local contractor, Reed Munson, and he explained that the trusses come in prefabricated sizes, so we agreed upon a dimension of 11 feet x 15 feet for the size of the building. Reed would not start pouring the cement foundation until the ground thawed in April. Serenidad Gallery would live on!

My brothers, John and George, came to Philp's funeral late in January. This is a photo of them with mom, who was doing well at that time.

George, Mom and John.

Early in February, five ladies indicated that they wanted me to teach them art lessons from the book "Drawing from the Right Side of the Brain" by Betty Edwards. I had taught this process of "learning how to see" for the past twenty years to people of many different ages. The book has been translated into at least 18 languages by then. It is a very effective tool for getting in touch with the creative abilities of the brain that may have been shut down in childhood when the person could not draw what they were seeing.

My friends joined mom and me around the dining room table and we began to work through the exercises. I must admit that it was a real confront for me to teach my mother. She was a special education teacher for many years and had written textbooks on the subject including the concept of mainstreaming and she had earned a master's degree in that field. It was possibly equally hard for her to take instructions from me as well! However, we proceeded and eventually she got *"it!"* The light went on in her mind and she understood at long last how to draw what she was seeing. The other four ladies had similar success.

Mid-February, I was contacted by a man who offered to sell me a painting by Rachel Bentley. This seemed to be an encouragement to me to continue selling her work. I purchased it right away. Later he posted a photo of a chicken on Facebook that really caught my attention. I drew it from the computer screen and did a painting of it using watercolor pencils mom had given me. It was quite challenging and kept me preoccupied during the long winter months. The breed was called "Blue Laced Red Wyandotte." The painting became famous on Facebook, and I eventually printed cards and prints of it, too.

Red Laced Blue Wyandotte

Jim Poteet, a retired lumberman, advised me to have the over 60 year old Blue Spruce pine tree beside my home cut down because he said that was about the length of the tree's life, and he could tell it needed to come down. Early the morning that the tree men were coming, I realized that I needed to post an ad on our local Facebook page to get the chain link fence removed that was right beside trunk before the tree could be cut down. My neighbor across the street came over with his backhoe right away and took apart the fence and removed the cement collar it was set in. The tree was indeed rotten in the core, and I was glad I it did not fall on my kitchen! Thankfully I got a nice stack of firewood out from it for my fireplace the next winter. The removal of the fence had an interesting effect on me, I had a new openness visually and mentally! The summer before, I had painted the front of our house with Philip walking in the front door without a fence even though it was still there at the time!

Blue Spruce beside my house being felled.

Painting I did of our house with Philip walking in the front door.

Early in March, mom and I took a trip out of town to do some shopping. At his funeral, I had been presented with a large American flag for Philip's service in the army in France in 1960. We wanted to learn how we might have it fly on top of a tall hill near Henriville. We stopped at the Post Office there and the postmistress, said that the lady who just walked out the door could take us to the man who would put the flag on that pole! It was a wonderful series of events.

We followed him to a spot on the highway where he got out of his car and began the forty five minute climb up the precipice. The final assent included a ladder and then a rope ladder to get to the flagpole constructed by a Boy Scout for his Eagle project. The pole had been set into the ground and then a sliding pole went down over the top of it. This was lifted straight up and off the bottom pole and the flag was then attached to it and slid back over the first pole. The man told us that because it was military flag and was made of heavy material, it would not last more than two months in the wind. The one he removed was all wrapped up in a tight wad!

We were jubilant to look up and see the flag as we drove by. Many people from Escalante were blessed to see it there, too, and we all had special memories of Philip because of the flag.

View of the precipice from Highway 12.

Flagpole up close.

The rest of that day on the return trip home mom kept saying that she wanted a flagpole for Escalante as well. We were not sure how to put one up, but she was determined to have it done!

I continued to give Art lessons to the five ladies. By mid-March we came to the lesson where they had to draw an object in their other hand . It was pencil and wipeout exercise and I decided to join in with them. Quoting Shakespear, I titled mine, "Sleep that knits up the raveled sleeve of care." I was slowly getting the "end of life details" competed for Philip and gradually moving on with my life!

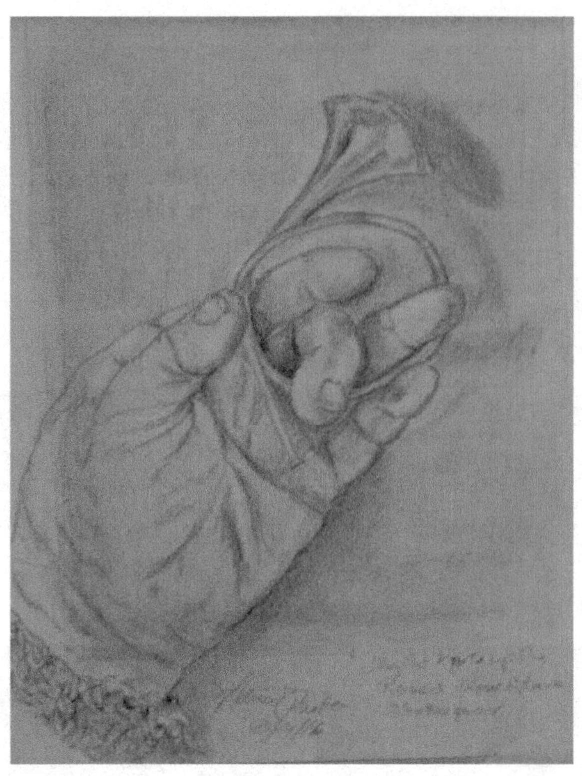

My pencil drawing: "Sleep that knits up the raveled sleeve of care."

I knew I had to ask mom if she wanted to travel to California again. She eagerly agreed and we began to design a trip to Pasadena to see her friends at Monte Vista Grove, and then on to the coast to meet John and his wife at Morro Bay. Unfortunately, just before we got to the ocean, mom's digestive system gave out, and she was not very well for the rest of the trip.

After visiting John's family in Fresno, we stayed with my friends, Teddi and Drummond McCunn, in Granite Bay. Then stopped briefly to visit my cousins in Truckee and Reno. By the time we got most of the way across Nevada, mom finally surrendered to me as her caregiver. This was a big step for her because she was a very self-determined person. When we got home, she revived to some degree.

I had committed to do a painting for my friend Kathy who was totally remodeling a very old brick pioneer home not far away from our house. I told her that when she and Jacob Croft finished rebuilding the porch, I would do a painting of the house. So, I set out each morning and worked on drawing and then painting it.

Kathy's house with the porch completed.

On Monday the 18th of April I was out working on the painting and a lady walked up the driveway from the house next door I knew that she had recently moved into town. As we chatted, she told me that she was a retired nurse, and she was kind enough to offer her services should mom need assistance.

I got back home around noon and went downstairs to check on mom and discovered that she had gotten up out of bed and was sitting on her cedar chest that her father had made for her many years ago. She said: "I have lost my soup." That was her family's way of saying that she could hardly move. I helped her back into bed and called the nurse at the clinic who informed Hospice.

Then Cathie, the retired nurse, came and assisted mom for the rest of the week. Winnie requested that our Pastor, Dale Richards, and the Pastor from Cedar City Presbyterian Church come and discuss her two memorial services with her. Dale recalls that she asked them to preach on "Christ's Resurrection." Dale read First Corinthians 15:20: "But now is Christ risen from the dead and become the first fruits of them that slept. For since by man came death, by man came also the resurrection of the dead." Then he read Job 19:25: "I know that my Redeemer lives, and that he shall stand at the last day upon the earth." The other pastor delivered a similar message at the church in Cedar City some days later.

By the middle of the week, when she could still say a few words, mom told me that she was sorry that she could not take any more art lessons from me! She wrote her last wishes on her legal yellow notepad. The main thing she stressed was having a flagpole in Escalante. Drew Parkin, who had helped design the new clinic the year before and I assured her that we would make sure that it happened.

Late Thursday afternoon, she told me that she had had a dream. I put my ear close to her mouth and she whispered to me that she had dreamed that she was waltzing into heaven with Tony whom we had met from Vienna many years ago. He was a handsome man dressed in a formal uniform. She told me that she was wearing a flowing purple velvet gown. She described how they waltzed into a grand room with many people around the sides. Then they went up and bowed low before the Lord, who was seated on a golden throne. Mom and dad had always loved Strauss Waltzes and Winnie had been the lead in "The Merry Widow" many years before. So, it was natural for her to have this dream.

My brothers arrived by Friday morning and we sang and prayed with her until she passed peacefully on Friday evening.

Later when Cathie and her daughter were preparing her body for burial, they discovered a swath of purple velvet packed with her nightgown that she wanted to be buried in. We buried her directly the next day and the next week we held the two memorial services that she requested.

We were able to raise $6,000 for the flagpole and base which was built beside the Kazan Clinic east of town. On November 11th, Veterans Day and mom's birthday, a nice group of friends and members of the Daughter's of the American Revolution attended the dedication. Students from the High School sang the Star Spangled Banner. She would have been very proud.

Winnie's Flagpole.

Exodus 20:12 Honor thy father and thy mother: that thy days may be long upon the land which the Lord thy God giveth thee.

Chapter 41 – "At Last!"

By the 2nd of May 2016, I had buried my husband at the age of 75 ½ years. We had been married for 35 ½ years. Three months later we buried my mother aged 98 ½. At the time, I never dreamed that this ordeal would be an opportunity for me to emphasize with others who have lost loved ones, particularly since I experienced their unexpected demise so close to one another. Now I can give a hug to anyone suffering loss and they know I understand their grief! My walk of faith continued as the Lord lead me day by day.

Work on the new gallery beside my home progressed as the weather got warmer and it was ready for me to move in by August. My brother, John, came from Fresno to help me get situated. Several men in town carried the one glass display case that I had not sold over to my new gallery. We hung fifteen large, framed watercolors by Rachel Bentley. Once again, our collection of her work gave direction in the early days of my new location. I had the building painted to match our brick home and installed the original carved wooden Serenidad Gallery sign in front. Then it was open for business a block and a half off Main Street.

Serenidad Gallery

By June, I knew I needed a fresh start with my painting and gave myself permission to spend the funds to attend a watercolor workshop led by Spike Ress at the Maynard Dixon Thunderbird Gallery near Mount Carmel Junction on Highway 89 south west of me in Utah. The class went out to several locations to paint. At one point, I just froze up and was unable to proceed. Spike advised me to go back to the Dixon studio and do value studies of the paintings on the walls. Somehow, I worked through the mental block and was able to produce a couple of paintings.

When I got back home, I continued to paint houses in town. I was doing a painting of a home that my dear friend Vicki Crawford had finally been able to purchase. I wanted to acknowledge her for all her hard work to get it and to include her lovely wild roses that were thriving beside the road.

Vickie's dream house.

As I was out standing on the sidewalk painting, Bruce Chesler came up and suggested that I come over to his home next. I did several paintings on his property including a backhouse which was part of the original Napoleon Bonepart Roundy estate where Escalante historian, Jerry Roundy, grew up! I entered my plein air painting of their home at the art festival that fall.

Back House built by the Roundy Family.

Early in September, I happened to see a very dramatic sunrise with a beam of sunlight piercing straight up through the clouds which gave a marvelous glow to the fence by the Waggoners' house. I sat in front of their property to capture the moment.

Sunning Sunrise and light!

While I was working three chickens walked in front of me pecking at the grass, so I added them to the painting and then their goat came over by the fence to investigate me and he was painted as well. When people saw the finished work, everyone loved the chickens so much that I decided to use the painting on my business card, which it still is to this day!

The Waggoner's house and their chickens and goat.

In October, I stood beside the original brick home built by Napoleon Boneparte Roundy in 1905. Jerry Roundy had told me that the family decided to remove the two upper stories in the 1950's because it was difficult to heat the large house. Napoleon, also known as Pole, had the ambition of building the tallest house south of Salt Lake City and added a tower to achieve his goal. Pole had two wives and sometimes used that vantage point to watch for polygamist hunters who were looking for him to put him in jail. There are many stories. Sadly, all that was left of the grandeur of the Queen Anne Style Victorian house was some lovely decorative woodwork on the porches. I stood outside drawing with my watercolor pencils to capture the essence of the place. Marie, from Paris, lived there at the time and had a French flag draped on one side of the porch. As I worked, I kept looking up as if to see what was not there anymore.

Side porch on the Napoleon Bonepart Roundy home built in 1905.

Finally, I said to myself, I must paint the whole thing! I found a black and white photo of the house taken early in the 1900's and eventually did a painting of it including the people in the photo who were standing out in front of the house, probably Napoleon and sons.

Napoleon Bonepart Roundy home was built in 1905.

In April 2017, I attended the Utah Daughters of the American Revolution State Conference in Salt Lake City. I was seated beside my friends Allan and Cindy Toone at a banquet the first evening. Striking up a conversation with Allan, I asked him what he was doing in his retirement years. He pulled out his phone and scrolled it to show me a photo of a large Victorian mansion they recently purchased in Ogden, just north of Salt Lake City. The amazing image was taken the previous December on the first evening they were finally able to turn on the electricity. Cindy had hung Christmas wreaths in all the windows! I immediately exclaimed, "I have to paint it!" They excitedly agreed and sent me historic photographs of the house in the early years. I did two studies from those black and white images to give me a better understanding of what the house had looked like in the past.

Black and white sketch from early photo of the Helfrich Healy home.

It was very challenging and finally they invited me to come and visit them in June of 2017 and get a good firsthand experience of how it appeared since they started working on it.

Color Study from another photo of the Helfrich Healy Home.

Their labors had created incredible results. I was very inspired by all their efforts to restore "The Helfrich/Healey Home" back to 1891. It reminded me of my Great Aunt Harriet's house above the Hudson River in New York state!

Final Painting of the Helfrich Healy home with Christmas Wreaths in the windows.

I must confess that while I knew that the Ten Commandments clearly state that: "Thou shalt not covet," I had yearned for years to be chosen by the Escalante Canyons Art Festival committee to be their "Featured Artist." I helped to create that concept at the beginning in 2004 to showcase the work of local artists and was always very pleased with their choices over the years. *At last*, the committee chose me! I was delighted and began gathering my work together to have a collection of my paintings including two of my wraparound scenic vases and recent watercolors to be shown in the exhibit hall during the festival.

When we were beginning the Everett Ruess Days Art Festival, I asked Dr. Paula McNeal from Valdosta State University in Valdosta, Georgia to create a slide presentation for each featured artist. Paula's family owned a vacation home in Escalante, and she had been living there for many summers after she taught art education and art history during the school year. She came to my home and worked with me on a presentation that included doing a video of one of my scenic vases turned on a lazy Susan. Friends kindly lent me paintings that they had purchased, and I had a very nice display. It was a very gratifying experience and I was truly grateful to be acknowledged.

Featrued Artist – 2017 – Escalante Canyons Art Festival.

I had two of my vases to display.

Note the tile painting in the upper right of the Kiva Koffee House.

Hebrews 11: 1. Now faith is the substance of things hoped for, the evidence of things not seen. 3. Through faith we understand that the worlds were framed by the word of God, so that things which are seen were not made of things which do appear.

6. But without faith it is impossible to please Him: for he that cometh to God must believe that He is, and that He is a rewarder of them that diligently seek Him.

Chapter 42 – "I will frame you free for life."

In the early 1960's when I was taking art classes at the University of Wyoming, I learned how to cut mats and frame my own watercolor paintings. I had a steady hand, but cutting mats was always a challenge. When I married Philip and later began to paint watercolors, Philip was very gracious to cut my mats and frame all my work.

After Philip passed away, I had quite a bit of framing materials in our house and I decided to give them all to our artist friend, Howard Hutchison. We had been selling Howard's drawings and cards in the gallery for several years. He gladly accepted all the supplies. Then he came to me and said: *"I will frame you free for life."* That was a most amazing gift! He continues frame my work to this very day! When needed, I purchased mats and other materials and we both found frames at garage sales and occasionally people have given them to us.

His support was the key to my future! After my "Featured Artist" exhibit at the Art Festival in 2017, a light went on in my head and I realized that I could show my work at various locations in this area. I was given the opportunity to have a small exhibit at the Red Canyon Visitor Center on Highway 12 in May of 2018, and then I was assigned two months to show my paintings at the Anasazi Museum in Boulder in August of 2018.

It was such a blessing to have these dates as goals to paint forward to.

I always knew that having a business a block and a half off of Main Street was challenging in any retail setting. Highway 12 is a National Scenic Road, so no advertising signs were allowed on Main Street. However, legislation was passed and for a fee I could pay a company to jump through the hoops and get permission for them to put up signs on Main Street advertising my business. The cost was $500 for their services and installation of two signs. Then $40 a month a year in advance for the signs to be in public view a half of a block before the turn up on 100 West. I finally got up the courage to spend the money and had two of them installed in the spring of 2017. It has paid off and I am always grateful when a customer tells me they came to the gallery because of the signs.

Sign on Main Street.

After I moved out of our gallery on Main Street, I discovered that the insurance on a vacant business building was a financial challenge. IF an insurance company would even cover it, the rate doubled! I was paying about $5000 a year for that vacant building including insurance, property taxes and utilities, with no tax credit. My small business paid those fees for several years. Eventually, a couple asked me sell the building to them carrying their loan. They put money down and worked on the building for few months, however they walked away from it leaving it in a sad state of repairs. So, I got it back and continued paying those fees for several more years!

In the past, I enjoyed creating calendars as gifts for my family, so in the summer of 2016, I printed my first calendar with my paintings for 2017 and sold it to people who liked my work and wanted something for the next year.

My friend, Beckie had an antique store in Panguitch and recently went out of business. She had a lot of nice Navajo silver jewelry which I took on consignment along with her collection of local rocks. Slowly as I built up my inventory with my watercolors, I sold all of Rachel's paintings to collectors in California so now I had room to show my own work. Beckie asked me to do a painting of "Factory Butte" on Highway 24 near Hanksville. She gave me a great photograph to work from. After much study I did a large painting. I knew she did not have a lot of money, so I traded the painting for her rock collection! Rocks for rocks!

Factory Butte north of Highway24 near Hanksville, Utah.

In December of 2017, Gibbs Simth, the publisher who had seen so instrumental in starting the Art Festival and who purchased six of my vases, passed away. I spoke with his wife, Catherine, and she agreed that the vases should be seen by the public. She gave them to me with the understanding that I could exhibit them with my paintings. We agreed that I was to find them a permanent home.

In May of 2018, I set up my first exhibit at the Red Canyon Visitor Center with paintings that I had done of that area.

Red Canyon Visitor Center Exhibit in 2018.

Then I dedicated my time to painting images about the history of Boulder. I found photographs of Hell's Back Bone Bridge spanning the one thousand foot gap to complete the first road connecting Escalante and Boulder. It was constructed of logs by the Civilian Conservation Corps and local men in 1933. The bridge was a unique structure and an amazing feat of engineering. I wanted to salute those early pioneers who took on that arduous task!

From Original Photo of Hells Back Bone Bridge built by local men and the CCCs-1933.

View of the 1000' drop the bridge was built over.

Note the three original logs that spanned the gap as they started. They are still there today!

I was very intrigued by the unique fencing around Boulder referred to as "Rip Gut" or "Stake and Rider" fences. In order for the early pioneers to have open fields to raise hay for their livestock, the men removed the cedar trees growing there and made long poles out of them which they wove back and forth making barriers so that deer would not jump over them, hence the name" Rip Gut." Many of the interesting fences still stand along the fields that were created in the Boulder and Salt Gulch areas.

Rip Gut Fencing in Boulder, Utah.

In July of 2018 I found a home for my Aunt Marion's seven bronze sculptures at the new Southern University Museum of Art in Cedar City. It is very difficult to donate art with the stipulation that the items will always be on display. Fortunately, the museum had just been built and in the back of the display was the archives for all the paintings that were donated. The front wall of the archive area was glass, so the sculptures were set inside and are always visible to the public while still in storage. Over time, art instructors have brought their students to view her work and study them which would have really pleased Marion.

I painted pictures of Boulder and Escalante showing the interdependency between the two towns, especially carrying the mail and milk back and forth on horseback and mules across the slick rock trails until the Hell's Back Bone Bridge was completed. After that they drove a mail truck that way for many years.

I hung my paintings in the exhibit room at the Anasazi State Park Museum in August of 2018 and displayed the five scenic vases that Catherine Smith donated along with two of mine. I did a painting of the replica of an Anasazi dwelling located behind the Museum. The Curator purchased the painting when the exhibit ended. The show was well attended by people from around the country and across the globe!

Replica of Anasazi structure behind the museum.

Later in August, I had occasion to visit the Fremont Indian State Park and Museum off Interstate 70 west of Richfield, Utah about three hours away from Escalante. I was amazed to discover all the Petroglyphs on the rock walls in the canyon which had been discovered and preserved when the freeway came through that area in the 1960's. I spoke with the curator and was invited to do an exhibit there the following March.

Now I really was in a fix! Rocks!!! The petroglyphs were all on rocks! What was I to do? Fortunately, there was an artist at the festival that September, named Ward Stroud, and he had a product to share with watercolor artists called Brusho. It was invented in England forty years before. The concept was to get watercolor paper wet and then shake the Brusho ink crystals on the surface and watch to see what would happen! It was a perfect solution for me. I made accurate representations of the petroglyphs, shapes chiseled onto the stone, and then made the rock background with the Brusho. It was a lot of fun and very freeing in many ways!

Fremont Petroglyphs and Brusho paint in the background.

One of the five ladies who took lessons from me in the spring of 2016 was Irit Reed. I first met her when she stayed the other bedroom in our basement with mom in 2015. Her eyesight was failing, and she did not want to live in California anymore where her husband was employed in the construction industry in the Bay Area.

After six weeks with us Irit found more permanent housing, and she was very happy to live in Escalante. Irit was originally from Jerusalem and had traveled and hiked extensively in the southwest taking photographs of many of the wonderful sights in this area. When she took the "Drawing from the Right Side of the Brain" instructions from me, she got "IT" and went on to work in pastels. In October of 2018, I invited Irit to have her first showing of her work in my gallery. She brought her dynamic pastels and her photographs to hang on my walls. She was very excited to begin showing her work to the public. Even though her eyesight continues to grow worse, she persists to this day to paint the images that have caught her imagination and inspired her to "keep on keeping on!"

Irit Reed and her first exhibit in Serenidad Gallery.

In November, my dear friend Sheila married Norm Godfrey in Marysvale. While I was attending their wedding, I did a photographic study of the early buildings from the Goldrush era there in the late 1800's. When I came home, I painted nine buildings to add to my display at the Fremont Museum in March 2019. The museum had nice display cases for my 7 scenic vases. Without Howard Hutchison's generous offer to "*frame me free for life*" none of this would have been possible!

Six of my "Wrap Around Vases" at the Fremont Museum.

Pictographs at the Fremont Museum.

Ephesians1: 4 According as God has chosen us before the foundation of the world, that we should be holy and without blame before Him in love: 5 God having predestinated us unto the adoption of children by Jesus Christ to himself, according to the good pleasure of His will, 6 to the praise of the glory of his grace where in God hath made us accepted in the beloved.

Chapter 43 – Keeping on Keeping on

Early each year I was fortunate to be assigned the dates to exhibit my work at the Anasazi Museum. This gave me a goal as I went forward with my paintings. By 2019, I had chosen to study pictographs and petroglyphs here in the Escalante area. There are many famous rock art sites in other regions such as "Newspaper Rock" south of Moab, Utah. However not much is known about sites here and there are no real public access markers for people to follow.

I had seen some locations because friends had taken me places over the years, but I knew there were many more that the local hikers had seen. I put out a request on Facebook and got some nice photos. One of my favorites which I had already painted several times was what I call the "Circle of Friends" in Main Canyon northwest of Escalante. When I visited it, I observed that the early pioneers also added their marks and names. I omitted those inscriptions and stayed with the older marks, mostly done in a red pigment. There were also some petroglyphs, and I included what I could in the painting.

"Circle of Friends" in Main Canyon.

I have a friend who owns property at North Creek west of town which has been designated by archeologists as the earliest site of habitation in Utah. On one wall are four horsemen and on a rock face further up the hill there is another pictograph of twelve horsemen. I had been shown a pictograph on up Main Canyon where two horsemen and other figures were painted under on overhanging rock. I came to surmise that these were all talking about the Spanish when they came into this area and possibly were capturing people for their slave trade in the 1600's. I painted all three panels on one page to show what I saw.

Eighteen horsemen on three different panels in the Escalante area.

My goal was to do as many paintings as I could by my date at the Anasazi Museum early in July 2019. I received many interesting photos to work from. One that particularly intrigued me was a long panel that I had to do in three paintings to get it all in. I was experimenting with painting on a plastic paper called Yupo. First using the Brusho ink crystals as the basis, I could then wipe out the figures easily after the paper was dry! This was a huge set of petroglyphs, and the male figures were at least six feet high! I made note that one of the footprints had eight toes! (Lots of speculation about what that means, I am not going there! I am just a recorder of what is seen!)

Pictographs in the Escalante River Canyon.

Another part of that Panel, note the number of toes on the footprints on the right!

Yet another part of the extensive panel in the Escalante River Canyon.

The show was well received and while at the Anasazi Museum I asked the curator if I might photograph the pottery that was stored in the back room. I knew from my own experience with the museums where I had worked in at the University of Wyoming and San Francisco State College that most of what an institution collected was never seen by the public. I was given permission to photograph some of the collection and then began to recreate pieces to show what they might have looked like when the women made them before the people disappeared from this area around 1250 AD. I learned that the clay was gathered, and the shape formed with the coil method and then smoothed and then the clay was painted and fired. This was all in one process! I have great respect for the women who created these amazing pieces.

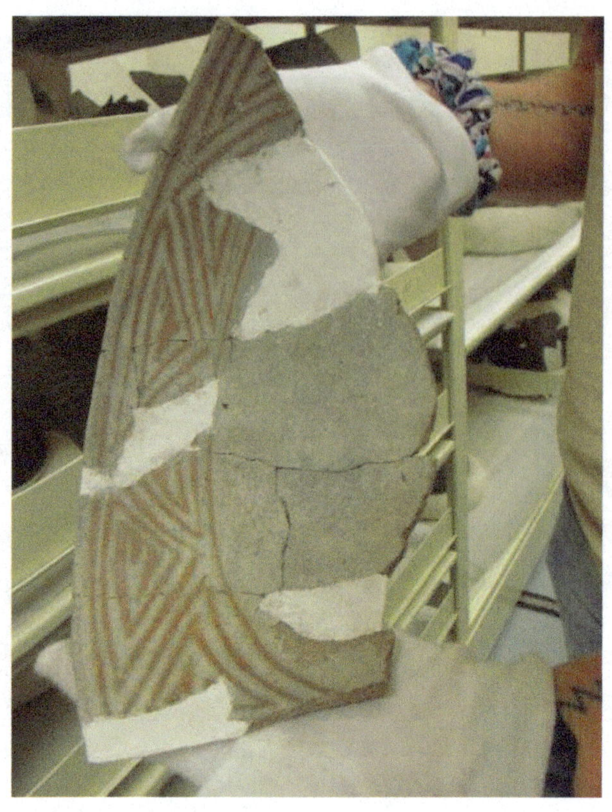

Fragment assembled at the Anasazi Museum.

My recreation of that large platter as it could have looked.

Some of the pieces simply did not give me guidance as to what the entire item would have looked like, and some did. Here is a painting of various "potsherds" and then a very large platter with an amazing design. The fate of these "Muckwich" people is unknown. This is the Paiute word for the "ancient ones" as opposed to the labels like Anasazi and Fremont given to them by the white explorers who came into the area in the 1800's.

Fragments of pottery at the Anasazi Museum.

A very large platter at the Anasazi Museum.

In February of 2020, I flew to Florida to visit some of my relatives and had a great time seeing the Kenedy Space Center. I was awestruck by all the missiles that had sent men into space. I had dreamed of that achievement in the 1960's and even built a model that resembled the one used in the movie 2001! My cousin took me to a museum to see artwork done of Florida. And we saw a Giant Sloth that had been excavated out of the swamp near Orlando! As always, I enjoyed flying across the country and seeing the amazing expanses of our wonderful land.

Early March I boarded Amtrak at the Green River, Utah station and traveled east to see Philip's sister and family in Battle Creek, Michigan. I was so glad I made the effort because she passed away that summer. Then I went on into Ontario, Canada, to meet David, the quadriplegic I had been communicating with since his fall in 2015. He took me to visit the Mennonite community near Windsor where he lived. We attended their church service that Sunday. The ladies sat on one side and the men on the other. They sang acapella. Their 250 voices were wonderful, and I was engulfed in Praise to the Lord. David arranged for his caregivers to take me to the Canadian side of Niagara Falls. I had been there at the age of 4 and had very little recall of the experience, so it was really a treat to stand right next to the roaring river as it plunged down into the falls directly below us!

Niagara Falls from the Canadian Side with a lovely rainbow!.

Then they took me to the train station on the New York side to catch Amtrak to return home. While we were waiting, we caught up on the news on March 12th and learned that a virus called Covid had hit New York City, and people were fearful that it would spread throughout the country. By the time I got home, the world had been shut down!

I hung my "What's in Back" exhibit at the Anasazi Museum mid-April. I am not sure how many people visited it.

Tourism declined steadily in those days. However, I "Kept on Keeping on" and gathered photos of ancient ruins in this area. Except certain ones near the highway most are seen only by ardent hikers. The ruins, called granaries, are mostly unknown. Friends including Bill Wolverton kindly gave me images to work from and I made a point of not remembering where they were!

Ruins of dwellings south of Escalante.

My exhibit at Red Canyon Visitor Center in the summer of 2020 featured some of the pictographs, petroglyphs, ruins and pottery paintings I had completed thus far.

Late in December we had a marvelous snowstorm, and I went out in my back yard to take photos in the early morning light. When the sunlight hit this tree, I quickly snapped a shot. Later I realized what a gem I had gotten, and it won a Sweepstakes Reserve Award at the Garfield County Fair the following August!

Sunlight on neighbors Blue Spruce.

In March 2021, I finally found a permanent home for my seven scenic vases at the Cedar City Public Library. I also was invited to show my 85 prehistoric paintings for "Archaeology Month" there at the Library in April. Then I hung the prehistoric paintings again at the Anasazi Museum in June.

Presenting 6 vases to the Cedar City Public Library on Permanent Display.

The vases are now on display at the Cedar City Public Library.

My friend Tad Lostlen had used his Covid time well. He came up from Southern California with some friends and built a large barn on his property southwest of town. He asked me to do a painting of it showing the two forty-foot containers he used as support on either side and had me paint his friends in various stages of construction including local contractor, Reed Munson, with his forklift placing another truss while Tad looked on.

Tad's friends helping to build his barn during Covid.

I knew that the 100th Anniversary of the creation of Bryce Canyon as a National Monument would be celebrated in the fall. I was amused when I looked at my photos that I took in 1956 when we visited Bryce Canyon and saw a shot of the twisted tree that a friend of mine had just insisted that I paint! I also painted the iconic "Thor's Hammer" with my favorite Powell Point in the distance! These were all exhibited at Red Canyon Visitor Center in the summer of 2022.

Twisted Tree at Bryce Canyon National Park.

Thor's Hammer at Bryce Canyon with Powell Point in the distance.

For several years I had been driving to Green River, Utah and catching Amtrak to travel to California to see friends and family . I loved the trip over the California Sierras and gazed down fondly at Donner Lake and looked for the house where I lived in the late 1960's when I taught art at the high school there. On this trip we were in a blizzard which also brought back many memories of the deep six foot snowstorms I had experienced there. I recalled hearing the trains slowly whining up to the summit with their snowplow engine in front of them.

Somewhere after the summit that day in November of 2022, our train came to a stop. I gazed out the window at the tall pines laden with snow and took out my pen and began to draw one of them. We were there for quite a while, so I was able to finish the picture. My goal was to do something about my art every day.

Pine tree laden with snow on Donner summit.

Psalm 139: 1 – 24 O LORD, thou hast searched me and known me, Thou knowest my down sitting and mine uprising, thou understand my thought afar off. Thou compassest my path and my lying down, and art acquainted with all my ways. For there is not a word in my tongue, but, lo O LORD, thou knowest it altogether. Thou hast beset me behind and before and laid thine hand upon me. Such knowledge is too wonderful for me; it is high, I cannot attain unto it. Wither shall I go from the spirit? Or wither shall I flee from thy presence? If I ascend up into heaven, thou are there: if I make my bed in hell, behold thou are there. If I take the wings of the morning, and dwell in the uttermost parts of the sea: even there shall thy hand lead me, and they right hand shall hold me. If I say, surely the darkness shall cover me; even the night shall be light about me. Yea, the darkness hideth not from thee; but the night shineth as the day: the darkness and light are both alike to thee. For thou hast possessed my reins; thou hast covered me in my mother's womb. I will praise thee; for I am fearfully and wonderfully made; marvelous are thy works; and that my soul knoweth right well. My substance was not hid from thee, when I was made in secret, and curiously wrought in the lowest parts of the earth. Thine eyes did see my substance, yet being unperfect; and in thy book all my members were written, which in continuance were fashions, when as yet there was none of them. How precious also are thy thoughts unto me, O God! How great is the sum of them! If I should count them, they are more in number than the sand; when I awake, I am still with thee. Surely, thou wilt slay the wicked, O God; depart from me therefore, ye bloody men, for they speak against thee wickedly, and thine enemies take thy name in vain. Do I not hate them, O LORD, that hate thee? And am I not grieved with those that rise up against thee? I hate them with perfect hatred: I count them mine enemies. **Search me, O God, and know my heart: try me and know my thoughts: and see if there be any wicked way in me and lead me in the way everlasting.**

Chapter 44 – "Where did you grow up?"

After the Art Festival in 2022, I literally came up against a brick wall! I had no more projects that I wanted to paint, I fiddled around for a while sorting through my mammoth collection of photos I have taken in Escalante since we moved here in 1991, but nothing struck my fancy.

Finally, I concluded that I could publish books using my paintings to illustrate the history of this area, first prehistoric and then historic. I contacted two publishing companies here in Utah and got the reply that they did not do "picture books." While having lunch with my dear friend Jana Hasset one day, I bemoaned my dilemma and she said, "Amazon publishes books!" And they certainly did. I connected with their office and began to understand the dynamics of publishing. They walked me through all the phases. My friend Joe Baughman taught me how to upload my images to their page and I was off and running so to speak.

For advice on Volume One: "The Peoples of South-Central Utah and the Land they lived on" - Prehistoric, I contacted two archeologists in this area to get more information on the people who were here and learn how to word my commentary about those years. By January 2023, I had Volume 1 completed. This covered up to the time that the archeologists said that the people disappeared from this area in South Central Utah about 1250AD. I included my paintings of pictographs- paintings on rocks, petrographs – carvings on rocks, various ruins here and pottery stored at the Anasazi State Park Museum in Boulder, Utah. I added some more paintings about the recent Paiute people by gathering information from a Paiute lady in Nevada. It is available on Amazon.

Then I went on to write Volume 2 "The Peoples of South-Central Utah and the Land they lived on." - Historic. I included my paintings about the history of the early exploration and settlement of Escalante, Boulder and the surrounding area including Bryce Canyon and Marysvale. I have now republished it in 2024, and it is available on Amazon.

Early in 2023, I was contacted by the committee that was presenting the 100th Anniversary of Escalante's first High School graduating class in 1923. They asked me to do paintings of the early schools, so, these were included in the book as well.

I did do more paintings in 2023, and I am looking forward to returning to painting views taken from a friend's drone of the dramatic rock formations in this area like the one I did of Upper Calf Creek Falls.

Upper Calf Creek Falls

I still have my Gallery and am in my eighth year in this building! I just celebrated my eighty first birthday and was given three different parties by dear friends in three days. I realized that I am very rich in friendships both here and around the world!

I still get the questions when customers walk in the door: "Are you from here?" and "Why did you move here?" I have been thinking about why people ask those questions. I find that when I ask them where they are from, I can often discover a connection with them since I have lived in so many places. It is a helpful way to begin our conversation and get acquainted.

So where did I grow up? That is a profound question. What is Growing Up? Do we ever arrive?

There are eight very large black locust trees in front of my home. They were probably planted in 1948 when this house was built by Leo Wilson. At that time, there were ditches running all along the city streets to bring irrigation water to the homes in town and the trees were watered that way. There are still a few other lines of locust trees in Escalante that were also planted along the ditches. Over the years and five boys later, the trees have grown and been pruned. One branch intrigued me, and I did a painting of it. First it grew the natural way and then for whatever reason it got pruned back, but it continued to grow in an upward direction, then it got pruned again, and again, and again. If you trace it carefully you can see that the branch was persistent despite its many happenstances!

The story of my life in this branch! Perseverance!

I relate to this branch in many ways. My life had many turns and changes that I had no control over. The "Normal growing up years "that people think of when they ask those questions simply did not exist for me! I sowed my wild oats in my twenties. I never did find someone who wanted me to settle down with him and have a family. My first husband was fifteen years older than me and had two adult children not much younger than myself, and they each had children as well.

The 1970's were a time of discovery for me as I became an antique dealer in 1974 and began to paint on porcelain in 1977. After I divorced in 1979, I immediately met Philip, and we married in 1980 with the understanding that we would not have children.

When the Lord called us to live in Escalante in 1988, we did not own property in California, so we saved money to start our new life here in 1991 in a town where we knew just a few people. When we opened the Serenidad Gallery in 1993, we continued to step out in faith, moment by moment.

I guess if you want to know what growing up meant to us, it was that life of faith and trust that the Lord had a plan for us since before the beginning of time. Upon reflection, I see that we were guided and provided for every step of the way and in circumstances that we did not anticipate!

My anthropology teacher used to tell us when we were complaining about standing in the hot Wyoming sun sifting dirt at the archeology dig that it was "Character building!" In many ways our day to day life was indeed character-building. Is that "growing up?" I think so.

So perhaps the answer is that I grew up here in Escalante and I have been growing up in my walk with the Lord all my life! Where the Lord guides, he provides. Thank you, Father!

Isaiah 58:11 And the LORD shall guide thee continually, and satisfy thy soul in drought, and make fat they bone: and thou shalt be like a watered garden, and like a spring of water, whose waters fail not.

POSTSCRIPT

After the arduous task of reviewing all these chapters and reliving my life yet again, I now come to an even clearer view of the Lord's hand in my life, and I am very grateful to Him for all His plans and provisions for our lives!

Our dear friend Tony's health is failing so I asked him recently if I could bring Philip's model of the Seguin home. Tony agreed and the tugboat is now sitting in the front room beside Rachel's seascape, which is the only one of all her paintings that I kept. I still enjoy it to this day. It seems fitting to have the work of these two very important people in my life together here showing Rachel's dedication to preserving the past with her watercolors and Philip's superb craftmanship with wood.

I am challenged and encouraged use each moment to fully and glorify God in my living!

The Seguin is home again!

Italian Tourists came visit me at the gallery in August of 2024.

Romans 16:27 To God only wise, be glory through Jesus Christ forever. Amen.

Made in the USA
Monee, IL
27 September 2024

65997156R10177